GRANDMA'S

ALL-TIME FAVORITE RECIPES

Copyright © 1997 Publications International, Ltd.
All rights reserved. This publication may not be reproduced or quoted in whole or in part by any means whatsoever without written permission from:

Louis Weber, CEO
Publications International, Ltd.
7373 North Cicero Avenue
Lincolnwood, Illinois 60646

Permission is never granted for commercial purposes.

All recipes and photographs that contain specific brand names are copyrighted by those companies and/or associations, unless otherwise specified. All photographs *except* those on pages 6, 11, 15, 19, 21, 25, 31, 35, 43, 45, 49, 51, 53, 55, 57, 65, 67, 79, 89, 99, 107, 109, 111, 113, 115, 119, 125, 137, 141, 151, 153, 155, 167, 169, 171, 173, 177, 179, 181, 185, 203, 221, 241, 245, 253, 271, 275, 289, 291, 293, 305, 309, 317, 319, 325, 327, 329, 331, 337, 339 and 345 copyright © Publications International, Ltd.

DOLE® is a registered trademark of Dole Food Company, Inc.

LIBBY'S, NESTLÉ and TOLL HOUSE are registered trademarks © 1997 Nestlé.

Some of the products listed in this publication may be in limited distribution.

Front cover photography by Sanders Studios, Inc., Chicago.

Pictured on the front cover *(clockwise from top right)*: Golden Hearty Cornbread *(page 16)*, Flaky Southern Biscuits *(page 16)*, Baked Country Cured Ham *(page 40)*, Corn Relish *(page 32)*, Green Beans with Pine Nuts *(page 28)*, Acorn Squash with Maple Butter *(page 30)*, Quick Dills *(page 33)*, Pickled Peaches *(page 84)* and Berry Cobbler *(page 84)*.

Pictured on the back cover: Raspberry Fudge Brownies *(page 314)*.

ISBN: 0-7853-2562-X

Library of Congress Catalog Card Number: 97-67948

Manufactured in U.S.A.

8 7 6 5 4 3 2 1

Nutritional Analysis: In the case of multiple choices, the first ingredient, the lowest amount and the lowest serving yield are used to calculate the nutritional analysis. "Serve with" suggestions are not included unless otherwise stated.

Microwave Cooking: Microwave ovens vary in wattage. Use the cooking times as guidelines and check for doneness before adding more time.

GRANDMA'S

ALL-TIME FAVORITE RECIPES

PUBLICATIONS INTERNATIONAL, LTD.

CONTENTS

DOWN HOME COOKIN'

Hearty Soups & Breads • 8
Harvest Vegetable Dishes • 22
Heartwarming Home-Style Suppers • 38
Country Chicken & Turkey • 54
Savory Seafood • 68
Old-Fashioned Delightful Desserts • 82

CASSEROLES & ONE-DISH MEALS

Home-Style Meaty Meals • 98
Fantastic Potluck Poultry • 112
Spectacular Deep Sea Dinners • 128
Dazzling Pasta Dishes • 140
Country Vegetables & Grains • 154
Hearty International Fare • 168

COUNTRY BAKING

Sensational Morning Glories • 184
Tasty Team-Ups • 204
Terrific Light Delights • 224
Sweet Snackin' Treats • 244

OLD-FASHIONED COOKIES

Traditional Cookie-Jar Favorites • 266
Classic Chips & Chunks • 284
Keepsake Bar Cookies • 298
Time-Honored Brownies • 312
Grandkids' Delights • 324
Old-World Holiday Treats • 334

Acknowledgments • 348

Index • 349

DOWN HOME

COOKIN'

CONTENTS

Hearty Soups & Breads • 8

Harvest Vegetable Dishes • 22

Heartwarming Home-Style Suppers • 38

Country Chicken & Turkey • 54

Savory Seafood • 68

Old-Fashioned Delightful Desserts • 82

Dairyland Confetti Chicken (page 66)

Hearty SOUPS & BREADS

POTATO & CHEDDAR SOUP

2 cups water
2 cups peeled red potato cubes
3 tablespoons butter or margarine
1 small onion, finely chopped
3 tablespoons all-purpose flour
Red and black pepper to taste
3 cups milk
½ teaspoon sugar
1 cup shredded Cheddar cheese
1 cup cubed cooked ham

Bring water to a boil in large saucepan. Add potatoes and cook until tender. Drain, reserving liquid. Measure 1 cup, adding water if necessary. Melt butter in saucepan over medium heat. Add onion; cook and stir until tender but not brown. Add flour; season with red and black pepper. Cook 3 to 4 minutes. Gradually add potatoes, reserved liquid, milk and sugar to onion mixture; stir well. Add cheese and ham. Simmer over low heat 30 minutes, stirring frequently. *Makes 12 servings*

— Hearty —

SOUPS & BREADS

BACON BRUNCH BUNS

- 1 loaf (1 pound) frozen bread dough
- 2 tablespoons (½ package) HIDDEN VALLEY RANCH® Original Ranch® with Bacon salad dressing mix
- ¼ cup unsalted butter or margarine, melted
- 1 cup shredded Cheddar cheese
- 2 egg yolks
- 1½ tablespoons cold water
- 3 tablespoons sesame seeds

Thaw bread dough according to package directions. Preheat oven to 375°F. On floured board, roll dough into rectangle about 18×7 inches. In small bowl, whisk together salad dressing mix and butter. Spread mixture on dough; sprinkle with cheese. Roll up tightly, jelly-roll style, pinching seam to seal. Cut into 16 slices.

Place slices cut-side down on greased jelly-roll pan. Cover with plastic wrap and let rise until doubled in bulk, about 1 hour. In small bowl, beat egg yolks and water; brush mixture over buns. Sprinkle with sesame seeds. Bake until golden brown, 25 to 30 minutes. Serve warm.

Makes 16 buns

ORANGE PECAN BREAD

- 1¾ cups all-purpose flour
- ¾ cup sugar
- 1 teaspoon baking powder
- ½ teaspoon baking soda
- ½ teaspoon salt
- ¾ cup Florida orange juice
- 1 egg, lightly beaten
- 2 tablespoons butter or margarine, melted and cooled
- 1 tablespoon grated fresh orange peel
- ½ teaspoon almond extract
- ½ cup chopped pitted dates
- ½ cup chopped pecans

Preheat oven to 350°F.

In large bowl, combine flour, sugar, baking powder, baking soda and salt. In separate bowl, combine orange juice, egg, butter, orange peel and almond extract.

Make a well in center of flour mixture and pour in orange juice mixture; stir until just combined. Stir in dates and pecans.

Pour batter into greased 9×5×3-inch loaf pan. Bake at 350°F for 50 minutes or until wooden pick inserted in center comes out clean. Cool in pan 10 minutes. Remove from pan. Cool completely on wire rack.

Makes 1 loaf

Favorite recipe from **Florida Department of Citrus**

Bacon Brunch Buns

Hearty

Soups & Breads

NAVAJO LAMB STEW WITH CORNMEAL DUMPLINGS

- 2 pounds lean lamb stew meat with bones, cut into 2-inch pieces *or* 1½ pounds lean boneless lamb, cut into 1½-inch cubes
- 1 teaspoon salt
- ½ teaspoon pepper
- 2½ tablespoons vegetable oil, divided
- 1 large onion, chopped
- 1 clove garlic, minced
- 4 cups water
- 2 tablespoons tomato paste
- 2 teaspoons chili powder
- 1 teaspoon ground coriander
- 3 small potatoes, cut into 1½-inch chunks
- 2 large carrots, cut into 1-inch pieces
- 1 package (10 ounces) frozen whole kernel corn
- ⅓ cup coarsely chopped celery leaves
- Cornmeal Dumplings (recipe follows)
- Whole celery leaves for garnish

Sprinkle meat with salt and pepper. Heat 2 tablespoons oil in 5-quart Dutch oven over medium-high heat. Add meat a few pieces at a time; cook until browned. Transfer meat to medium bowl. Heat remaining ½ tablespoon oil over medium heat. Add onion and garlic; cook until onion is tender. Stir in water, tomato paste, chili powder and coriander. Return meat to Dutch oven. Add potatoes, carrots, corn and chopped celery leaves. Bring to a boil. Cover; reduce heat and simmer 1 hour and 15 minutes or until meat is tender. During last 15 minutes of cooking, prepare Cornmeal Dumplings. Drop dough onto stew to make 6 dumplings. Cover and simmer 18 minutes or until dumplings are firm to the touch and wooden pick inserted in center comes out clean. To serve, spoon stew onto individual plates; serve with dumplings. Garnish with whole celery leaves.

Makes 6 servings

Cornmeal Dumplings
- ½ cup yellow cornmeal
- ½ cup all-purpose flour
- 1 teaspoon baking powder
- ¼ teaspoon salt
- 2½ tablespoons cold butter or margarine
- ½ cup milk

Combine cornmeal, flour, baking powder and salt in medium bowl. Cut in butter with fingers, pastry blender or 2 knives until mixture resembles coarse crumbs. Make a well in center; pour in milk all at once and stir with fork until mixture forms dough.

Navajo Lamb Stew with Cornmeal Dumplings

Hearty

SOUPS & BREADS

CHEDDAR CHOWDER

- 2 cups boiling water
- 2 cups cauliflowerets
- 1 cup diced potatoes
- ½ cup sliced carrots
- ½ cup sliced celery
- ¼ cup chopped onion
- 1½ teaspoons salt
- ¼ teaspoon pepper
- ¼ cup butter or margarine
- ¼ cup flour
- 2 cups milk
- 2 cups (8 ounces) SARGENTO® Classic Supreme® or Fancy Supreme® Shredded Mild or Sharp Cheddar Cheese
- 1 cup cubed cooked ham (optional)

In large saucepan, combine water, cauliflower, potatoes, carrots, celery, onion, salt and pepper. Bring to a boil over medium-high heat; cover and simmer 10 minutes. Do not drain. In large saucepan, melt butter. Stir in flour, then milk; heat to boiling. Continue simmering, stirring constantly, until thickened. Add Cheddar cheese; stir until melted. Add undrained vegetable mixture and ham, if desired. Heat through, but do not boil.

Makes about 8 servings

APPLE CHEDDAR MUFFINS

- 1 egg, slightly beaten
- ½ cup milk
- ¼ cup vegetable oil
- 1 cup applesauce
- ¼ cup sugar
- 1½ cups all-purpose flour
- 2 teaspoons baking powder
- ½ teaspoon salt
- ½ teaspoon ground cinnamon
- ½ cup (2 ounces) SARGENTO® Classic Supreme® Shredded Mild or Sharp Cheddar Cheese

In large bowl, combine egg, milk, oil, applesauce and sugar. Sift flour, baking powder, salt and cinnamon together; add all at once with Cheddar cheese to egg mixture. Stir only until flour mixture is moistened (batter will be lumpy). Divide batter evenly among 12 greased muffin cups. (Cups will be more than ⅔ full.) Bake at 400°F for about 20 minutes or until wooden pick inserted in center comes out clean. Let cool in muffin pan 5 minutes. Run knife around outer edges of each muffin; turn out onto rack to cool completely.

Makes 12 muffins

Left to right: Cheddar Chowder; Apple Cheddar Muffins

Hearty

SOUPS & BREADS

GOLDEN HEARTY CORNBREAD

- 1¼ cups cornmeal
- ½ cup all-purpose flour
- ½ teaspoon baking soda
- ⅛ teaspoon salt (optional)
- ½ cup KELLOGG'S® ALL-BRAN® cereal
- ¾ cup skim milk
- 2 egg whites, slightly beaten
- 3 tablespoons vegetable oil
- 1 cup no-salt-added whole kernel corn, drained
- ½ cup reduced fat Cheddar cheese
- ½ cup chopped green onions
- Nonstick cooking spray

1. Stir together cornmeal, flour, baking soda and salt. Set aside.

2. In large mixing bowl, combine Kellogg's® All-Bran® cereal and milk. Let stand 2 minutes or until cereal is slightly softened. Add egg whites, oil, corn, cheese and onions. Add flour mixture, stirring just until combined. Spread batter into 8×8×2-inch baking pan coated with cooking spray.

3. Bake at 400°F about 40 minutes or until golden brown. Serve warm. *Makes 9 servings*

FLAKY SOUTHERN BISCUITS

- 2 cups all-purpose flour
- 1 tablespoon baking powder
- ½ teaspoon salt
- ½ cup chilled vegetable shortening
- ¾ cup cold milk

Preheat oven to 425°F. In large bowl, combine flour, baking powder and salt. With pastry blender, cut in shortening until mixture resembles coarse meal. Stir in milk until dough holds together. Knead gently about 1 minute. Roll dough ½ inch thick. With 2½- to 3-inch biscuit cutter, cut dough. Place 1 inch apart on ungreased cookie sheet. Bake 12 to 15 minutes or until lightly browned. *Makes 10 biscuits*

Favorite recipe from **McIlhenny Company**

OLD-FASHIONED CARROT SOUP

- 1 (46-fluid ounce) can COLLEGE INN® Chicken Broth
- 1½ pounds carrots, cut in 1-inch pieces
- 4 large onions, coarsely chopped
- 3 stalks celery, cut in 1-inch pieces
- ¼ cup chopped parsley
- ¼ cup margarine
- ¼ cup all-purpose flour
- 2 cups milk*

*For thinner soup, add additional milk until desired consistency.

Hearty

Soups & Breads

In large heavy pot, over medium-high heat, bring broth, carrots, onions, celery and parsley to a boil. Cover; reduce heat and simmer until vegetables are tender, about 30 minutes. Cool slightly. In blender container or food processor, blend mixture in batches until smooth; set aside.

In same saucepan, melt margarine; blend in flour. Stir in carrot mixture and milk. Cook, stirring occasionally, until heated through. Garnish with additional parsley if desired. *Makes 8 servings*

QUICK & EASY CHILI

- 1½ pounds ground beef
- 1 large onion, chopped
- 1 clove garlic, minced
- 2 (16-ounce) cans kidney beans, drained
- 2 (12-ounce) jars ORTEGA® Mild or Medium Thick and Chunky Salsa
- 2 teaspoons chili powder
- ½ teaspoon dried oregano leaves
- ½ teaspoon ground cumin
- Shredded Cheddar cheese (optional)

In 4-quart saucepan, over medium heat, cook beef, onion and garlic until beef is no longer pink, stirring occasionally to break up meat; drain. Add beans, salsa, chili powder, oregano and cumin. Cover; simmer for 30 minutes, stirring occasionally. Serve topped with cheese if desired. *Makes 6 servings*

CORNSTICKS

- ⅔ cup yellow or blue cornmeal
- ⅓ cup all-purpose flour
- 3 tablespoons sugar
- 1½ teaspoons baking powder
- ½ teaspoon LAWRY'S® Seasoned Salt
- 1 cup milk
- 2 tablespoons butter or margarine, melted
- 1 egg, well beaten
- 2 tablespoons diced green chiles

Preheat oven to 425°F. In medium bowl, combine cornmeal, flour, sugar, baking powder and Seasoned Salt. In 4-cup measure, combine milk, butter and egg; blend well. Slowly pour into flour mixture, stirring until well blended. Stir in green chiles. Spoon batter into lightly greased corn-shaped molds. Bake on lowest rack in 425°F oven 20 to 25 minutes or until golden brown. Serve warm with whipped butter. *Makes 12 cornsticks*

TIP: For a wonderful flavor variation, try adding ¼ cup grated Cheddar cheese. If cornstick molds are not available, use an 8-inch square baking pan. Spoon batter into lightly greased pan and bake as directed.

— Hearty —

SOUPS & BREADS

MINESTRONE SOUP

- ½ cup finely chopped leeks
- 3 tablespoons finely chopped onion
- 1 clove garlic, finely chopped
- 2 tablespoons vegetable oil
- 1½ cups chopped zucchini
- 1½ cups chopped carrots
- 1½ cups chopped potatoes
- ½ cup thinly sliced celery
- 1 can (28 ounces) whole tomatoes, chopped and undrained
- 5 cups chicken broth
- 1 can (16 ounces) Great Northern beans
- ½ teaspoon salt
- ½ teaspoon dried basil leaves
- ¼ teaspoon black pepper
- 1 bay leaf
- 2 sprigs fresh parsley
- 1 package (10 ounces) frozen peas
- 1 cup KELLOGG'S® ALL-BRAN® cereal
- 3 tablespoons grated Parmesan cheese
- Snipped fresh parsley

In 8-quart saucepan, cook and stir leeks, onion and garlic in oil. Add zucchini, carrots, potatoes and celery. Cook for 5 minutes, stirring frequently. Add tomatoes with liquid, broth, beans and seasonings. Cover; bring to a boil. Simmer 20 minutes; stir occasionally. Add peas; simmer 10 minutes or until tender.

Remove bay leaf and parsley. Stir in Kellogg's® All-Bran® cereal. Serve hot garnished with Parmesan cheese and snipped fresh parsley.
Makes 9 servings (1½ cups each)

BAYOU JAMBALAYA

- 1 medium onion, sliced
- ½ cup chopped green bell pepper
- 1 clove garlic, minced
- 1 cup uncooked white rice
- 2 tablespoons vegetable oil
- 1 cup water
- ¾ cup HEINZ® Tomato Ketchup
- 1 tablespoon HEINZ® Vinegar
- ⅛ teaspoon black pepper
- ⅛ teaspoon ground red pepper
- 1 cup cubed cooked ham
- 1 medium tomato, coarsely chopped
- ½ pound raw medium shrimp, shelled, deveined

In large skillet, cook and stir onion, green pepper, garlic and rice in oil until onion is tender. Stir in water, ketchup, vinegar, black pepper, red pepper, ham and tomato. Cover; simmer 20 to 25 minutes or until rice is tender. Add shrimp; simmer, uncovered, 3 to 5 minutes or until shrimp turn pink, stirring occasionally.
Makes 4 to 6 servings (about 6 cups)

Bayou Jambalaya

Hearty

Soups & Breads

Classic Banana Bread

- 2 extra-ripe, medium DOLE® Bananas, peeled
- ¾ cup brown sugar, packed
- ½ cup margarine, softened
- 1 egg
- ¼ cup dairy sour cream
- 1 teaspoon vanilla extract
- 2¼ cups all-purpose flour
- 1 teaspoon baking powder
- ½ teaspoon baking soda
- ½ teaspoon salt
- ½ teaspoon ground cinnamon
- 1 cup DOLE® Chopped Almonds

- Preheat oven to 350°F.

- Process bananas in blender; measure 1 cup.

- Beat sugar and margarine until light and fluffy. Beat in egg. Beat in processed bananas, sour cream and vanilla until blended.

- Combine flour, baking powder, baking soda, salt and cinnamon. Stir into banana mixture. Stir in almonds.

- Pour into greased 9×5-inch loaf pan. Bake in preheated oven 65 to 70 minutes or until wooden pick inserted in center comes out clean. Cool in pan 10 minutes. Invert onto wire rack to cool completely.

Makes 1 loaf

Poppy Seed Bread

- 1 cup sugar
- ½ cup margarine, softened
- 2 eggs
- 1 teaspoon grated lemon peel
- 2 extra-ripe, medium DOLE® Bananas, peeled
- 2 cups all-purpose flour
- 2 teaspoons baking powder
- ½ teaspoon salt
- ¼ teaspoon ground cinnamon
- ¼ cup poppy seeds

- Preheat oven to 350°F.

- In large bowl, beat sugar and margarine until light and fluffy. Beat in eggs and lemon peel. Process bananas in blender; measure 1 cup.

- In small bowl, combine flour, baking powder, salt and cinnamon. Add flour mixture to egg mixture alternately with processed bananas, ending with flour mixture. Stir in poppy seeds. Spoon into greased 9×5-inch loaf pan.

- Bake in preheated oven 60 to 70 minutes or until wooden pick inserted in center comes out clean. Cool slightly in pan. Invert onto wire rack to cool completely.

Makes 1 loaf

Classic Banana Bread

Harvest VEGETABLE DISHES

FRESH VEGETABLE CASSEROLE

- 8 small new potatoes
- 8 baby carrots
- 1 small cauliflower, broken into florets
- 4 stalks asparagus, cut into 1-inch pieces
- 3 tablespoons butter or margarine
- 3 tablespoons all-purpose flour
- 2 cups milk
- Salt
- Pepper
- ¾ cup (3 ounces) shredded Cheddar cheese
- Chopped fresh cilantro

Cook vegetables until crisp-tender. Arrange vegetables in buttered 2-quart casserole. To make sauce, melt butter in medium saucepan over medium heat. Stir in flour until smooth. Gradually stir in milk. Cook until thickened, stirring constantly. Season to taste with salt and pepper. Add cheese, stirring until cheese is melted. Pour sauce over vegetables and sprinkle with cilantro. Bake in preheated 350°F oven 15 minutes or until heated through.   *Makes 4 to 6 servings*

— Harvest —

VEGETABLE DISHES

CREAMY CORN AU GRATIN

- ½ cup green onion slices
- ½ cup chopped red pepper
- ¼ cup margarine, divided
- 2 (10-ounce) packages sweet corn, thawed, drained
- ½ pound VELVEETA® Pasteurized Process Cheese Spread, cubed
- ⅔ cup crushed tortilla chips
- ½ teaspoon Mexican seasoning
- 2 tablespoons chopped cilantro

- Cook and stir onions and pepper in 2 tablespoons margarine. Reduce heat to low.

- Stir in corn and process cheese spread. Cook 5 to 7 minutes or until process cheese spread is melted and mixture is thoroughly heated, stirring occasionally.

- Melt remaining margarine in separate pan; stir in tortilla chips and seasoning. Cook over medium heat 3 minutes; stir in cilantro.

- Spoon corn mixture into serving bowl; sprinkle with tortilla mixture. Garnish with additional cilantro and red pepper. *Makes 6 servings*

Preparation Time: 25 minutes

MICROWAVE DIRECTIONS: Microwave onions, peppers and 2 tablespoons margarine in 1½-quart microwavable bowl on HIGH 2 to 3 minutes or until vegetables are tender. Stir in corn and process cheese spread. Microwave 5 to 7 minutes or until process cheese spread is melted and mixture is thoroughly heated, stirring every 3 minutes. Microwave remaining margarine in 1-quart microwavable bowl 1 minute. Stir in tortilla chips and seasoning. Microwave 2 minutes, stirring after 1 minute; stir in cilantro. Continue as directed.

Microwave Cooking Time: 13 minutes

VARIATION: Substitute ¼ teaspoon ground cumin and ¼ teaspoon chili powder for Mexican seasoning.

COUNTRY-STYLE POTATO SALAD

- 2 pounds cooked red potatoes, peeled and diced
- 3 green onions, cut into ½-inch pieces
- 10 cherry tomatoes, halved
- 2 hard-cooked eggs, chopped
- ⅓ cup mayonnaise
- ⅓ cup GREY POUPON® Dijon or Country Dijon Mustard
- 2 tablespoons red wine vinegar
- ½ teaspoon garlic powder
- ⅛ teaspoon ground black pepper

In large bowl, combine potatoes, green onions, tomatoes and eggs; set aside.

In small bowl, blend remaining ingredients; stir into potato mixture, tossing to coat well. Cover; chill at least 2 hours to blend flavors.

Makes 6 (1¼-cup) servings

Creamy Corn au Gratin

SPINACH BAKE

- 2 eggs, beaten
- ¾ cup MIRACLE WHIP® Salad Dressing, divided
- 2 (10-ounce) packages frozen chopped spinach, thawed, well drained
- 1 (14-ounce) can artichoke hearts, drained, cut into quarters
- ½ cup sour cream
- ¼ cup (1 ounce) KRAFT® 100% Grated Parmesan Cheese
- 6 crisply cooked bacon slices, crumbled

• Combine eggs and ½ cup salad dressing, mixing until well blended. Add spinach and artichokes; mix lightly. Spoon mixture into lightly greased 10×6-inch baking dish. Combine remaining salad dressing, sour cream and cheese; mix well. Spoon over spinach mixture. Bake at 350°F 30 minutes or until set. Sprinkle with bacon.

Makes 8 servings

Prep Time: 10 minutes
Bake Time: 30 minutes

MICROWAVE DIRECTIONS: Substitute 1½-quart microwavable casserole for 10×6-inch baking dish. Combine eggs and ½ cup salad dressing in casserole, mixing until well blended. Add spinach and artichokes; mix lightly. Microwave on HIGH (100% power) 8 to 9 minutes or until thoroughly heated, stirring every 3 minutes. Combine remaining salad dressing, sour cream and cheese; mix well. Spoon over spinach mixture. Microwave on HIGH (100% power) 1½ to 2 minutes or until sour cream mixture is warmed. (*Do not overcook.*) Sprinkle with bacon. Let stand 5 minutes.

MICROWAVE TIP: To thaw spinach, place frozen spinach in 1½-quart microwavable casserole; cover. Microwave on HIGH (100% power) 5 minutes. Break apart with fork; drain well.

CAJUN-STYLE GREEN BEANS

- 2 pounds green beans, trimmed
- ½ cup diced salt pork
- 1 clove garlic, minced
- 2 tablespoons white wine vinegar
- 1 tablespoon Dijon-style mustard
- 1 teaspoon sugar
- ½ teaspoon TABASCO® pepper sauce
- ¼ cup chopped celery leaves

In medium saucepan, in 1 inch boiling salted water, cook beans covered 10 minutes or until crisp-tender. Drain. In small skillet over medium-high heat, cook salt pork 2 to 3 minutes to render fat. Reduce heat; add garlic and cook 1 minute. Stir in vinegar, mustard, sugar and TABASCO® sauce. Remove from heat; stir in celery leaves. Toss with beans to coat.

Makes 8 servings

VEGETABLE DISHES

CREAMY BAKED MASHED POTATOES

- 1 envelope LIPTON® Recipe Secrets® Vegetable Soup Mix
- 4 cups hot mashed potatoes*
- 1 cup shredded Cheddar or Swiss cheese (about 4 ounces), divided
- ½ cup chopped green onions (optional)
- 1 egg, slightly beaten
- ⅛ teaspoon LAWRY'S® Seasoned Pepper

*Do not use salt when preparing hot mashed potatoes.

MICROWAVE DIRECTIONS: In lightly greased 1½-quart microwavable casserole, thoroughly combine all ingredients except ¼ cup cheese. Microwave, covered, at HIGH (100% power), turning casserole occasionally, 7 minutes or until heated through. Top with remaining cheese, then let stand covered 5 minutes.

Makes about 8 servings

CONVENTIONAL DIRECTIONS: Preheat oven to 375°F. In lightly greased 1½-quart casserole, thoroughly combine all ingredients except ¼ cup cheese. Bake 40 minutes. Top with remaining cheese and bake an additional 5 minutes or until cheese is melted.

OKRA-BACON CASSEROLE

- 1½ pounds young fresh okra
- 3 large tomatoes, chopped
- 1 medium onion, chopped
- 1 small green pepper, chopped
- ½ teaspoon TABASCO® pepper sauce
- 5 slices bacon

Preheat oven to 350°F. Slice okra into thin rounds. In greased 2½-quart casserole, arrange okra, tomatoes, onion and green pepper. Season with TABASCO® sauce. Place bacon on top. Bake uncovered 1½ hours or until okra is tender.

Makes 6 to 8 servings

NOTE: Two (10-ounce) packages frozen okra, thawed, may be substituted for fresh okra. Bake casserole 1 hour.

MICROWAVE DIRECTIONS: In 2½-quart microwavable casserole place bacon; cover with paper towel. Cook on HIGH (100% power) 4 to 5 minutes or until crisp; remove to paper towel to cool, then crumble and set aside. Into drippings in same casserole place okra, onion and green pepper; season with TABASCO® sauce. Cover loosely with plastic wrap; cook on HIGH (100% power) 15 to 18 minutes or until okra is just tender. Add tomatoes. Cover; cook on HIGH (100% power) 1 to 2 minutes or until tomatoes are tender. Sprinkle with reserved bacon before serving.

Harvest

VEGETABLE DISHES

GREEN BEANS WITH PINE NUTS

- 1 pound green beans, ends removed
- 2 tablespoons butter or margarine
- 2 tablespoons pine nuts
- Salt
- Pepper

Cook beans in 1 inch water in covered 3-quart saucepan 4 to 8 minutes or until crisp-tender; drain. Melt butter in large skillet over medium heat. Add pine nuts; cook, stirring frequently, until golden. Add beans; stir gently to coat beans with butter. Season with salt and pepper to taste.

Makes 4 servings

FRESH CORN WITH ADOBE BUTTER

- ½ teaspoon chili powder
- 1 teaspoon lime juice
- ¼ cup butter or margarine, softened
- Salt
- 4 ears yellow or white corn, husks and silk removed

Moisten chili powder with lime juice in small bowl. Add butter; stir until well blended. Season to taste with salt. Place in small crock or bowl. Place corn in 5-quart pan; cover with cold water. Cover; bring to a boil. Boil 1 minute. Turn off heat; let stand 2 minutes or until corn is tender. Drain. Serve with butter mixture. *Makes 4 servings*

GLAZED SWEET POTATOES AND TURNIPS

- 4 medium sweet potatoes, peeled, cut in chunks
- 4 medium turnips, peeled, cut in chunks
- 1 cup Florida orange juice
- ⅓ cup brown sugar
- ¼ cup butter or margarine, melted
- ½ teaspoon mace
- ½ teaspoon salt
- 2 Florida oranges, peeled, sliced

In large saucepan in 1 inch boiling water, cook potatoes and turnips until crisp-tender, about 30 minutes.

Preheat oven to 400°F.

Place vegetables in 2-quart shallow baking dish. In small bowl, combine orange juice, sugar, butter, mace and salt. Pour over vegetables.

Bake, uncovered, in 400°F oven about 30 minutes. Baste often with pan juices. Vegetables are done when pan juices are reduced and vegetables are glazed. Garnish with orange slices.

Makes 8 servings

Favorite recipe from **Florida Department of Citrus**

Top to bottom: Green Beans with Pine Nuts;
Fresh Corn with Adobe Butter

VEGETABLE DISHES

ACORN SQUASH WITH MAPLE BUTTER

   2 medium acorn squash*
     LAWRY'S® Seasoned Salt
   3 tablespoons margarine or butter
   3 tablespoons maple syrup
   ¼ teaspoon ground nutmeg (optional)

*Butternut squash can be substituted for acorn squash.

Pierce squash with fork. Bake in 375°F oven 1 to 1½ hours or until fork-tender. Cut squash in half crosswise. Slice off ends, if necessary, so halves will be level. Remove seeds. Sprinkle squash with Seasoned Salt. In baking dish, place squash cut-side up. Divide margarine and syrup among halves. Bake 5 minutes. Sprinkle with Seasoned Salt and nutmeg. *Makes 4 servings*

PRESENTATION: Serve in quarters or sliced ½ inch thick.

MICROWAVE DIRECTIONS: Pierce squash in several places; microwave whole squash on HIGH (100% power) 10 to 12 minutes or until fork-tender; let stand 2 minutes and cut in half crosswise. Slice off ends, if necessary, so halves will be level. Remove seeds. Sprinkle squash with Seasoned Salt. In 13×9×2-inch microwavable baking dish, place squash cut-side up. Divide margarine and maple syrup among halves. Cover with plastic wrap, venting one corner. Microwave on HIGH (100% power) 30 seconds; brush syrup mixture over cut surface and microwave on HIGH (100% power) 30 seconds longer. Sprinkle with Seasoned Salt and nutmeg; let squash stand 3 minutes before serving.

CHEDDAR BROCCOLI CORN BAKE

   ¼ cup margarine, divided
   2 tablespoons all-purpose flour
   ¼ teaspoon salt
   1½ cups skim milk
   1½ cups (6 ounces) shredded Cheddar cheese
   2 cups KELLOGG'S CORN FLAKES® cereal, crushed, divided
   1 can (16 ounces) corn, drained
   2 packages (10 ounces each) frozen broccoli spears, cooked and drained

1. Melt 2 tablespoons margarine in large saucepan over low heat. Stir in flour and salt. Add milk gradually, stirring until smooth. Increase heat to medium and cook until bubbly and thickened, stirring constantly. Add cheese, stirring until melted. Stir in ¼ cup crushed Kellogg's Corn Flakes® cereal and corn and remove from heat.

2. Arrange broccoli in 12×7½×2-inch (2-quart) glass baking dish. Pour cheese sauce over broccoli.

3. Melt remaining margarine in saucepan; stir in remaining cereal. Sprinkle over casserole. Bake at 350°F 30 minutes or until heated. *Makes 7 cups*

Acorn Squash with Maple Butter

CORN RELISH

16 to 20 medium-size ears fresh corn in husks (about 10 cups fresh whole kernel corn)
1½ cups chopped green bell peppers
1½ cups chopped red bell peppers
1 cup chopped celery
1 cup chopped onions
4 cups white vinegar (labeled 5% acidity)
2¼ cups sugar
1 cup water
2 tablespoons mustard seed
1 tablespoon plus 1 teaspoon KERR® Pickling Salt
1 teaspoon celery seed
½ teaspoon ground turmeric

Husk corn; remove silk and wash. Drop in boiling water. Return to a boil; boil 5 minutes. Immediately dip in cold water. Cut kernels from cobs. (Do not scrape cobs.) Measure 10 cups cut corn. Combine corn, peppers, celery, onions, vinegar, sugar, water, mustard seed, pickling salt, celery seed and turmeric in 8-quart saucepan. Bring to a boil over medium-high heat; boil 15 minutes, stirring occasionally.

Immediately fill hot pint jars with corn mixture, leaving ½-inch headspace. Carefully run nonmetal spatula down inside of jars to remove trapped air bubbles. Wipe jar tops and threads clean. Place hot lids on jars; screw bands on firmly. Process in Boiling Water Canner (directions follow) 15 minutes.
Makes 6 to 7 pints

Boiling Water Canner Directions: Examine jar tops. Tops with defects will prevent jar from sealing. Wash jars and keep hot to prevent breakage when filled with hot food and placed in canner for processing. Jars to be processed in Boiling Water Canner for less than 10 minutes need to be sterilized. To sterilize, cover jars with water; boil for 10 minutes. Leave in hot water until ready to use.

Examine screwbands. Use only those free from rust and dents. Examine lids. Use only those free from dents and scratches, with a complete ring of sealing compound in the groove. Wash lids; pour boiling water over lids and leave them in hot water for at least 3 minutes or until ready to use. Do not boil or reuse lids.

Fill hot jars as directed, leaving appropriate headspace. Prepare only enough jars of food at one time to fill canner. Place hot lids on jars with sealing compound next to jar top. Center on jars. Screw bands on firmly.

Partially fill canner with water; bring to a simmer. Using jar lifter, place jars, without tipping, onto rack in canner. Increase heat to high; bring to a boil. Cover; reduce heat slightly to maintain gentle, steady boil. Begin timing. Be sure water stays boiling and that it covers jars by 2 inches, adding more boiling water if needed.

VEGETABLE DISHES

When proper time is reached, turn off heat. Remove jars with jar lifter, making sure food does not touch lid. Place on rack or dry towel at least 1 inch apart, free from drafts. Cool overnight. Do not cover while cooling. Do not retighten screwbands after processing.

QUICK DILLS

- 6 pounds 3- to 5-inch pickling cucumbers
- 6 cups water
- 3 cups white vinegar (labeled 5% acidity)
- ½ cup KERR® Pickling Salt
- 12 to 24 heads fresh dill
- 6 to 12 cloves garlic (optional)

Wash cucumbers and remove ¹⁄₁₆ inch from blossom end. Soak in ice water for 24 hours. Drain. Combine water, vinegar and pickling salt in 6-quart saucepan. Bring to a boil over high heat. Meanwhile, place 1 to 2 heads of dill and 1 to 2 cloves garlic in hot quart jars. Firmly pack cucumbers into jars, leaving ½-inch headspace. Top with additional 1 to 2 heads of dill. Immediately fill jars with hot vinegar mixture, leaving ½-inch headspace. Carefully run nonmetal spatula down inside of jars to remove trapped air bubbles. Wipe jar tops and threads clean. Place lids on hot jars and screw bands on firmly. Process in Boiling Water Canner (page 32) for 15 minutes. For best flavor, let stand 2 to 3 weeks in jars before serving.

Makes 6 quarts

WONDERFULLY FLAVORED SKILLET GREENS

- 4 tablespoons margarine
- 2 cups chopped onions
- 2 tablespoons Chef Paul Prudhomme's SEAFOOD MAGIC®, in all
- ½ pound smoked (preferably not water-cured) picnic ham or lean smoked ham, cut into ½-inch pieces
- 2 cups peeled, chopped tomatoes
- 1 teaspoon minced garlic
- 2 bay leaves
- 1¼ pounds cleaned and picked over mustard and/or collard greens, torn into pieces (about 12 packed cups)
- 2 cups water, in all

Melt margarine in 4-quart saucepan over high heat. Add onions and sauté about 4 minutes, stirring occasionally. Add 1 tablespoon of the Seafood Magic®, stirring well. Cook until onions start to brown, about 3 minutes, stirring occasionally. Add ham and cook about 2 minutes, stirring fairly often. Add tomatoes, garlic and bay leaves, stirring well; cook about 1 minute. Add greens and cook about 7 minutes, stirring occasionally. Stir in remaining Seafood Magic® and cook about 2 minutes. Add ½ cup water; reduce heat to low and simmer about 20 minutes, stirring occasionally. Add remaining water and continue simmering until greens are tender and flavors blend, about 25 minutes more, stirring occasionally. Discard bay leaves and serve immediately.

Makes 6 servings

Harvest

VEGETABLE DISHES

BAKED POTATO SPEARS

3 large baking potatoes
¼ cup MIRACLE WHIP® Light Reduced Calorie Salad Dressing
Onion salt
Pepper
Parma Dip (recipe follows)
Hearty Barbecue Dip (recipe follows)

- Cut potatoes lengthwise into wedges. Brush with salad dressing. Season with onion salt and pepper.
- Place on greased 15×10×1-inch jelly roll pan.
- Bake at 375°F, 50 minutes or until tender and golden brown.
- Prepare Parma Dip and Hearty Barbecue Dip. Serve with potatoes. *Makes 4 servings*

Parma Dip
1 cup MIRACLE WHIP® Light Reduced Calorie Salad Dressing
¼ cup (1 ounce) KRAFT® 100% Grated Parmesan Cheese
¼ cup milk
1 tablespoon chopped chives

- Combine ingredients; mix well. *Makes 1¼ cups*

Hearty Barbecue Dip
½ cup MIRACLE WHIP® Light Reduced Calorie Salad Dressing
¼ cup KRAFT® Thick 'n Spicy Barbecue Sauce with Honey
2 tablespoons chopped onion
2 tablespoons chopped green pepper

- Combine ingredients; mix well. *Makes 1 cup*

Preparation Time: 10 minutes
Baking Time: 50 minutes

TIP: For a more blended flavor, prepare dips ahead of time. Cover; chill.

OLD-FASHIONED COLE SLAW

½ cup reduced calorie mayonnaise
2 tablespoons milk
1 tablespoon white vinegar
½ teaspoon sugar
Salt and pepper to taste
1 bag (1 pound) DOLE® Cole Slaw Blend

- Combine mayonnaise, milk, vinegar, sugar, salt and pepper in glass measure.
- Place Cole Slaw Blend in large bowl. Pour dressing over mixture. Toss to coat with dressing.
- Cover; refrigerate at least 1 hour for flavors to blend. *Makes 8 servings*

Baked Potato Spears

VEGETABLE DISHES

CORN PUDDING SOUFFLÉ

  2 tablespoons butter or margarine
  2 tablespoons all-purpose flour
     Half-and-half
  1 can (17 ounces) whole kernel corn, drained, liquid reserved
  ¼ cup canned chopped green chilies, drained
     Dash garlic powder
  2 eggs, separated
  ¼ cup cream-style cottage cheese

Melt butter in medium saucepan over medium heat. Stir in flour until smooth. Add enough half-and-half to corn liquid to measure 1 cup. Gradually stir liquid into saucepan. Continue stirring until sauce is smooth and hot. Stir in corn, chilies and garlic powder.

Bring to a boil over medium heat, stirring constantly. Reduce heat to low. Beat egg yolks in small bowl. Stir about ¼ cup of the hot sauce into egg yolks, beating constantly. Stir egg yolk mixture back into sauce. Remove from heat; stir in cottage cheese. Beat egg whites in narrow bowl until stiff peaks form. Fold egg whites into corn mixture. Pour into ungreased 1½-quart soufflé dish. Bake in preheated 350°F oven 30 minutes or until wooden pick inserted in center comes out clean.

Makes 4 to 6 servings

TOMATO GINGER APPLE SALAD

  2 Golden Delicious or Granny Smith apples, cored and sliced into ¼-inch rings
  4 medium tomatoes, sliced into ¼-inch rings
  ¼ cup thinly sliced radishes
  ¼ cup chopped parsley
  ¼ cup vegetable oil
  2 teaspoons grated fresh ginger
  1 teaspoon sugar
  1 teaspoon lemon juice
  ½ teaspoon grated lemon peel
     Salt and pepper to taste
     Parsley or cilantro sprigs (optional)

Arrange apple and tomato slices alternately on serving platter; sprinkle with radishes and parsley. In small bowl, combine oil, ginger, sugar, lemon juice and lemon peel; season to taste with salt and pepper. Drizzle mixture over arranged salad. Marinate salad in refrigerator 1 to 2 hours. Garnish with parsley or cilantro sprigs, if desired.

Makes 4 servings

Favorite recipe from **Washington Apple Commission**

Corn Pudding Soufflé

Heartwarming HOME-STYLE SUPPERS

HICKORY BEEF KABOBS

1 pound boneless beef top sirloin or
   tenderloin steak, cut into 1¼-inch pieces
4 small ears thawed frozen corn, cut into
   1-inch pieces
1 green or red bell pepper, cut into 1-inch pieces
1 small red onion, cut into ½-inch wedges
½ cup beer or nonalcoholic beer
½ cup chili sauce
1 teaspoon dry mustard
2 cloves garlic, minced
1½ cups hickory chips
   Hot cooked rice (optional)

Place beef and vegetables in plastic bag. Combine next 4 ingredients in bowl; pour into bag. Seal; turn to coat. Refrigerate 1 to 8 hours; turn occasionally. Soak hickory chips in cold water 20 minutes. Drain beef and vegetables; reserve marinade. Alternately thread beef and vegetables onto skewers. Brush with marinade. Drain chips; sprinkle over medium-hot coals. Grill kabobs 10 to 12 minutes or until desired doneness. Brush with marinade and turn over once; discard remaining marinade. Serve over rice.

Makes 4 servings

– Heartwarming –

HOME-STYLE SUPPERS

PATCHWORK CASSEROLE

- 2 pounds ground beef
- 2 cups chopped green bell pepper
- 1 cup chopped onion
- 2 pounds frozen Southern-style hash-brown potatoes, thawed
- 2 cans (8 ounces each) tomato sauce
- 1 cup water
- 1 can (6 ounces) tomato paste
- 1 teaspoon salt
- ½ teaspoon dried basil, crumbled
- ¼ teaspoon ground black pepper
- 1 pound pasteurized process American cheese, thinly sliced

Preheat oven to 350°F.

Cook and stir beef in large skillet over medium heat until crumbled and brown, about 10 minutes; drain off fat.

Add green pepper and onion; cook and stir until tender, about 4 minutes. Stir in potatoes, tomato sauce, water, tomato paste, salt, basil and black pepper.

Spoon ½ mixture into 13×9×2-inch baking pan or 3-quart baking dish; top with half of cheese. Spoon remaining meat mixture evenly on top of cheese. Cover pan with aluminum foil. Bake 45 minutes.

Cut remaining cheese into decorative shapes; place on top of casserole. Let stand loosely covered until cheese melts, about 5 minutes.

Makes 8 to 10 servings

BAKED COUNTRY CURED HAM

- 1 country cured ham, 10 to 14 pounds
  Whole cloves
- 6 cups hot water
- 1 cup vinegar
- 1 cup cider
- 1 tablespoon Worcestershire sauce
- 2 bay leaves
- 1 cup molasses

Remove rind or skin from ham without removing the delicate layer of fat. Gently wash ham under running water. Pat dry and score fat into diamond shapes. Place a whole clove in each diamond. Insert meat thermometer into meaty part of ham, being careful not to touch fat or bone. Place ham, fat side up, in large roasting pan with cover. Use heavy duty aluminum foil to make a cover, if necessary. In large bowl, combine water, vinegar, cider and Worcestershire sauce; pour over ham. Place bay leaves in liquid. Bake at 325°F 20 minutes per pound or to an internal temperature of 160°F. Baste often during cooking time with molasses. Bake uncovered last 30 minutes. Decorate with fruit, if desired. Cool before slicing.

Makes 20 to 25 servings

Favorite recipe from **National Pork Producers Council**

Patchwork Casserole

– *Heartwarming* –

Home-Style Suppers

TEXAS-STYLE DEEP-DISH CHILI PIE

- 1 pound beef stew meat, cut into ½-inch cubes
- 1 tablespoon vegetable oil
- 2 cans (14½ ounces *each*) Mexican-style stewed tomatoes, undrained
- 1 medium green bell pepper, diced
- 1 package (1 ounce) LAWRY'S® Taco Spices & Seasonings
- 1 tablespoon yellow cornmeal
- 1 can (15¼ ounces) kidney beans, drained
- 1 package (15 ounces) flat refrigerated pie crusts
- ½ cup (2 ounces) shredded Cheddar cheese, divided

In Dutch oven, brown beef in oil; drain fat. Add stewed tomatoes, bell pepper, Taco Spices & Seasonings and cornmeal. Bring to a boil; reduce heat and simmer, uncovered, 20 minutes. Add kidney beans.

In 10-inch pie plate, unfold 1 crust and fill with chili mixture and ¼ cup cheese. Top with remaining crust, fluting edges. Bake, uncovered, in 350°F oven 30 minutes. Sprinkle remaining cheese over crust; return to oven and bake 10 minutes longer.

Makes 6 servings

PORK ROAST WITH CORN BREAD & OYSTER STUFFING

- 1 (5- to 7-pound) pork loin roast*
- 2 tablespoons butter or margarine
- ½ cup chopped onion
- ½ cup chopped celery
- 2 cloves garlic, minced
- ½ teaspoon fennel seeds, crushed
- 1 teaspoon TABASCO® pepper sauce
- ½ teaspoon salt
- 2 cups packaged corn bread stuffing mix
- 1 can (8 ounces) oysters, undrained, chopped

*Have butcher crack backbone of pork loin roast.

Preheat oven to 325°F. Make a deep slit in back of each chop on pork loin. In large saucepan, melt butter; add onion, celery, garlic and fennel seeds. Cook 5 minutes or until vegetables are tender; stir in TABASCO® sauce and salt. Add stuffing mix, oysters and oyster liquid; toss to mix well.

Stuff corn bread mixture into slits in pork. (Any leftover stuffing may be baked in covered baking dish during last 30 minutes of roasting.) Place meat in shallow roasting pan. Cook 30 to 35 minutes per pound or until meat thermometer inserted into meat registers 170°F. Remove to heated serving platter. Allow meat to stand 15 minutes before serving.

Makes 10 to 12 servings

Texas-Style Deep-Dish Chili Pie

— Heartwarming —

HOME-STYLE SUPPERS

SAUSAGE SKILLET DINNER

- 12 ounces fully cooked smoked pork link sausage, cut diagonally into 1-inch pieces
- 2 tablespoons water
- 1 medium onion
- 2 small red apples
- 2 tablespoons butter, divided
- 12 ounces natural frozen potato wedges
- ¼ cup cider vinegar
- 3 tablespoons sugar
- ½ teaspoon caraway seeds
- 2 tablespoons chopped fresh parsley

Place sausage and water in large nonstick skillet; cover tightly and cook over medium heat 8 minutes, stirring occasionally. Meanwhile, cut onion into 12 wedges; core and cut each apple into 8 wedges. Remove sausage to warm platter. Pour off drippings. Cook and stir onion and apples in 1 tablespoon of butter in same skillet, 4 minutes or until apples are crisp-tender. Remove to sausage platter.

Heat remaining 1 tablespoon butter; add potatoes and cook, covered, over medium-high heat 5 minutes or until potatoes are tender and golden brown, stirring occasionally. Combine vinegar, sugar and caraway seeds. Reduce heat; return sausage, apple mixture and vinegar mixture to skillet. Cook 1 minute or until heated through, stirring gently. Sprinkle with parsley.

Makes 4 servings

Favorite recipe from **National Cattlemen's Beef Association**

CORNED BEEF, POTATO AND PEPPER HASH

- Water
- 1 teaspoon salt
- 1 pound Russet potatoes, cut into ½-inch cubes
- 2 tablespoons butter, divided
- 1 medium onion, coarsely chopped
- ⅓ cup *each* chopped red, yellow and green bell peppers
- 12 ounces cooked corned beef, cut into ½-inch cubes
- 3 tablespoons chopped parsley
- ¼ cup half-and-half
- 3 tablespoons dry white wine
- ½ teaspoon dry mustard
- ⅛ teaspoon black pepper

Bring water to a boil in large saucepan; add salt and potatoes. Return to a boil. Cook 5 minutes; drain well. Melt 1 tablespoon butter in cast-iron or large heavy skillet over medium-high heat; add onion and bell peppers. Cook and stir 2 minutes or until crisp-tender; remove from pan. Add corned beef, potatoes and parsley to onion mixture; mix lightly. Combine half-and-half, wine, mustard and pepper; add to corned beef mixture and mix well. Wipe out cast-iron skillet with paper towel; place over medium heat until hot. Add remaining butter. Add beef mixture, pressing down firmly. Cook 15 minutes or until browned; turn with spatula several times.

Makes 4 servings

Favorite recipe from **National Cattlemen's Beef Association**

Sausage Skillet Dinner

— Heartwarming —

Home-Style Suppers

STRING PIE

- 1 pound ground beef
- ½ cup chopped onion
- ¼ cup chopped green pepper
- 1 jar (15½ ounces) spaghetti sauce
- 8 ounces spaghetti, cooked and drained
- ⅓ cup grated Parmesan cheese
- 2 eggs, beaten
- 2 teaspoons butter
- 1 cup cottage cheese
- ½ cup (2 ounces) shredded mozzarella cheese

Cook beef, onion and green pepper in large skillet over medium-high heat until meat is brown, stirring to separate meat. Drain fat. Stir in spaghetti sauce; mix well. Combine spaghetti, Parmesan cheese, eggs and butter in large bowl; mix well. Place in bottom of 13×9-inch pan. Spread cottage cheese over top. Pour sauce mixture over cottage cheese. Sprinkle mozzarella cheese over top. Bake in preheated 350°F oven until cheese melts, about 20 minutes.

Makes 6 to 8 servings

Favorite recipe from **North Dakota Beef Commission**

HAM WITH FRUITED MUSTARD SAUCE

- 1 fully cooked ham slice (1 to 1¼ pounds), cut ½ inch thick*
- 1 tablespoon butter or margarine
- 1 can (8 ounces) pineapple slices, undrained
- ¼ cup HEINZ® 57 Sauce
- 2 tablespoons honey
- 1 tablespoon prepared mustard
- 1½ teaspoons cornstarch
- Dash ground allspice

*A 1-pound piece of Canadian bacon, cut into 4 slices, may be substituted.

Cut ham into 4 serving portions. In large skillet, cook ham in butter 3 to 4 minutes on each side or until heated through. Meanwhile, drain pineapple, reserving juice. In small bowl, combine juice, 57 Sauce, honey, mustard, cornstarch and allspice. Remove ham from skillet; keep warm. Pour 57 Sauce mixture into skillet and cook until thickened. Return ham to skillet. Top each ham portion with pineapple slice and spoon sauce over; heat through.

Makes 4 servings (about ⅔ cups sauce)

String Pie

— Heartwarming —

T-BONE STEAKS WITH VEGETABLE KABOBS

- 4 beef T-bone steaks, cut 1 to 1½ inches thick
- Salt and pepper
- Vegetable Kabobs (recipe follows)

Grill steaks over medium coals. When first sides are browned, turn and season with salt and pepper; finish cooking second sides. Turn and season. Steaks cut 1 inch thick require about 16 minutes for rare; 20 minutes for medium. Steaks cut 1½ inches thick require about 22 minutes for rare; 30 minutes for medium. Serve with Vegetable Kabobs.

Makes 4 servings

Vegetable Kabobs
- 2 large potatoes (about 1½ pounds)
- 1 large sweet onion
- 3 tablespoons butter, melted
- 1 teaspoon paprika
- ½ teaspoon celery salt
- ¼ teaspoon garlic powder
- ⅛ teaspoon freshly ground pepper

Cook potatoes (do not peel) in boiling salted water 20 minutes; drain. Cut each potato crosswise into four 1-inch-thick slices. Cut onion crosswise into four 1-inch-thick slices. Alternately thread 2 potato slices and 1 onion slice, through skin of vegetables, on each of four 8-inch skewers. Combine butter, paprika, celery salt, garlic powder and pepper. Brush both sides of vegetables with seasoned butter. Grill kabobs over medium coals 20 minutes, turning after 10 minutes and brushing with seasoned butter occasionally.

Makes 4 servings

Favorite recipe from **National Cattlemen's Beef Association**

FAMILY BAKED BEAN DINNER

- 1 can (20 ounces) DOLE® Pineapple Chunks in Juice
- ½ DOLE® Green Bell Pepper, julienne-cut
- ½ cup chopped onion
- 1 pound Polish sausage or frankfurters, cut into 1-inch chunks
- ⅓ cup packed brown sugar
- 1 teaspoon dry mustard
- 2 cans (16 ounces each) baked beans

- **MICROWAVE DIRECTIONS:** Drain pineapple; reserve juice for beverage. Add green pepper and onion to 13×9-inch microwavable dish.

- Cover; microwave on HIGH (100% power) 3 minutes. Add sausage, arranging around edges of dish. Cover; continue microwaving on HIGH (100% power) 6 minutes.

- In bowl, combine brown sugar and mustard; stir in beans and pineapple. Add to sausage mixture. Stir to combine. Microwave, uncovered, on HIGH (100% power) 8 to 10 minutes, stirring after 4 minutes.

Makes 6 servings

T-Bone Steaks with Vegetable Kabobs

Heartwarming

HOME-STYLE SUPPERS

LAMB & PORK CASSOULET

- **1 package (1 pound) dry white navy beans, rinsed**
- **Water**
- **½ pound salt pork, sliced**
- **1½ pounds boneless lamb shoulder or leg, cut into 1-inch cubes**
- **4 large pork chops**
- **½ pound pork sausages**
- **Salt**
- **Pepper**
- **2 large onions, chopped**
- **1 can (28 ounces) tomatoes, drained**
- **½ cup dry red wine**
- **3 cloves garlic, finely chopped**
- **¼ cup chopped fresh parsley**
- **1 teaspoon dried thyme, crushed**
- **1 bay leaf**

Place beans in large bowl. Cover with cold water; soak overnight. Drain and rinse beans. Place beans in Dutch oven; cover with cold water. Bring to a boil over high heat. Skim foam as necessary. Reduce heat to low. Cover and simmer about 1 hour. Drain beans, reserving liquid.

Fry salt pork in large skillet over medium-high heat until some of the fat is rendered. Remove salt pork. In batches, brown lamb, pork chops and sausages in fat. Remove from skillet; drain on paper towels. Cut chops and sausages into 1-inch pieces. Sprinkle meat with salt and pepper. Remove all but 2 tablespoons of the fat from skillet. Add onions. Cook and stir over medium-high heat until onions are tender. Add tomatoes, wine, garlic, parsley, thyme and bay leaf. Combine tomato mixture, drained beans and meats in large bowl. Spoon into large casserole. Pour reserved bean liquid over mixture just to cover. Bake at 350°F about 1½ hours or until meat is fork-tender. Remove bay leaf before serving.

Makes 6 to 8 servings

Favorite recipe from **American Lamb Council**

SPICY BARBECUE BEEF

- **½ cup A.1.® Steak Sauce**
- **⅓ cup chili sauce**
- **3 tablespoons GREY POUPON® Dijon Mustard**
- **¼ cup water**
- **1 pound beef top round steak**
- **1 tablespoon vegetable oil**
- **1 large onion, sliced**
- **Hot cooked wide noodles (optional)**

In small bowl, combine steak sauce, chili sauce, mustard and water; set aside.

In large skillet, over medium-high heat, brown steak in oil. Add onion, stirring until lightly browned. Stir in sauce mixture; heat to a boil. Cover; reduce heat and simmer 1½ hours or until steak is tender. Slice steak and serve with noodles if desired.

Makes 4 servings

Lamb & Pork Cassoulet

HOME-STYLE SUPPERS

TEXAS-STYLE BEEF BRISKET

- **6 to 8 pounds boneless beef brisket**
- **¾ cup finely chopped onion**
- **2 teaspoons paprika**
- **½ teaspoon freshly ground pepper**
- **Water**
- **1 cup prepared steak sauce**
- **Special Sauce (recipe follows)**

Trim fat covering on brisket to ¼ inch. Combine onion, paprika and pepper. Rub mixture evenly over surface of brisket. Place brisket, fat side up, in large disposable aluminum pan. Add ½ cup water. Cover pan tightly with aluminum foil. Place in center of grid over very low coals. (Single layer of coals with space in between each.) Place cover on cooker and cook 5 hours, turning brisket over every 1½ hours. (Remove fat from pan with baster as it accumulates.) Add ½ cup water, as needed, to pan. (Be sure to add briquets as needed to keep coals at very low temperature.)

Remove foil from pan. Remove brisket; place on grid directly over very low coals. Combine pan drippings with steak sauce; reserve 1 cup for Special Sauce. Brush part of remaining steak sauce mixture over brisket. Replace cover and continue cooking 1 hour, brushing occasionally with steak sauce mixture. Serve brisket with Special Sauce.

Makes 24 to 30 servings

Special Sauce: Cook ½ cup finely chopped onion in 2 tablespoons butter until tender. Stir in 1 cup reserved steak sauce/beef drippings mixture, 1 cup ketchup, 1 tablespoon brown sugar and ¼ to ½ teaspoon crushed red pepper. Simmer 10 minutes.

Makes 2 cups

Favorite recipe from **National Cattlemen's Beef Association**

SHEPHERD'S PIE

- **2 cups diced cooked leg of American lamb**
- **2 large potatoes, cubed and cooked**
- **3 green onions, sliced**
- **1 cup cooked peas**
- **1 cup cooked carrot slices**
- **1 clove garlic, minced**
- **2 cups prepared brown gravy**
- **1 teaspoon black pepper**
- **2 sheets prepared pie dough***

*Or, use mashed potatoes on top in place of second crust.

In large bowl, combine lamb, potatoes, green onions, peas, carrots, garlic, brown gravy and black pepper.

Place 1 sheet pie dough in pie plate; fill with lamb mixture. Cover with second sheet of pie dough. Crimp edges; cut slits in top to allow steam to escape.

Bake 30 minutes at 350°F or until pie crust is golden brown.   *Makes 4 to 6 servings*

Favorite recipe from **American Lamb Council**

Texas-Style Beef Brisket

Country CHICKEN & TURKEY

CHICKEN AND HAM WITH RICE

- ¾ pound boned chicken breasts, cut into strips
- 4 ounces boiled ham, cut into strips
- 2 tablespoons butter or margarine
- 1 can (10¾ ounces) condensed cream of chicken soup
- 1 cup water
- 2 tablespoons Dijon-style mustard (optional)
- 1 package (10 ounces) asparagus cuts, thawed
- 1½ cups MINUTE® Rice
- 2 slices Swiss cheese, cut into wedges or small cubes

- Cook and stir chicken and ham in hot butter in large skillet until lightly browned.

- Stir in soup, water and mustard; add asparagus. Bring to a boil. Stir in rice and top with cheese. Cover; remove from heat.

- Let stand 5 minutes. Fluff with fork.

Makes 4 servings

Country

Tasty turkey pot pie

- ½ cup MIRACLE WHIP® Salad Dressing
- 2 tablespoons flour
- 1 teaspoon instant chicken bouillon
- ⅛ teaspoon pepper
- ¾ cup milk
- 1½ cups chopped cooked turkey or chicken
- 1 (10-ounce) package frozen mixed vegetables, thawed, drained
- 1 (4-ounce) can refrigerated crescent rolls

- Combine salad dressing, flour, bouillon and pepper in medium saucepan. Gradually add milk.

- Cook, stirring constantly, over low heat until thickened. Add turkey and vegetables; heat thoroughly, stirring occasionally.

- Spoon into 8-inch square baking dish. Unroll dough into two rectangles. Press perforations together to seal. Place rectangles side-by-side to form square; press edges together to form seam. Cover turkey mixture with dough.

- Bake at 375°F 15 to 20 minutes or until browned.

Makes 4 to 6 servings

Preparation Time: 15 minutes
Baking Time: 20 minutes

VARIATIONS: Combine 1 egg, beaten and 1 tablespoon cold water, mixing until well blended. Brush dough with egg mixture just before baking.

Substitute one chicken bouillon cube for instant chicken bouillon.

Substitute 10×6-inch baking dish for 8-inch square baking dish.

Substitute 12×8-inch baking dish for 8-inch square dish. Double all ingredients. Assemble recipe as directed, using three dough rectangles to form top crust. Decorate crust with cutouts from remaining rectangle. Bake as directed.

MICROWAVE TIP: To prepare sauce, combine salad dressing, flour, bouillon and pepper in 1-quart microwavable measure or bowl; gradually add milk. Microwave on HIGH 4 to 5 minutes or until thickened, stirring after each minute.

Tasty Turkey Pot Pie

Country

DOWN-HOME CORN AND CHICKEN CASSEROLE

- **2 chickens (2 to 3 pounds each), each cut into 10 pieces**
- **3 tablespoons Chef Paul Prudhomme's POULTRY MAGIC®, in all**
- **⅓ cup vegetable oil**
- **8 cups fresh corn, cut off cob (about twelve 8-inch ears), in all**
- **3½ cups finely chopped onions**
- **1½ cups finely chopped green bell peppers**
- **1 pound tomatoes, peeled, chopped**
- **3½ cups water**
- **2 cups uncooked rice**

Remove excess fat from chickens; season chicken pieces with 2 tablespoons of the Poultry Magic® and place in plastic bag. Seal and refrigerate overnight.

Heat oil in an 8-quart roasting pan over high heat until it just starts to smoke, about 6 minutes. Add the 10 largest pieces of chicken (skin side down first) and brown, cooking 5 minutes on each side. Remove chicken and reheat oil about 1 minute or until oil stops sizzling. Brown remaining chicken 5 minutes on each side. Remove and keep warm.

Add half of corn to hot oil. Scrape bottom of pan well to get up all browned chicken bits and stir to mix well. Let corn cook, without stirring, about 6 minutes. You want it to brown and to start breaking down starch. Add ½ tablespoon Poultry Magic® and stir to combine. Let mixture cook, without stirring, about 7 minutes to continue browning process. Stir in onions, bell peppers and remaining ½ tablespoon Poultry Magic®. Cover with tight-fitting lid and cook about 5 minutes. Add remaining corn and tomatoes. Stir to mix well; cover and cook 10 minutes. Transfer corn mixture to another pan and keep warm. Preheat oven to 400°F.

Add water and rice to roasting pan. Bring to a boil, stirring occasionally. Layer chicken pieces on top of rice and cover chicken layer with corn mixture. Cover and bake 25 minutes.

Remove casserole from oven. Let stand 10 minutes, covered, then serve. *Makes 8 servings*

Down-Home Corn and Chicken Casserole

— Country —

TURKEY COTTAGE PIE

- ¼ cup butter or margarine
- ¼ cup all-purpose flour
- 1 envelope LIPTON® Recipe Secrets® Golden Onion Soup Mix
- 2 cups water
- 2 cups cut-up cooked turkey or chicken
- 1 package (10 ounces) frozen mixed vegetables, thawed
- 1¼ cups shredded Swiss cheese (about 5 ounces), divided
- ⅛ teaspoon pepper
- 5 cups hot mashed potatoes

Preheat oven to 375°F.

In large saucepan, melt butter and add flour; cook, stirring constantly, 5 minutes or until golden. Stir in golden onion soup mix thoroughly blended with water. Bring to a boil, then simmer 15 minutes or until thickened. Stir in turkey, vegetables, 1 cup cheese and pepper. Turn into lightly greased 2-quart casserole; top with hot potatoes, then remaining ¼ cup cheese. Bake 30 minutes or until bubbling. *Makes about 8 servings*

MICROWAVE DIRECTIONS: In 2-quart casserole, heat butter at HIGH (100% power) 1 minute. Stir in flour and heat uncovered, stirring frequently, 2 minutes. Stir in golden onion soup mix thoroughly blended with water. Heat uncovered, stirring occasionally, 4 minutes or until thickened. Stir in turkey, vegetables, 1 cup cheese and pepper. Top with hot potatoes, then remaining ¼ cup cheese. Heat uncovered, turning casserole occasionally, 5 minutes or until bubbling. Let stand uncovered 5 minutes. For additional color, sprinkle, if desired, with paprika.

GOLDEN CHICKEN NORMANDY-STYLE

- 1 (2½- to 3-pound) chicken, cut-up
- Salt and pepper
- ¼ cup flour
- 2 tablespoons butter or margarine
- 2 Golden Delicious apples (about 12 ounces), cored and sliced
- ¾ cup half-and-half
- ⅓ cup dry white wine
- 1 tablespoon lemon juice
- 2 tablespoons chopped fresh parsley

Season chicken with salt and pepper; coat in flour. In large skillet, melt butter. Brown chicken on all sides; remove from skillet. Add apples; brown lightly. Place chicken and apples in shallow 2½-quart baking dish. Bake at 350°F 20 minutes or until chicken is tender. Reserve 2 tablespoons pan drippings in skillet. Add half-and-half to skillet; cook and stir until thickened. Blend in wine and lemon juice. Add salt and pepper to taste; pour over chicken and apples. Sprinkle with chopped parsley. *Makes 4 servings*

Favorite recipe from **Washington Apple Commission**

Turkey Cottage Pie

CHICKEN & TURKEY

POTLUCK POCKETS

    Nonstick cooking spray
½ **pound lean ground turkey**
¾ **cup chopped onions**
1 **clove garlic, minced**
½ **cup sliced mushrooms**
1 **jar (14 ounces) spaghetti sauce**
2½ **cups all-purpose flour, divided**
½ **cup cornmeal**
2 **teaspoons baking powder**
½ **teaspoon dried oregano leaves**
¼ **cup margarine**
1¼ **cups KELLOGG'S® ALL-BRAN® cereal**
1 **cup skim milk**
½ **cup (2 ounces) shredded part-skim mozzarella cheese**

In large skillet coated with nonstick cooking spray, cook turkey, onions and garlic over medium heat. Stir in mushrooms and spaghetti sauce. Cover; simmer an additional 20 minutes, stirring occasionally.

In medium bowl, stir together 2 cups flour, cornmeal, baking powder and oregano. With pastry blender, cut in margarine until mixture resembles coarse crumbs.

In small bowl, combine Kellogg's® All-Bran® cereal and milk. Let stand 3 minutes or until milk is absorbed. Add cereal mixture to flour mixture, stirring with fork until dough forms ball.

On lightly floured surface, knead in remaining flour until dough is smooth and elastic. Divide dough in half; roll to ⅛-inch thickness. With pastry cutter or small saucepan lid, cut dough into 6-inch rounds. Cover each round with 2 teaspoons cheese; top with ¼ cup turkey mixture. Fold rounds in half, pinching dough with fork to seal. Repeat with remaining dough. Place on baking sheet coated with nonstick cooking spray.

Bake at 350°F 20 minutes or until lightly browned. Serve warm. *Makes 12 servings*

FANCY CHICKEN PUFF PIE

4 **tablespoons butter or margarine**
¼ **cup chopped shallots**
¼ **cup all-purpose flour**
1 **cup chicken stock or broth**
¼ **cup sherry**
    Salt to taste
⅛ **teaspoon white pepper**
    Pinch ground nutmeg
¼ **pound ham, cut into 2×¼-inch strips**
3 **cups cooked PERDUE® chicken, cut into 2¼-inch strips**
1½ **cups fresh asparagus pieces *or* 1 (10-ounce) package frozen asparagus pieces**
1 **cup (½ pint) heavy cream**
    Chilled pie crust for a 1-crust pie *or* 1 sheet frozen puff pastry
1 **egg, beaten**

CHICKEN & TURKEY

In medium saucepan over medium-high heat, melt butter; cook and stir shallots lightly. Stir in flour; cook 3 minutes. Add broth and sherry. Heat to boiling, stirring constantly; season to taste with salt, pepper and nutmeg. Reduce heat to low and simmer 5 minutes. Stir in ham, chicken, asparagus and cream. Pour chicken mixture into ungreased 9-inch pie plate.

Preheat oven to 425°F. Cut 8-inch circle from crust. Cut hearts from extra dough with cookie cutter, if desired. Place circle on cookie sheet moistened with cold water. Pierce with fork, brush with egg and decorate with hearts; brush hearts with egg.

Bake crust and filled pie plate 10 minutes; reduce heat to 350°F and bake additional 10 to 15 minutes or until pastry is golden brown and filling is hot and set. With spatula, place pastry over hot filling and serve immediately.

Makes 4 servings

TASTY TURKEY ROLL

- **1 pound ground turkey**
- **½ cup soft bread crumbs**
- **¼ cup tomato juice**
- **1 egg, beaten**
- **2 cloves garlic, minced**
- **¼ teaspoon dried oregano**
- **¼ teaspoon pepper**
- **¼ pound shaved turkey ham**
- **1 cup grated mozzarella cheese**
- **2 tablespoons chili sauce (optional)**

In medium bowl, combine ground turkey, bread crumbs, juice, egg, garlic, oregano and pepper.

On rectangular 16×12-inch piece of waxed paper, shape turkey mixture into 12×9-inch rectangle. Place turkey ham over top of turkey mixture and sprinkle cheese over turkey ham. Roll turkey, jelly-roll style, using waxed paper to help make roll. Lightly press ends of roll to seal. Place turkey roll, seam side down, on baking sheet lightly coated with nonstick cooking spray.

Bake at 350°F 1 hour or until center of turkey roll reaches 160°F on meat thermometer and ground turkey is no longer pink.

To serve, drizzle 2 tablespoons chili sauce over top of roll, if desired, and cut into 12 equal pieces.

Makes 12 servings

Favorite recipe from **National Turkey Federation**

Country

GRILLED ROASTER WITH INTERNATIONAL BASTING SAUCES

1 PERDUE® Oven Stuffer Roaster
   (5 to 7 pounds)
Salt
Ground pepper
1 cup vegetable oil
⅓ cup red wine vinegar
1 teaspoon paprika

Remove and discard giblets from roaster; rinse bird and pat dry with paper towels. Sprinkle inside and out with salt and pepper; set aside. To prepare basting sauce, in small covered jar, combine oil, vinegar, paprika, 1 teaspoon salt and ½ teaspoon pepper. Shake well; set aside.

If using a gas grill, follow manufacturer's directions. If using a covered charcoal grill, prepare coals at least 30 minutes before grilling. Open all vents and place a drip pan at center in bottom of grill. Arrange 25 to 30 hot coals at either end of drip pan. For added smoky flavor, soak 1 cup mesquite, hickory, oak, apple or cherry wood chips in water and scatter onto hot coals.

When coals are covered with gray ash and are medium-hot (you can hold your hand over them 3 to 4 seconds), place roaster on grill over drip pan. Cover with grill lid and cook roaster about 2 hours until Bird Watcher thermometer pops up and juices run clear with no hint of pink when thigh is pierced. (Note: Smoking may cause meat to remain slightly pink.) Begin checking roaster for doneness after 1½ hours. If thermometer has popped, brush on basting sauce and grill 30 minutes longer. In small saucepan, bring remaining basting sauce to a boil; serve with carved roaster. Do not reuse sauce.

Makes 6 servings

SAUCE VARIATIONS:

Italian Roaster: Prepare basting sauce as directed, adding 2 cloves minced garlic, 1 cup ketchup, 1 teaspoon dried oregano and ½ teaspoon dried basil to mixture. Use only in last 10 minutes of grilling.

French Roaster: Prepare basting sauce as directed, adding ⅓ cup minced shallots, ⅓ cup Dijon-style mustard and 1 teaspoon crumbled dried tarragon to mixture.

German Roaster: Prepare basting sauce as directed, adding ½ cup beer, 2 tablespoons molasses and 2 tablespoons caraway seeds to mixture. Use only in last 10 minutes of grilling.

Chinese Roaster: Prepare basting sauce as directed, adding ⅓ cup soy sauce, 2 cloves minced garlic and 1 teaspoon ground ginger or 1 tablespoon grated fresh ginger root to mixture.

Grilled Roaster with International Basting Sauces

DAIRYLAND CONFETTI CHICKEN

- 1 cup diced carrots
- ¾ cup chopped onion
- ½ cup diced celery
- ¼ cup chicken broth
- 1 can (10½ ounces) cream of chicken soup
- 1 cup dairy sour cream
- 3 cups cubed cooked chicken
- ½ cup (4 ounces) sliced mushrooms
- 1 teaspoon Worcestershire sauce
- 1 teaspoon salt
- ⅛ teaspoon pepper
- Confetti Topping (recipe follows)

For casserole: In saucepan, combine carrots, onion, celery and chicken broth. Simmer 20 minutes. In 3-quart casserole, mix soup, sour cream, chicken cubes, mushrooms, Worcestershire sauce, salt and pepper. Add simmered vegetables and liquid; mix well. Drop tablespoons of Confetti Topping onto casserole and bake in 350°F oven for 40 to 45 minutes or until golden brown. Sprinkle with remaining ¼ cup cheese and return to oven until melted. Garnish as desired.

Makes 6 to 8 servings

Confetti Topping
- 1 cup sifted all-purpose flour
- 2 teaspoons baking powder
- ½ teaspoon salt
- 2 eggs, slightly beaten
- ½ cup milk
- 1 tablespoon chopped green bell pepper
- 1 tablespoon chopped pimiento
- 1¼ cups (5 ounces) shredded Wisconsin Cheddar cheese, divided

In mixing bowl, combine flour, baking powder and salt. Add eggs, milk, green pepper, pimiento and 1 cup of the cheese. Mix just until well blended.

Favorite recipe from **Wisconsin Milk Marketing Board**

Dairyland Confetti Chicken

Savory SEAFOOD

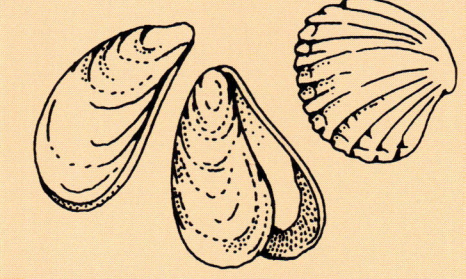

ZESTY CATFISH BAKE

  6 (4- to 5-ounce) farm-raised catfish fillets
  1 tablespoon butter
  ⅓ cup chopped onion
  1 (8-ounce) package cream cheese, softened
  ¼ cup dry white wine
  2 tablespoons shredded horseradish
  1 tablespoon Dijon-style mustard
  ½ teaspoon salt
  ⅛ teaspoon pepper
  4 strips bacon, cooked crisp, crumbled
  2 tablespoons finely chopped fresh parsley

If frozen, thaw fish fillets; rinse and pat dry. Preheat oven to 350°F. Grease large baking dish. Arrange fillets in single layer in dish. Melt butter in skillet over medium-high heat. Add onion; cook and stir until softened. Combine cream cheese, wine, horseradish, mustard, salt and pepper in small bowl; stir in onion. Pour mixture over fish and top with crumbled bacon. Bake 30 minutes or until fish flakes easily when tested with fork. Garnish with parsley. *Makes 6 servings*

Savory

SEAFOOD

SHRIMP IN ANGEL HAIR PASTA CASSEROLE

- 1 tablespoon butter
- 2 eggs
- 1 cup half-and-half
- 1 cup plain yogurt
- ½ cup (4 ounces) shredded Swiss cheese
- ⅓ cup crumbled feta cheese
- ⅓ cup chopped fresh parsley
- ¼ cup chopped fresh basil *or* 1 teaspoon dried basil leaves, crushed
- 1 teaspoon dried oregano leaves, crushed
- 1 package (9 ounces) uncooked fresh angel hair pasta
- 1 jar (16 ounces) mild, thick and chunky salsa
- 1 pound medium shrimp, peeled and deveined
- ½ cup (4 ounces) shredded Monterey Jack cheese

With 1 tablespoon butter, grease 12×8-inch pan. Combine eggs, half-and-half, yogurt, Swiss cheese, feta cheese, parsley, basil and oregano in medium bowl; mix well. Spread ½ the pasta on bottom of prepared pan. Cover with salsa. Add ½ the shrimp. Cover with remaining pasta. Spread egg mixture over pasta and top with remaining shrimp. Sprinkle Monterey Jack cheese over top. Bake in preheated 350°F oven 30 minutes or until hot. Let stand 10 minutes. Garnish as desired.

Makes 6 servings

Favorite recipe from **Southeast United Dairy Industry Association, Inc.**

LOUISIANA SEAFOOD BAKE

- ⅔ cup uncooked white rice
- 1 cup sliced celery
- 1 cup water
- 1 can (14½ ounces) whole tomatoes, undrained and cut up
- 1 can (8 ounces) tomato sauce
- 1⅓ cups (2.8-ounce can) FRENCH'S® French Fried Onions, divided
- 1 teaspoon FRANK'S® Original REDHOT® Cayenne Pepper Sauce
- ½ teaspoon garlic powder
- ¼ teaspoon oregano leaves
- ¼ teaspoon thyme leaves
- ½ pound white fish (thawed if frozen), cut into 1-inch chunks
- 1 can (4 ounces) shrimp, drained
- ⅓ cup sliced pitted ripe olives
- ¼ cup (1 ounce) grated Parmesan cheese

Preheat oven to 375°F. In 1½-quart casserole, combine uncooked rice, celery, water, tomatoes with juice, tomato sauce, ⅔ *cup* French Fried Onions, RedHot® sauce and seasonings. Bake, covered, at 375°F for 20 minutes. Stir in fish, shrimp and olives. Bake, covered, 20 minutes or until heated through. Top with cheese and remaining ⅔ *cup* onions; bake, uncovered, 3 minutes or until onions are golden.

Makes 4 servings

Shrimp in Angel Hair Pasta Casserole

Savory

SEAFOOD

TUNA WITH PEPPERCORNS ON A BED OF GREENS

- Salt
- 4 tuna steaks (about 1½ pounds)
- 2 teaspoons coarsely ground black pepper
- 1 large onion, thinly sliced
- 1 tablespoon butter or margarine
- ¼ cup dry white wine
- ½ pound fresh kale or spinach, cut into 1-inch strips
- ½ teaspoon sugar
- ¼ teaspoon black pepper
- 1 tablespoon olive oil
- Carrot strips (optional)

Preheat oven to 325°F. Lightly sprinkle salt over fish steaks, then press coarsely ground pepper onto both sides of steaks; set aside. Cook and stir onion in melted butter in large skillet over medium heat 5 minutes or until crisp-tender. Add wine; remove from heat. Spread onion mixture in 13×9-inch glass baking dish. Place fish on top. Bake 30 minutes or until fish flakes easily when tested with fork, turning fish over and basting with liquid halfway through baking time.

Cook and stir kale, sugar and black pepper in hot oil in medium skillet over medium-high heat 2 to 3 minutes or until tender. Place kale on plates; top with onion mixture, then fish. Place carrot strips over fish; garnish, if desired. *Makes 4 servings*

DILLED SALMON SUPPER

- 1 bottle (8 ounces) clam juice
- ½ cup dry vermouth
- ½ cup UNCLE BEN'S® CONVERTED® Brand Rice, uncooked
- 1 tablespoon lime juice
- 1 clove garlic, crushed
- 2 teaspoons chopped fresh dill *or* ½ teaspoon dried dill weed
- ⅛ teaspoon freshly ground black pepper
- 2 salmon steaks, ¾-inch thick* (about ¾ pound)
- ½ cup frozen peas, thawed
- ¼ cup plain low fat yogurt
- Paprika

*Haddock, halibut or red snapper fillets, ½- to ¾-inch thick, may be substituted.

Bring clam juice and vermouth to a boil in 10-inch skillet. Stir in rice, lime juice, garlic, dill and pepper. Arrange salmon steaks on top. Cover and simmer 20 minutes. Remove from heat. Gently stir peas into rice. Let stand covered until all liquid is absorbed, about 5 minutes. Top salmon with yogurt and sprinkle with paprika.

Makes 2 servings

Tuna with Peppercorns on a Bed of Greens

— Savory —

SEAFOOD

BAKED FISH WITH POTATOES AND ONIONS

- 1 pound baking potatoes, very thinly sliced
- 1 large onion, very thinly sliced
- 1 small red or green bell pepper, thinly sliced
- Salt
- Black pepper
- ½ teaspoon dried oregano leaves, crushed, divided
- 1 pound lean fish fillets, cut 1 inch thick
- ¼ cup butter or margarine
- ¼ cup all-purpose flour
- 2 cups milk
- ¾ cup (3 ounces) shredded Cheddar cheese

Preheat oven to 375°F.

Arrange ½ potatoes in buttered 3-quart casserole. Top with ½ onion and ½ bell pepper. Season with salt and black pepper. Sprinkle with ¼ teaspoon oregano. Arrange fish in 1 layer over vegetables. Arrange remaining potatoes, onion and bell pepper over fish. Season with salt, black pepper and remaining ¼ teaspoon oregano.

Melt butter in medium saucepan over medium heat. Stir in flour; cook until bubbly, stirring constantly. Gradually stir in milk. Cook until thickened, stirring constantly. Pour white sauce over casserole. Cover and bake at 375°F 40 minutes or until potatoes are tender. Sprinkle with cheese. Bake, uncovered, about 5 minutes more or until cheese is melted. *Makes 4 servings*

SEAFOOD PASTA SALAD

- 1 can (15¼ ounces) DOLE® Tropical Fruit Salad
- 6 ounces spiral pasta, hot, cooked
- 2 teaspoons toasted sesame oil
- Fruity Dressing (recipe follows)
- 12 ounces cooked baby shrimp
- 2 cups (4 ounces) bean sprouts
- 1 cup snow peas
- ½ cup chopped DOLE® Celery
- ½ cup chopped DOLE® Red Bell Pepper
- ¼ cup DOLE® Chopped Dates
- ¼ cup dry roasted peanuts, coarsely chopped

- Drain tropical fruit salad; reserve ⅓ cup juice for dressing.

- Toss hot pasta with sesame oil. When cool, mix with Fruity Dressing.

- Add tropical fruit salad and remaining ingredients; toss to combine. *Makes 8 servings*

Fruity Dressing
- ¼ cup rice or white vinegar
- 2 tablespoons light soy sauce
- 2 tablespoons chopped fresh cilantro or parsley
- 1 teaspoon minced jalapeño or serrano chile

- Combine ⅓ cup juice, reserved from Tropical Fruit Salad, vinegar, soy sauce, cilantro and jalapeño; whisk to blend.

Baked Fish with Potatoes and Onions

— Savory —

SEAFOOD

COMPANY CRAB

- 1 pound blue crabmeat, fresh, frozen or pasteurized
- 1 can (15 ounces) artichoke hearts, drained
- 1 can (4 ounces) sliced mushrooms, drained
- 2 tablespoons butter or margarine
- 2½ tablespoons all-purpose flour
- ½ teaspoon salt
- ⅛ teaspoon ground red pepper
- 1 cup half-and-half
- 2 tablespoons dry sherry
- 2 tablespoons crushed corn flakes
- 1 tablespoon grated Parmesan cheese
- Paprika

Thaw crabmeat if frozen. Remove any pieces of shell or cartilage. Cut artichoke hearts in half. Place artichokes in well-greased, shallow 1½-quart casserole. Add crabmeat and mushrooms; cover and set aside.

Melt butter over medium heat in small saucepan. Stir in flour, salt and ground red pepper. Gradually stir in half-and-half. Continue cooking until sauce thickens, stirring constantly. Stir in sherry. Pour sauce over crabmeat. Combine corn flakes and cheese in small bowl; sprinkle over casserole. Sprinkle with paprika. Bake in preheated 450°F oven 12 to 15 minutes or until bubbly.

Makes 6 servings

Favorite recipe from **Florida Department of Agriculture and Consumer Services, Bureau of Seafood and Aquaculture**

OYSTER-ARTICHOKE PAN ROAST

- 1 (14-ounce) can artichoke hearts, drained and quartered
- 4 tablespoons butter or margarine
- 1 cup chopped green onions
- ½ cup chopped onion
- 1 clove garlic, minced
- 3 tablespoons flour
- 1 quart oysters with their liquor
- ½ cup chopped fresh parsley
- 1 tablespoon lemon juice
- 1 teaspoon Worcestershire sauce
- ¼ teaspoon TABASCO® pepper sauce
- ½ teaspoon salt
- 2 tablespoons butter or margarine
- 1 cup fresh bread crumbs

In small saucepan, place artichoke hearts in water. Bring to a simmer; keep warm.

In medium skillet, heat 4 tablespoons butter; cook and stir green onions, onion and garlic until tender. Sprinkle with flour. Cook and stir another 3 minutes to cook flour.

While vegetables are cooking, in medium saucepan poach oysters in their liquor (add water, if necessary) until edges curl and oysters plump up. Drain, reserving liquid.

Add 1 to 1½ cups oyster liquid to vegetables. Add parsley, lemon juice, Worcestershire sauce, TABASCO® sauce and salt. Simmer until

SEAFOOD

thickened. Place oysters and artichokes in shallow casserole; cover with sauce. (Recipe may be prepared ahead of time up to this point.)

Heat oven to 350°F. In skillet, melt 2 tablespoons butter; stir in bread crumbs until well coated. Sprinkle over casserole. Bake at 350°F 15 to 20 minutes or until bread crumbs are browned and sauce is bubbly. *Makes 4 servings*

CRISPY CATFISH NUGGETS WITH CREOLE SAUCE

- 4½ cups KELLOGG'S CORN FLAKES® cereal, crushed to 2 cups
- ½ teaspoon paprika
- ½ teaspoon onion powder
- 1 cup skim milk
- 1 egg, beaten
- 1 pound catfish nuggets (about 36 nuggets)
- Nonstick cooking spray
- 1 clove garlic, minced
- 1 tablespoon olive oil
- ½ cup chopped onion
- ½ cup chopped green pepper
- ¼ cup chopped celery
- 1 tablespoon sugar
- ¼ teaspoon red pepper flakes
- 1 can (6 ounces) tomato paste
- ½ cup water

1. Stir together crushed Kellogg's Corn Flakes®, paprika and onion powder in shallow dish or pan. Set aside.

2. Combine milk and egg in second shallow dish or pan. Dip catfish nuggets into egg mixture. Coat with cereal mixture. Place on baking sheet coated with cooking spray.

3. Bake at 350°F about 20 minutes. Serve warm with Creole Sauce.

4. **To make Creole Sauce:** in saucepan, cook garlic in oil over medium heat until browned. Add onion, green pepper, celery, sugar and red pepper flakes. Cook until vegetables are tender. Stir in tomato paste and water. Cover; simmer 15 minutes. Serve with catfish nuggets.

Makes 3 dozen nuggets, 1⅔ cups sauce

QUICK AND EASY TUNA RICE WITH PEAS

- 1 package (10 ounces) green peas
- 1¼ cups water
- 1 can (11 ounces) condensed Cheddar cheese soup
- 1 can (12½ ounces) tuna, drained and flaked
- 1 chicken bouillon cube
- 1½ cups MINUTE® Rice

- Bring peas, water, soup, tuna and bouillon cube to a full boil in medium saucepan. Stir in rice. Cover; remove from heat. Let stand 5 minutes. Fluff with fork. *Makes 4 servings*

SEAFOOD

HERB-BAKED FISH & RICE

- 1½ cups hot chicken bouillon
- ½ cup uncooked white rice (not instant)
- ¼ teaspoon Italian seasoning
- ¼ teaspoon garlic powder
- 1 package (10 ounces) frozen chopped broccoli, thawed and drained
- 1⅓ cups (2.8-ounce can) FRENCH'S® French Fried Onions, divided
- 1 tablespoon grated Parmesan cheese
- 1 pound unbreaded fish fillets (thawed if frozen)
- Paprika
- ½ cup (2 ounces) shredded Cheddar cheese

Preheat oven to 375°F. In 12×8-inch baking dish, combine hot bouillon, uncooked rice and seasonings. Bake, covered, at 375°F for 10 minutes. Top with broccoli, *⅔ cup* French Fried Onions and Parmesan cheese. Place fish fillets diagonally down center of dish; sprinkle fish lightly with paprika. Bake, covered, at 375°F 20 to 25 minutes or until fish flakes easily with fork. Stir rice. Top fish with Cheddar cheese and remaining *⅔ cup* onions; bake, uncovered, 3 minutes or until onions are golden.

Makes 3 to 4 servings

OLD-FASHIONED TUNA NOODLE CASSEROLE

- ¼ cup plain dry bread crumbs
- 3 tablespoons butter or margarine, melted and divided
- 1 tablespoon finely chopped parsley
- ½ cup chopped onion
- ½ cup chopped celery
- 1 cup water
- 1 cup milk
- 1 package LIPTON® Noodles & Sauce–Butter
- 2 cans (6½ ounces each) tuna, drained and flaked

In small bowl, thoroughly combine bread crumbs, 1 tablespoon butter and parsley; set aside.

In medium saucepan, melt remaining 2 tablespoons butter. Cook onion and celery over medium heat, stirring occasionally, 2 minutes or until onion is tender. Add water and milk; bring to a boil. Stir in Noodles & Butter Sauce. Continue boiling over medium heat, stirring occasionally, 8 minutes or until noodles are tender. Stir in tuna. Turn into greased 1-quart casserole, then top with bread crumb mixture. Broil until bread crumbs are golden.

Makes about 4 servings

Herb-Baked Fish & Rice

Savory

SEAFOOD

CHESAPEAKE CRAB STRATA

- 4 tablespoons butter or margarine
- 4 cups unseasoned croutons
- 2 cups shredded Cheddar cheese
- 2 cups milk
- 8 eggs, beaten
- ½ teaspoon dry mustard
- ½ teaspoon seafood seasoning
- Salt and black pepper to taste
- 1 pound crabmeat, picked over to remove any shells

Preheat oven to 325°F. Place butter in 11×7×1½-inch baking dish. Heat in oven until melted, tilting to coat dish. Remove dish from oven; spread croutons over melted butter. Top with cheese; set aside.

Combine milk, eggs, dry mustard, seafood seasoning, salt and black pepper; mix well. Pour egg mixture over cheese in dish and sprinkle crabmeat on top. Bake for 50 minutes or until mixture is set. Remove from oven and let stand for about 10 minutes. Garnish with pepper rings, if desired.

Makes 6 to 8 servings

SHRIMP IN CAJUN RED GRAVY

- 1 tablespoon plus 2 teaspoons Chef Paul Prudhomme's SEAFOOD MAGIC®, in all
- 1 pound medium to large shelled, deveined shrimp
- 2 tablespoons unsalted butter
- 3 tablespoons olive oil
- 1 cup finely chopped onion
- ½ cup finely chopped green bell pepper
- ¼ cup finely chopped celery
- 2 bay leaves
- 1 tablespoon minced fresh garlic
- 2 cups canned crushed tomatoes
- 1 tablespoon dark brown sugar
- 1½ cups water
- Hot cooked rice or pasta

Add 2 teaspoons of the Seafood Magic® to shrimp and mix well. Reserve. Melt butter in 10-inch skillet over high heat. Add olive oil and heat 1½ minutes or until mixture comes to a hard sizzle. Stir in onion, bell pepper, celery, remaining 1 tablespoon Seafood Magic® and bay leaves. Cook, stirring occasionally, 5 to 6 minutes or until vegetables begin to soften. Add garlic and tomatoes; cook, stirring occasionally, about 8 minutes. Stir in brown sugar and water. Cook, stirring occasionally, 4 minutes or until mixture boils rapidly. Add shrimp and stir well. Cook 2 minutes or just until shrimp are plump and pink. Turn heat off. Cover skillet; let stand 5 minutes. Serve over hot cooked rice or pasta.

Makes 4 servings

Chesapeake Crab Strata

Old-Fashioned Delightful Desserts

Peanut Chocolate Surprise Pie

- 8 tablespoons (1 stick) butter, melted
- 1 cup granulated sugar
- 2 eggs
- ½ cup all-purpose flour
- ½ cup chopped peanuts
- ½ cup chopped walnuts
- ½ cup semisweet chocolate chips
- ¼ cup bourbon
- 1 teaspoon vanilla extract
- 1 (9-inch) unbaked deep-dish pie shell
- Whipped cream, for garnish
- Chocolate shavings, for garnish

Preheat oven to 350°F. Cream butter and sugar in large bowl. Add eggs and beat until well mixed. Gradually add flour, then stir in nuts, chips, bourbon and vanilla. Spread mixture evenly in unbaked pie shell. Bake 40 minutes. Cool pie on wire rack; decorate with whipped cream and chocolate shavings.

Makes one 9-inch pie

— Old-Fashioned —

BERRY COBBLER

- 1 pint fresh raspberries (2½ cups)*
- 1 pint fresh blueberries or strawberries, sliced (2½ cups)*
- ⅓ cup sugar
- 2 tablespoons cornstarch
- 1 cup all-purpose flour
- 1 tablespoon sugar
- 1½ teaspoons baking powder
- ¼ teaspoon salt
- ½ cup milk
- ⅓ cup butter or margarine, melted
- ¼ teaspoon ground nutmeg

*One (16-ounce) bag frozen raspberries and one (16-ounce) bag frozen blueberries or strawberries may be substituted for fresh berries. Thaw berries, reserving juices. Increase cornstarch to 3 tablespoons.

Preheat oven to 375°F. Combine berries, ⅓ cup sugar and cornstarch in medium bowl; toss lightly to coat. Spoon into 1½-quart or 8-inch square baking dish. Combine flour, 1 tablespoon sugar, baking powder and salt in medium bowl. Add milk and butter; mix just until dry ingredients are moistened. Drop six heaping tablespoonfuls of batter evenly over berries; sprinkle with nutmeg. Bake 25 minutes or until topping is golden brown and fruit is bubbly. Cool on wire rack. Serve warm or at room temperature.

Makes 6 servings

PICKLED PEACHES

- 6 pounds firm-ripe peaches, peeled, pitted and halved
- 6¾ cups sugar
- 3½ cups white vinegar (labeled 5% acidity)
- 4 (2½-inch) cinnamon sticks
- 1 tablespoon whole cloves
- 1 tablespoon ground ginger

Combine sugar and vinegar in a 6- to 8-quart saucepan. Bring to a boil; continue boiling 5 minutes. Tie spices in spice bag or cheesecloth. Add spice bag and peaches to syrup. Simmer 5 to 10 minutes or until peaches are cooked but not too soft, stirring peaches gently to cook all sides. Cover and let stand in cool place for 12 to 18 hours, stirring peaches 2 or 3 times.

Bring peaches and syrup to a boil. Remove from heat and remove spices. Skim off foam, if necessary. Immediately fill hot pint or quart jars with mixture, leaving ½-inch headspace.

Carefully run nonmetallic utensil down inside of jars to remove trapped air bubbles. Wipe jar tops and threads clean. Place hot lids on jars and screw bands on firmly. Process in Boiling Water Canner (page 32) 25 minutes for quarts or 20 minutes for pints.

Makes about 2 quarts or 4 to 5 pints

Favorite recipe from **Alltrista Corporation Kerr Brands®**

Berry Cobbler

Old-Fashioned

Delightful Desserts

MARVELOUS MACAROONS

- 1 can (8 ounces) DOLE® Crushed Pineapple in Juice
- 1 can (14 ounces) sweetened condensed milk
- 1 package (7 ounces) flaked coconut
- ½ cup DOLE® Chopped Almonds, toasted
- ½ cup margarine, melted
- Grated peel from 1 DOLE® Lemon
- ¼ teaspoon almond extract
- 1 cup all-purpose flour
- 1 teaspoon baking powder

- Drain pineapple well; reserve juice for beverage.

- Combine drained pineapple, sweetened condensed milk, coconut, almonds, margarine, 1 teaspoon lemon peel and almond extract.

- Combine flour and baking powder. Beat into pineapple mixture until blended.

- Drop by heaping tablespoonfuls, 1 inch apart, onto greased cookie sheets. Bake in 350°F oven 13 to 15 minutes. Remove to wire racks to cool. Store in refrigerator. *Makes 3½ dozen cookies*

APRICOT-PEAR STRUDEL

- 2 sheets frozen puff pastry
- 1 (17-ounce) can apricots, drained and sliced
- 1 (16-ounce) can pears, drained and cubed
- ½ cup blanched slivered almonds
- ¼ cup packed light brown sugar
- ½ teaspoon ground cinnamon
- ½ teaspoon nutmeg
- 1 egg
- 1 teaspoon water

Thaw pastry 20 minutes; unfold and place second sheet directly on top of first sheet. Roll on lightly floured surface to 14×10-inch rectangle. In large bowl, combine apricots, pears, almonds, brown sugar, cinnamon and nutmeg. Spoon fruit filling lengthwise down center third of pastry. Beat egg and water together. Brush edges with egg-water mixture. Fold left side of pastry over filling; fold right side of pastry over to enclose filling completely. Pinch edges to seal. Roll strudel over onto ungreased baking sheet; seal edges by pressing with fork. Brush top with egg-water mixture; refrigerate, covered, 30 minutes or overnight. Preheat oven to 425°F. With sharp knife, lightly score top of strudel. Bake 25 to 30 minutes or until puffed and golden brown. Cool on wire rack for 30 minutes. *Makes 8 servings*

Old-Fashioned

OLD-FASHIONED UPSIDE-DOWN CAKE

⅔ cup margarine, divided
⅔ cup brown sugar, packed
1 can (20 ounces) DOLE® Pineapple Slices in Syrup or Juice
10 maraschino cherries
¾ cup granulated sugar, divided
2 eggs, separated
1 teaspoon grated lemon peel
1 teaspoon lemon juice
1 teaspoon vanilla extract
1½ cups all-purpose flour
1¾ teaspoons baking powder
¼ teaspoon salt
½ cup dairy sour cream

- Melt ⅓ cup margarine in 10-inch cast iron skillet. Remove from heat. Add brown sugar and stir until blended.

- Drain pineapple well; reserve 2 tablespoons syrup. Arrange pineapple in sugar mixture. Place cherry in center of each slice.

- Beat remaining ⅓ cup margarine with ½ cup granulated sugar until light and fluffy. Beat in egg yolks, lemon peel, lemon juice and vanilla.

- Combine flour, baking powder and salt. Blend into creamed mixture alternately with sour cream and reserved 2 tablespoons pineapple syrup.

- Beat egg whites to soft peaks. Gradually beat in remaining ¼ cup granulated sugar until stiff peaks form. Fold into batter. Pour over pineapple in skillet. Bake in 350°F oven about 35 minutes or until wooden pick inserted in center comes out clean. Let stand 10 minutes, then invert onto serving plate. Serve warm or cold.

Makes 8 servings

BLACK BOTTOM BANANA CREAM PIE

2 tablespoons margarine
4 (1-ounce) squares semisweet chocolate
1 NILLA® Pie Crust
2 small bananas, sliced
1 (3⅜-ounce) package ROYAL® Instant Vanilla Pudding & Pie Filling
2 cups cold milk
Whipped topping, for garnish

In small saucepan, over low heat, melt margarine and chocolate, stirring until smooth. Spread evenly over bottom of crust. Arrange banana slices over chocolate; set aside.

Prepare pudding according to package directions for pie using milk; pour over bananas. Chill at least 1 hour. Garnish with whipped topping.

Makes 8 servings

Old-Fashioned

Delightful Desserts

FRESH LEMON MERINGUE PIE

- 1½ cups sugar
- ¼ cup plus 2 tablespoons cornstarch
- ½ teaspoon salt
- ½ cup cold water
- ½ cup fresh squeezed lemon juice
- 3 egg yolks, well beaten
- 2 tablespoons butter or margarine
- 1½ cups boiling water
- Grated peel of ½ SUNKIST® Lemon
- 2 to 3 drops yellow food coloring (optional)
- 1 (9-inch) baked pie crust
- Three-Egg Meringue (recipe follows)

In large saucepan, combine sugar, cornstarch and salt. Gradually blend in cold water and lemon juice. Stir in egg yolks. Add butter and boiling water. Bring to a boil over medium-high heat, stirring constantly. Reduce heat to medium and boil 1 minute. Remove from heat; stir in lemon peel and food coloring. Pour into baked pie crust. Top with Three-Egg Meringue, sealing well at edges. Bake at 350°F 12 to 15 minutes. Cool 2 hours before serving.
Makes 6 servings

Three-Egg Meringue
- 3 egg whites
- ¼ teaspoon cream of tartar
- 6 tablespoons sugar

In large bowl, with electric mixer, beat egg whites with cream of tartar until foamy. Gradually add sugar and beat until stiff peaks form.

PEACH COBBLER

- 4 cups sliced peeled peaches *or* 2 (29-ounce) cans sliced peaches, drained
- 1 cup fresh or frozen blueberries (optional)
- ⅔ cup all-purpose flour, divided
- ⅓ cup sugar, divided
- 2 tablespoons lemon juice
- ⅓ cup margarine, softened, divided
- 20 NILLA® Wafers, finely rolled (about ¾ cups crumbs)
- 2 tablespoons water

In large bowl, toss peaches and blueberries with 2 tablespoons flour, 3 tablespoons sugar and lemon juice. Place in greased 8×8×2-inch baking dish; dot with 1 tablespoon margarine.

In medium bowl, combine wafer crumbs with remaining flour and sugar; cut in remaining margarine until mixture resembles coarse crumbs. Stir in water until mixture holds together; shape into ball. Roll dough out between 2 sheets of lightly floured waxed paper to 7½-inch circle. Remove 1 sheet of waxed paper. Cut 1-inch circle out of center of dough. Invert dough over fruit mixture; peel off paper. Sprinkle with additional sugar if desired.

Bake at 400°F for 35 to 40 minutes or until pastry is browned. Cool slightly before serving.
Makes 8 servings

Fresh Lemon Meringue Pie

Old-Fashioned

Delightful Desserts

KAREN ANN'S LEMON CAKE

- 2 cups all-purpose flour
- 1½ teaspoons baking powder
- ½ teaspoon baking soda
- ¼ teaspoon salt
- ⅔ cup butter or margarine, softened
- 1¼ cups granulated sugar
- 3 eggs, separated
- ¾ cup sour cream
- Grated peel of 1 SUNKIST® Lemon
- Lemony Frosting (recipe follows)

Line two 8-inch round cake pans with waxed paper. Preheat oven to 350°F. In medium bowl, combine flour, baking powder, baking soda and salt. In large bowl, with electric mixer, cream together butter and sugar. Beat in egg yolks one at a time; continue beating until light in color. Add dry ingredients to creamed mixture alternately with sour cream, beating just until smooth. With clean beaters, beat egg whites until soft peaks form. Gently fold egg whites and lemon peel into batter. Pour into pans. Bake 30 to 35 minutes or until wooden pick inserted in center comes out clean. Cool 10 minutes. Remove from pans; peel off waxed paper. Cool on wire racks. Fill and frost with Lemony Frosting. *Makes 12 servings*

Lemony Frosting

- ½ cup butter or margarine, softened
- 3 cups confectioners' sugar, divided
- Grated peel of ½ SUNKIST® Lemon
- 2 tablespoons fresh squeezed lemon juice

In medium bowl, cream together butter and 1 cup confectioners' sugar. Add lemon peel, lemon juice and remaining 2 cups sugar; beat until smooth.
Makes about 1¾ cups frosting

APPLE-BUTTERMILK PIE

- 2 medium-size Granny Smith apples
- 3 eggs
- 1½ cups sugar, divided
- 1 cup buttermilk
- ⅓ cup margarine or butter, melted
- 2 tablespoons all-purpose flour
- 2 teaspoons vanilla extract
- 1 tablespoon ground cinnamon, divided
- 2 teaspoons ground nutmeg, divided
- 1 (9-inch) unbaked pie shell

Preheat oven to 350°F. Peel and core apples; cut into small chunks. Place apples in bowl; cover with cold water and set aside. Beat eggs briefly at low speed of electric mixer until mixed. Reserve 1 tablespoon sugar. Add remaining sugar, buttermilk, margarine, flour, vanilla, 2 teaspoons cinnamon and 1½ teaspoons nutmeg; mix at low speed until well blended. Drain apples thoroughly and place in unbaked pie shell. Pour buttermilk mixture over apples. Combine reserved 1 teaspoon sugar, 1 teaspoon cinnamon and ½ teaspoon nutmeg; sprinkle over top. Bake 50 to 60 minutes. Serve warm or at room temperature for the best flavor. Store in refrigerator. *Makes one 9-inch pie*

Apple-Buttermilk Pie

Old-Fashioned

Delightful Desserts

PRALINE PUMPKIN TART

- 1¼ cups all-purpose flour
- 1 tablespoon granulated sugar
- ¾ teaspoon salt, divided
- ¼ cup vegetable shortening
- ¼ cup butter or margarine
- 2 to 3 tablespoons cold water
- 1 can (16 ounces) solid-pack pumpkin
- 1 can (13 ounces) evaporated milk
- 2 eggs
- ⅔ cup packed brown sugar
- 1 teaspoon ground cinnamon
- ½ teaspoon ground ginger
- ¼ teaspoon ground cloves
- Praline Topping (recipe follows)
- Sweetened Whipped Cream (recipe follows)
- Additional ground cinnamon and pecan halves for garnish

Combine flour, granulated sugar and ¼ teaspoon salt in large bowl. Cut in shortening and butter with pastry blender until mixture forms pea-sized pieces. Sprinkle water, 1 tablespoon at a time, over flour mixture, tossing with fork after each addition until mixture holds together. Form into a ball. Wrap in plastic wrap; refrigerate 1 hour or until chilled.

Roll out dough on lightly floured surface 1 inch larger than inverted 10-inch tart pan with removable bottom. Place dough in tart pan; cut dough even with edge. Cover; refrigerate 30 minutes.

Preheat oven to 400°F. Prick crust with fork. Bake 15 minutes or until set. Place pan on wire rack to cool completely.

Preheat oven to 400°F. Beat pumpkin, milk, eggs, brown sugar, 1 teaspoon cinnamon, remaining ½ teaspoon salt, ginger and cloves in large bowl until blended. Pour into cooled tart crust. Bake 35 minutes.

Meanwhile, prepare Praline Topping and Sweetened Whipped Cream. Sprinkle topping over center of tart, leaving 1½-inch rim around edge. Bake 15 minutes or until knife inserted 1 inch from center comes out clean. Cool completely on wire rack. Remove side of pan. Pipe edge of tart with Sweetened Whipped Cream; sprinkle with additional cinnamon and garnish with pecans. *Makes 8 servings*

Praline Topping
- ⅓ cup *each* packed brown sugar, chopped pecans and uncooked quick-cooking oats
- 1 tablespoon butter or margarine, softened

Place sugar, pecans and oats in small bowl. Cut in butter with pastry blender until crumbs form.

Sweetened Whipped Cream
- 1 cup whipping cream
- 2 tablespoons powdered sugar
- ½ teaspoon vanilla

Place all ingredients in chilled bowl. Beat until soft peaks form. *Do not overbeat.* Refrigerate.

Praline Pumpkin Tart

Old-Fashioned

Delightful Desserts

CALIFORNIA APRICOT-CHERRY CORNMEAL COBBLER

- 2 cups sliced fresh apricots (about 1 pound)
- ⅓ cup plus 5½ teaspoons granulated sugar, divided
- 2 cups pitted fresh cherries
- 1 cup plus 1 tablespoon all-purpose flour, divided
- ½ cup yellow cornmeal
- 2 teaspoons baking powder
- ¼ teaspoon salt
- ½ teaspoon grated orange peel
- 5 tablespoons unsalted butter, chilled
- ¾ cup low-fat milk

Preheat oven to 375°F. In bowl, mix apricots and ⅓ cup sugar. In separate bowl, mix cherries and 1 tablespoon flour. In large bowl, mix remaining 1 cup flour, cornmeal, 1½ tablespoons sugar, baking powder and salt; add orange peel. Cut in butter until mixture resembles coarse meal. Add milk; combine until just moistened. Combine fruit in 1½-quart baking dish; spoon batter over top. Sprinkle with remaining 1 teaspoon sugar. Bake 25 to 30 minutes or until golden brown. Cool slightly.

Makes 8 servings

GOLDEN APPLE CHEESECAKE

- Pastry (recipe follows)
- 4 to 5 Golden Delicious apples
- 1 package (8 ounces) cream cheese, softened
- Sugar
- 1 egg
- ½ teaspoon grated lemon peel
- ¼ teaspoon vanilla
- ⅛ teaspoon salt
- ½ teaspoon ground cinnamon
- ¼ cup sliced almonds

Prepare pastry; set aside. Peel, core and slice apples to measure 4 cups. Place apples in shallow pan; cover with foil. Bake at 400°F 15 minutes. Meanwhile, beat cream cheese with ¼ cup sugar. Beat in egg, lemon peel, vanilla and salt until smooth; spoon into partially baked pastry. Arrange warm, partially cooked apple slices on top. Combine ⅓ cup sugar and cinnamon; sprinkle over apples. Top with almonds. Bake at 400°F 35 to 40 minutes or until crust is brown and apples are tender. Cool before cutting.

Makes 8 to 10 servings

Pastry: Combine ⅓ cup sugar, 6 tablespoons butter, ¼ teaspoon vanilla and ⅛ teaspoon salt. Blend in 1 cup flour. Pat onto bottom and 1¼ inches up sides of lightly greased 9-inch springform pan. Bake at 400°F 10 minutes. Cool.

Favorite recipe from **Washington Apple Commission**

California Apricot-Cherry Cornmeal Cobbler

CASSEROLES

& ONE-DISH MEALS

CONTENTS

Home-Style Meaty Meals • 98

Fantastic Potluck Poultry • 112

Spectacular Deep Sea Dinners • 128

Dazzling Pasta Dishes • 140

Country Vegetables & Grains • 154

Hearty International Fare • 168

Fresh Vegetable Lasagna (page 156)

Home-Style
MEATY MEALS

SUCCESS IN A SKILLET

 1 bag SUCCESS® Rice
 1 teaspoon reduced-calorie margarine
½ cup chopped onion
½ pound chopped turkey-ham
¼ pound sliced fresh mushrooms
½ cup green peas
½ cup chopped tomatoes
¾ teaspoon lemon pepper seasoning
¼ cup water

Prepare rice according to package directions.

Melt margarine in large skillet over medium heat. Add onion; cook and stir until tender. Stir in turkey-ham, mushrooms, peas, tomatoes, lemon pepper and water. Reduce heat to low; simmer until water is absorbed, about 5 minutes. Stir in rice; heat thoroughly, stirring occasionally.
Makes 4 servings

— Home-Style —

Meaty Meals

BEEF BOURGUIGNON

- **1 boneless beef sirloin steak, ½ inch thick, trimmed, cut into ½-inch pieces (about 3 pounds)**
- **½ cup all-purpose flour**
- **4 slices bacon, diced**
- **3 cups Burgundy wine or beef broth**
- **2 medium carrots, diced**
- **1 teaspoon dried marjoram leaves, crushed**
- **½ teaspoon dried thyme leaves, crushed**
- **½ teaspoon salt**
- **Pepper to taste**
- **1 bay leaf**
- **2 tablespoons vegetable oil**
- **20 to 24 fresh pearl onions**
- **8 small new red potatoes, cut into quarters**
- **8 to 10 mushrooms, sliced**
- **3 cloves garlic, minced**

Coat beef with flour, shaking off excess. Set aside.

Cook and stir bacon in 5-quart Dutch oven over medium-high heat until partially cooked. Brown half of beef with bacon in Dutch oven over medium-high heat. Remove with slotted spoon; set aside. Brown remaining beef. Pour off drippings. Return beef and bacon to Dutch oven.

Stir in wine, carrots, marjoram, thyme, salt, pepper and bay leaf. Bring to a boil over high heat. Reduce heat to low. Cover and simmer 10 minutes.

Meanwhile, heat oil in large saucepan over medium-high heat. Cook and stir onions, potatoes, mushrooms and garlic about 10 minutes. Add to Dutch oven. Cover and simmer 50 minutes or until meat is fork-tender. Discard bay leaf before serving. *Makes 10 to 12 servings*

CIDER STEW

- **2 pounds stew beef, cut into 1-inch cubes**
- **2 tablespoons margarine**
- **¼ cup all-purpose flour**
- **2 cups water**
- **1 cup apple cider**
- **½ cup A.1.® Steak Sauce**
- **2 teaspoons dried thyme leaves**
- **½ teaspoon ground black pepper**
- **1 bay leaf**
- **3 medium potatoes, peeled and cut into 1-inch cubes**
- **3 medium carrots, sliced**
- **1 medium onion, chopped**
- **1 (10-ounce) package frozen cut green beans**

In large heavy saucepan, over medium-high heat, brown beef in margarine. Stir in flour. Gradually stir in water, cider and steak sauce. Bring to a boil over high heat; stir in thyme, pepper and bay leaf. Reduce heat to low; cover and simmer 2 hours.

Add potatoes, carrots, onion and beans. Cover and cook 30 minutes or until vegetables are tender. Discard bay leaf before serving.

Makes 6 to 8 servings

Beef Bourguignon

SOUTHWESTERN BEEF AND BEAN LASAGNA

- ½ pound extra lean ground beef
- 1 can (16 ounces) pinto beans, drained
- 1 teaspoon cumin seeds *or* ½ teaspoon ground cumin
- 1 teaspoon olive oil
- 1½ cups chopped onions
- 1 tablespoon seeded and minced jalapeño pepper
- 1 clove garlic, minced
- 4 cups no-salt-added tomato sauce
- 1 can (4 ounces) diced green chilies, undrained
- 2 teaspoons chili powder
- 1 teaspoon dried oregano leaves
- 1 container (8 ounces) nonfat cottage cheese
- 1½ cups (6 ounces) shredded reduced fat Cheddar cheese, divided
- 1 egg white
- ¼ cup chopped fresh cilantro
- ½ teaspoon salt
- ¼ teaspoon black pepper
- 8 ounces uncooked lasagna noodles
- 1 cup water

Brown beef in large skillet. Drain off fat. Stir in beans; set aside. Place cumin seeds in large nonstick skillet. Cook and stir over medium heat 2 minutes or until fragrant. Remove from skillet.

In same skillet, heat oil. Add onions, jalapeño and garlic; cook until onions are soft. Add tomato sauce, green chilies, chili powder, oregano and cumin seeds. Bring to a boil; reduce heat. Simmer, uncovered, 20 minutes.

Preheat oven to 350°F. Combine cottage cheese, ½ cup Cheddar cheese, egg white, cilantro, salt and black pepper in medium bowl.

Spray 13 × 9-inch baking pan with cooking spray. Cover bottom with ¾ cup tomato sauce mixture. Place layer of noodles on sauce. Spread half the beef mixture over noodles, then place another layer of noodles on top. Spread cheese mixture over noodles. Spread with remaining beef mixture. Layer with remaining noodles. Pour remaining sauce mixture over all; sprinkle with remaining 1 cup Cheddar cheese. Pour water around edges. Cover tightly with foil. Bake 1 hour and 15 minutes or until pasta is tender. Cool 10 minutes before serving. *Makes 6 servings*

Southwestern Beef and Bean Lasagna

Home-Style

MEATY MEALS

VEGETABLE BEEF POT PIE

FILLING
- ⅓ cup all-purpose flour
- 1 teaspoon salt
- ¼ teaspoon black pepper
- 2 pounds lean stewing beef, cut into cubes
- ¼ BUTTER FLAVOR* CRISCO® Stick or ¼ cup BUTTER FLAVOR CRISCO all-vegetable shortening, divided
- 1 medium onion, peeled and finely chopped
- 2 cups beef stock or broth
- ½ cup red cooking wine
- 2 tablespoons tomato paste or ketchup
- 2 tablespoons finely chopped parsley
- 1 teaspoon minced garlic
- ¼ teaspoon dried thyme leaves
- 1 package (32 ounces) or 1½ packages (20 ounces each) frozen vegetables for stew

9-INCH CLASSIC CRISCO® SINGLE CRUST
- 1⅓ cups all-purpose flour
- ½ teaspoon salt
- ½ CRISCO® Stick or ½ cup CRISCO all-vegetable shortening
- 3 tablespoons cold water

GLAZE
- 1 egg, lightly beaten

*Butter Flavor Crisco® is artificially flavored.

1. For filling, combine flour, salt and pepper in paper or plastic bag. Add meat pieces; shake until well coated.

2. Melt 3 tablespoons shortening in Dutch oven. Brown meat on all sides in batches. Remove beef with slotted spoon to separate container.

3. Melt remaining 1 tablespoon shortening in Dutch oven. Saute onion until soft. Add stock, wine, tomato paste, parsley, garlic and thyme. Stir to combine.

4. Return meat to Dutch oven. Bring to a boil. Reduce heat. Simmer, uncovered, 2 to 2½ hours or until meat is tender, stirring occasionally. Add frozen vegetables. Mix to combine. Keep warm.

5. Heat oven to 375°F. Grease 13×9×2-inch pan with shortening.

6. For crust, combine flour and salt in medium bowl. Cut in shortening using pastry blender (or two knives) until flour is blended to form pea-size pieces.

7. Sprinkle with water, 1 tablespoon at a time. Toss lightly with fork until dough forms a ball.

8. Press dough between hands to form 5-inch square. Roll dough into 13×9-inch rectangle between sheets of waxed paper. Peel off top sheet.

9. Spoon beef mixture into pan. Flip pastry carefully over filling. Remove other sheet of waxed paper. Tuck in pastry or flute edge. Cut slits in crust for escape of steam.

10. For glaze, brush crust with beaten egg.

11. Bake at 375°F 30 to 45 minutes or until lightly browned. Serve hot. *Makes 8 servings*

Home-Style

MEATY MEALS

MEAT AND POTATO PIE

FILLING
- ¼ CRISCO® Stick or ¼ cup CRISCO all-vegetable shortening
- 1 pound sirloin steak, trimmed and cut into ½-inch cubes
- ½ cup ½-inch diced onion
- ½ cup ½-inch diced carrots
- ¼ cup tomato paste
- ½ teaspoon dried basil leaves
- ½ teaspoon dried thyme leaves
- ½ teaspoon garlic powder
- 1 can (10½ ounces) condensed double strength beef broth
- 4½ cups peeled, ¾-inch cubed Idaho (russet) potatoes
- 1 tablespoon cornstarch
- 2 tablespoons cold water
- ½ cup frozen green peas, thawed

9-INCH CLASSIC CRISCO® DOUBLE CRUST
- 2 cups all-purpose flour
- 1 teaspoon salt
- ¾ CRISCO® Stick or ¾ cup CRISCO all-vegetable shortening
- 5 tablespoons cold water

1. For filling, melt shortening in large saucepan. Add steak. Brown over medium-high heat. Add onion and carrots. Cook until onion starts to brown, stirring often. Add tomato paste, basil, thyme and garlic powder. Cook 2 to 3 minutes, stirring constantly. Add broth and potatoes. Reduce heat to low; cover and simmer until potatoes are cooked through but still firm.

2. Dissolve cornstarch in water. Add to mixture in saucepan. Cook and stir until thickened. Remove from heat. Stir in peas. Cool to room temperature.

3. Heat oven to 375°F.

4. For crust, combine flour and salt in medium bowl. Cut in shortening using pastry blender (or two knives) until flour is blended to form pea-size pieces.

5. Sprinkle with water, 1 tablespoon at a time. Toss lightly with fork until dough forms a ball.

6. Divide dough in half. Roll and press bottom crust into 9-inch deep-dish pie plate or casserole. Spoon in filling. Moisten pastry edge with water. Roll out top crust. Lift onto filled pie. Cut slits in top crust to allow steam to escape. Bake at 375°F for 30 to 35 minutes or until browned. Serve hot.

Makes one 9-inch pie

Home-Style

MEATY MEALS

SAVORY PORK & APPLE STIR-FRY

- 1 package (7.2 ounces) RICE-A-RONI® Rice Pilaf
- 1⅓ cups apple juice or apple cider
- 1 pound boneless pork loin, pork tenderloin or skinless, boneless chicken breast halves
- 1 teaspoon paprika
- 1 teaspoon dried thyme leaves
- ½ teaspoon ground sage or poultry seasoning
- ½ teaspoon salt (optional)
- 2 tablespoons margarine or butter
- 2 medium apples, cored and sliced
- 1 teaspoon cornstarch
- ⅓ cup coarsely chopped walnuts

1. Prepare Rice-A-Roni® Mix as package directs, substituting 1 cup water and 1 cup apple juice for water in directions.

2. While Rice-A-Roni® is simmering, cut pork into 1½×¼-inch strips. Combine seasonings; toss with meat.

3. In second large skillet, melt margarine over medium heat. Stir-fry meat 3 to 4 minutes or just until pork is no longer pink.

4. Add apples; stir-fry 2 to 3 minutes or until apples are almost tender. Add combined remaining ⅓ cup apple juice and cornstarch. Stir-fry 1 to 2 minutes or until thickened to form glaze.

5. Stir in nuts. Serve rice topped with pork mixture.
Makes 4 servings

MINI MEAT LOAVES & VEGETABLES

- 1½ pounds lean ground beef
- 1 egg
- 1 can (8 ounces) tomato sauce
- 1⅓ cups (2.8-ounce can) FRENCH'S® French Fried Onions, divided
- ½ teaspoon salt
- ½ teaspoon Italian seasoning
- 6 small red potatoes, thinly sliced (about 1½ cups)
- 1 bag (16 ounces) frozen vegetable combination (broccoli, corn, red pepper), thawed and drained
- Salt and freshly ground black pepper

Preheat oven to 375°F. In medium bowl, combine ground beef, egg, ½ *can* tomato sauce, ⅔ *cup* French Fried Onions, ½ *teaspoon* salt and Italian seasoning. Shape into 3 mini loaves and place in 13×9-inch baking dish. Arrange potatoes around loaves. Bake, covered, at 375°F 35 minutes. Spoon vegetables around meat loaves; stir to combine with potatoes. Lightly season vegetables with salt and black pepper, if desired. Top meat loaves with remaining tomato sauce. Bake, uncovered, 15 minutes or until meat loaves are done. Top loaves with remaining ⅔ *cup* onions; bake, uncovered, 3 minutes or until onions are brown.
Makes 6 servings

Savory Pork & Apple Stir-Fry

Home-Style

MEATY MEALS

CHILI MEATLOAF & POTATO CASSEROLE

MEATLOAF
- 1½ pounds lean ground beef
- ¾ cup finely chopped onion
- ⅓ cup saltine cracker crumbs
- 1 egg, slightly beaten
- 3 tablespoons milk
- 1 tablespoon chili powder
- ¾ teaspoon salt

POTATO TOPPING
- 3 cups prepared mashed potatoes
- 1 can (11 ounces) whole kernel corn with red and green peppers, drained
- ¼ cup thinly sliced green onions
- ½ to 1 cup shredded taco-seasoned cheese

1. Preheat oven to 375°F. In large bowl combine ground beef, onion, crumbs, egg, milk, chili powder and salt; mix well. Gently press mixture on bottom of 9-inch square baking pan. Bake 20 to 25 minutes or until no longer pink in center and juices run clear. Carefully pour off juices.

2. Meanwhile, in medium bowl, combine mashed potatoes, corn with peppers and onions. Spread over meatloaf to edges of pan; sprinkle with cheese. Broil 3 to 4 inches from heat 3 to 5 minutes or until top is lightly browned.

Makes 6 servings

Favorite recipe from **National Cattlemen's Beef Association**

OLD-FASHIONED BEEF POT PIE

- 1 pound ground beef
- 1 can (11 ounces) condensed beef with vegetables and barley soup
- ½ cup water
- 1 package (10 ounces) frozen peas and carrots, thawed and drained
- ½ teaspoon seasoned salt
- ⅛ teaspoon garlic powder
- ⅛ teaspoon ground black pepper
- 1 cup (4 ounces) shredded Cheddar cheese
- 1⅓ cups (2.8-ounce can) FRENCH'S® French Fried Onions, divided
- 1 package (7.5 ounces) refrigerated biscuits

Preheat oven to 350°F. In large skillet, brown ground beef in large chunks; drain. Stir in soup, water, vegetables and seasonings; bring to a boil. Reduce heat and simmer, uncovered, 5 minutes. Remove from heat; stir in *½ cup* cheese and *⅔ cup* French Fried Onions.

Pour mixture into 12×8-inch baking dish. Cut each biscuit in half; place, cut side down, around edge of casserole. Bake, uncovered, 15 to 20 minutes or until biscuits are done. Top with remaining cheese and *⅔ cup* onions; bake, uncovered, 5 minutes or until onions are golden brown.

Makes 4 to 6 servings

Chili Meatloaf & Potato Casserole

Home-Style

Meaty Meals

COUNTDOWN CASSEROLE

- 1 jar (8 ounces) pasteurized process cheese spread
- ¾ cup milk
- 2 cups (12 ounces) cubed cooked roast beef
- 1 bag (16 ounces) frozen vegetable combination (broccoli, corn, red pepper), thawed and drained
- 4 cups frozen hash brown potatoes, thawed
- 1⅓ cups (2.8-ounce can) FRENCH'S® French Fried Onions, divided
- ½ teaspoon seasoned salt
- ¼ teaspoon freshly ground black pepper
- ½ cup (2 ounces) shredded Cheddar cheese

Preheat oven to 375°F. Spoon cheese spread into 12×8-inch baking dish; place in oven just until cheese melts, about 5 minutes. Using fork, stir milk into melted cheese until well blended. Stir in beef, vegetables, potatoes, ⅔ cup French Fried Onions and seasonings. Bake, covered, at 375°F 30 minutes or until heated through. Top with Cheddar cheese; sprinkle remaining ⅔ cup onions down center. Bake, uncovered, 3 minutes or until onions are golden brown. *Makes 4 to 6 servings*

MICROWAVE DIRECTIONS: In 12×8-inch microwave-safe dish, combine cheese spread and milk. Cook, covered, on HIGH 3 minutes; stir. Add ingredients as directed. Cook, covered, 14 minutes or until heated through, stirring beef mixture halfway through cooking time. Top with Cheddar cheese and remaining onions as directed. Cook, uncovered, 1 minute or until cheese melts. Let stand 5 minutes.

PRIZE POTLUCK CASSEROLE

- 1 cup lentils, rinsed and drained
- 2 cups water
- 1 can (16 ounces) whole tomatoes, cut up, undrained
- ¼ cup minced onion
- ¼ cup chopped green pepper
- 1 teaspoon salt
- ½ teaspoon dry mustard
- ¼ teaspoon Worcestershire sauce
- ¼ teaspoon pepper
- ⅛ teaspoon thyme
- 1 pound Polish sausage, cut into 1½-inch-thick slices

Cook lentils in water until tender, about 30 minutes; drain if necessary. Preheat oven to 350°F. Combine lentils with tomatoes, onion, green pepper and seasonings. Turn into 13 × 9-inch casserole. Top with sausage. Cover casserole and bake 45 minutes. Uncover and bake 15 minutes longer. *Makes 6 servings*

Favorite recipe from USA Dry Pea & Lentil Council

Countdown Casserole

— *Fantastic* —
POTLUCK POULTRY

ORANGE GINGER CHICKEN & RICE

1 package (6.9 ounces) RICE-A-RONI® With
⅓ Less Salt Chicken Flavor
1 tablespoon margarine or butter
1 cup orange juice
¾ pound skinless, boneless chicken
breasts, cut into thin strips
2 cloves garlic, minced
¼ teaspoon ground ginger
Dash crushed red pepper flakes (optional)
1½ cups carrots, cut into short thin strips *or*
3 cups broccoli flowerets

1. In large skillet, sauté Rice-A-Roni® mix and margarine over medium heat, stirring frequently until vermicelli is golden brown.

2. Stir in 1½ cups water, orange juice, chicken, garlic, ginger, red pepper flakes and contents of seasoning packet; bring to a boil over high heat.

3. Cover; reduce heat. Simmer 10 minutes. Stir in carrots. Cover; continue to simmer 5 to 10 minutes or until liquid is absorbed and rice is tender.

Makes 4 servings

– Fantastic –

POTLUCK POULTRY

MICROWAVED GARLIC AND HERB CHICKEN

- 8 broiler-fryer chicken thighs (about 2 pounds)
- ½ cup olive oil
- 1 large tomato, chopped
- 1 rib celery, thinly sliced
- 2 tablespoons parsley flakes
- 6 cloves garlic, chopped
- 1 teaspoon salt
- ½ teaspoon ground black pepper
- ½ teaspoon dried oregano leaves
- ¼ teaspoon dried basil leaves
- ⅛ teaspoon ground nutmeg

MICROWAVE DIRECTIONS: In microwave-safe baking dish, mix together olive oil, tomato, celery, parsley, garlic, salt, pepper, oregano, basil and nutmeg. Microwave on HIGH (100% power) 3 minutes; stir. Add chicken; mix well. Cover; refrigerate 3 hours or overnight. Cover baking dish with waxed paper; microwave on HIGH 10 minutes. Turn chicken over; cover again with waxed paper and microwave on HIGH 10 minutes or until chicken is no longer pink in center. Let stand 5 minutes. To serve, remove garlic; discard. Spoon sauce over chicken. *Makes 4 servings*

Favorite recipe from **National Broiler Council**

CHICKEN TETRAZZINI

- 8 ounces uncooked spaghetti, broken in half
- 3 tablespoons butter, divided
- ¼ cup all-purpose flour
- 1 teaspoon salt
- ½ teaspoon paprika
- ½ teaspoon celery salt
- ⅛ teaspoon pepper
- 2 cups milk
- 1 cup chicken broth
- 3 cups chopped cooked chicken
- 1 can (4 ounces) mushrooms, drained
- ¼ cup pimiento strips
- ¾ cup (3 ounces) grated Wisconsin Parmesan cheese, divided

In large saucepan, cook spaghetti according to package directions; drain. Return to same saucepan; add 1 tablespoon butter. Stir until melted. Set aside. In 3-quart saucepan, melt remaining 2 tablespoons butter over medium heat; stir in flour, salt, paprika, celery salt and pepper. Remove from heat; gradually stir in milk and chicken broth. Cook over medium heat, stirring constantly, until thickened. Add chicken, mushrooms, pimiento, spaghetti and ¼ cup cheese; heat thoroughly. Place chicken mixture on ovenproof platter or in shallow casserole; sprinkle remaining ½ cup cheese over top. Broil about 3 inches from heat until lightly browned.
Makes 6 to 8 servings

Favorite recipe from **Wisconsin Milk Marketing Board**

Microwaved Garlic and Herb Chicken

– Fantastic –

TURKEY–TORTILLA BAKE

- 9 (6-inch) corn tortillas
- ½ pound 93% fat free ground turkey
- ½ cup chopped onion
- ¾ cup mild or medium taco sauce
- 1 can (4 ounces) chopped green chilies, drained
- ½ cup frozen whole kernel corn, thawed
- ½ cup (2 ounces) shredded reduced fat Cheddar cheese

Preheat oven to 400°F. Place tortillas on large baking sheet, overlapping tortillas as little as possible. Bake 4 minutes; turn tortillas. Continue baking 2 minutes or until crisp. Cool completely on wire rack.

Heat medium nonstick skillet over medium heat until hot. Add turkey and onion. Cook and stir 5 minutes or until turkey is browned and onion is tender. Add taco sauce, chilies and corn. Reduce heat and simmer 5 minutes.

Break 3 tortillas and arrange on bottom of 1½-quart casserole. Spoon half the turkey mixture over the tortillas; sprinkle with half the cheese. Repeat layers. Bake 10 minutes or until cheese is melted and casserole is heated through. Break remaining tortillas and sprinkle over casserole. Garnish with reduced fat sour cream, if desired.

Makes 4 servings

SAVORY CHICKEN & BISCUITS

- 2 tablespoons olive or vegetable oil
- 1 pound boneless, skinless chicken breasts, cut into 1-inch pieces
- 1 medium onion, chopped
- 1 cup thinly sliced carrots
- 1 cup thinly sliced celery
- 1 envelope LIPTON® Recipe Secrets® Savory Herb with Garlic Soup Mix*
- 1 cup milk
- 1 package (10 ounces) refrigerated flaky buttermilk biscuits

Preheat oven to 375°F.

In 12-inch skillet, heat oil over medium-high heat. Add chicken; cook 5 minutes or until no longer pink. Stir in onion, carrots and celery; cook, stirring occasionally, 3 minutes. Stir in Savory Herb with Garlic Soup Mix blended with milk. Bring to a boil over medium-high heat, stirring occasionally; cook 1 minute. Turn into lightly greased 2-quart casserole; arrange biscuits on top of chicken mixture with edges touching. Bake 15 minutes or until biscuits are golden brown.

Makes 4 servings

*Also terrific with LIPTON® Recipe Secrets® Golden Onion or Golden Herb with Lemon Soup Mix.

SESAME CHICKEN AND VEGETABLE STIR-FRY

- 1 tablespoon dark sesame oil
- 1 pound chicken tenders, cut into 1-inch pieces
- 2 cups broccoli flowerettes
- 1 small red bell pepper, sliced
- ½ cup onion slices (about 1 small)
- ½ cup snow peas
- 1 can (8 ounces) water chestnuts, sliced and drained
- 2 cloves garlic, minced
- 1 teaspoon five-spice powder
- 1 cup defatted low sodium chicken broth
- 2 teaspoons cornstarch
- 2 tablespoons cold water
- 2 cups hot cooked rice

Heat sesame oil in wok or large nonstick skillet over medium heat until hot. Add chicken; stir-fry about 8 minutes or until chicken is no longer pink in center. Remove chicken from wok.

Add broccoli, bell pepper, onion, peas, water chestnuts and garlic to wok; stir-fry 5 to 8 minutes or until vegetables are crisp-tender. Sprinkle with five-spice powder; cook and stir 1 minute.

Return chicken to wok. Add chicken broth; heat to a boil. Combine cornstarch and water in small bowl; stir into broth mixture. Boil 1 to 2 minutes, stirring constantly. Serve over rice.

Makes 4 servings

CHICKEN TABBOULEH

- 1 cup bulgur or cracked wheat
- 3 cups hot water
- 1½ to 2 pounds boneless, skinless chicken breasts or thighs, cut into ½-inch cubes
- 1 teaspoon salt, divided
- ¼ teaspoon pepper, divided
- ½ cup plus 2 teaspoons olive or vegetable oil, divided
- 1 teaspoon butter or margarine
- 1 to 2 cups minced fresh parsley
- ¼ cup finely chopped onion
- ¼ cup plus 3 tablespoons fresh lemon juice
- ¼ teaspoon garlic powder
- Thin lemon slices for garnish

Soak bulgur in hot water in medium bowl 30 minutes.

Sprinkle chicken with ½ teaspoon salt and ⅛ teaspoon pepper. Heat 2 teaspoons oil and butter in large skillet over medium heat. Add chicken; cook, stirring frequently, until chicken is no longer pink in center, 3 to 5 minutes. Set aside.

Drain bulgur; transfer to large bowl. Add chicken, parsley, onion, remaining ½ cup oil, lemon juice, remaining ½ teaspoon salt, remaining ⅛ teaspoon pepper and garlic powder. Toss well. Cover; refrigerate at least 1 hour. Garnish with lemon slices.

Makes 4 servings

— Fantastic —

POTLUCK POULTRY

CHICKEN RAGOÛT

- 1 package (4.9 ounces) RICE-A-RONI® Chicken & Broccoli Flavor
- 3 tablespoons all-purpose flour
- ¾ teaspoon salt (optional)
- ½ teaspoon black pepper
- 1 pound skinless, boneless chicken breasts or thighs, cut into 1-inch pieces
- 2 tablespoons margarine or butter
- 2 cups sliced mushrooms
- 1 cup thinly sliced carrots
- 1 cup coarsely chopped onion
- 2 cloves garlic, minced
- ½ cup reduced-sodium or regular chicken broth
- ¼ cup dry white wine or additional chicken broth
- 1 teaspoon dried thyme leaves

1. Prepare Rice-A-Roni® Mix as package directs.

2. While Rice-A-Roni® is simmering, combine flour, salt and pepper. Coat chicken with flour mixture.

3. In second large skillet, melt margarine over medium heat. Add mushrooms, carrots, onion and garlic; cook 5 minutes, stirring occasionally. Add chicken; continue cooking 4 minutes, stirring occasionally. Add chicken broth, wine and thyme. Reduce heat to low.

4. Simmer 5 to 7 minutes or until chicken is cooked through and carrots are tender.

5. Serve rice topped with chicken mixture.
Makes 4 servings

ONE-DISH CHICKEN 'N' RICE

- 1 cup uncooked regular or converted rice
- 1 medium red bell pepper, sliced
- 1 medium onion, cut into wedges
- 1 envelope LIPTON® Recipe Secrets® Golden Herb with Lemon or Savory Herb with Garlic Soup Mix
- 1½ cups water
- 1 cup orange juice
- ½ teaspoon salt
- 4 boneless skinless chicken breast halves (about 1 pound)

Preheat oven to 350°F.

In 13 × 9-inch casserole, combine uncooked rice, red pepper and onion. Add Golden Herb with Lemon Soup Mix blended with water, orange juice and salt. Arrange chicken on rice, spooning some liquid over chicken. Cover and bake 45 minutes or until chicken is no longer pink in center and rice is done. Garnish with orange slices and fresh chopped parsley.
Makes 4 servings

Chicken Ragoût

— Fantastic —

POTLUCK POULTRY

CHICKEN AND VEGGIE LASAGNA

        Tomato-Herb Sauce (recipe follows)
        Nonstick olive oil cooking spray
1½ cups thinly sliced zucchini
  1 cup thinly sliced carrots
  3 cups torn fresh spinach leaves
  ½ teaspoon salt
  1 package (15 ounces) fat free ricotta cheese
  ½ cup grated Parmesan cheese
  9 lasagna noodles, cooked and drained
  2 cups (8 ounces) reduced fat shredded mozzarella cheese, divided

Prepare Tomato-Herb Sauce. Preheat oven to 350°F. Spray large nonstick skillet with cooking spray; heat over medium heat until hot. Add zucchini and carrots; cook and stir about 5 minutes or until almost tender. Remove from heat; stir in spinach and salt.

Combine ricotta and Parmesan cheese in small bowl. Spread 1⅔ cups Tomato-Herb Sauce on bottom of 13 × 9-inch baking pan. Top with 3 noodles. Spoon half the ricotta cheese mixture over noodles; spread lightly with spatula. Spoon half the zucchini mixture over ricotta cheese mixture; sprinkle with 1 cup mozzarella cheese. Repeat layers; place remaining 3 noodles on top.

Spread remaining Tomato-Herb Sauce over noodles. Cover with aluminum foil; bake 1 hour or until sauce is bubbly. Let stand 5 to 10 minutes; cut into rectangles. Garnish as desired.

Makes 12 servings

Tomato-Herb Sauce
        Nonstick olive oil cooking spray
1½ cups chopped onions (about 2 medium)
  4 cloves garlic, minced
  1 tablespoon dried basil leaves
  1 teaspoon dried oregano leaves
  ½ teaspoon dried tarragon leaves
  ¼ teaspoon dried thyme leaves
2½ pounds ripe tomatoes, peeled and cut into wedges
  1 pound ground chicken, cooked, crumbled and drained
  ¾ cup water
  ¼ cup no-salt-added tomato paste
  ½ teaspoon salt
  ½ teaspoon pepper

Spray large nonstick skillet with cooking spray; heat over medium heat until hot. Add onions, garlic, basil, oregano, tarragon and thyme; cook and stir about 5 minutes or until onions are tender.

Add tomatoes, chicken, water and tomato paste; heat to a boil. Reduce heat to low and simmer, uncovered, about 20 minutes or until sauce is reduced to 5 cups. Stir in salt and pepper.

Makes 5 cups

Chicken and Veggie Lasagna

CHICKEN BOURGUIGNONNE

- 4 pounds skinless chicken thighs and breasts
- Flour
- Nonstick cooking spray
- 2 cups defatted low sodium chicken broth
- 2 cups dry white wine or defatted low sodium chicken broth
- 1 pound whole baby carrots
- ¼ cup tomato paste
- 4 cloves garlic, minced
- ½ teaspoon dried thyme leaves
- 2 bay leaves
- ¼ teaspoon salt
- ¼ teaspoon pepper
- 8 ounces fresh or thawed frozen pearl onions
- 8 ounces whole medium mushrooms
- 2 cups hot cooked white rice
- 2 cups hot cooked wild rice
- ¼ cup minced fresh parsley

Preheat oven to 325°F. Coat chicken very lightly with flour. Generously spray nonstick ovenproof Dutch oven or large nonstick ovenproof skillet with cooking spray; heat over medium heat until hot. Cook chicken 10 to 15 minutes or until browned on all sides. Drain fat from Dutch oven.

Add chicken broth, wine, carrots, tomato paste, garlic, thyme, bay leaves, salt and pepper to Dutch oven; heat to a boil. Cover; transfer to oven. Bake 1 hour. Add onions and mushrooms. Uncover; bake about 35 minutes or until vegetables are tender and chicken is no longer pink in center and juices run clear. Remove bay leaves. Combine white and wild rice; serve with chicken. Sprinkle with parsley.

Makes 8 servings

CHICKEN & WILD RICE

- 6 cups cooked wild rice (1½ cups uncooked)
- 1 can (10¾ ounces) cream of chicken soup
- 1 can (10¾ ounces) cream of celery soup
- 1 can (about 14 ounces) chicken broth
- 1 can (4 ounces) mushrooms, drained
- 3 cups diced cooked chicken
- ¼ cup chopped green bell pepper
- ¼ cup chopped red bell pepper
- ¼ teaspoon garlic powder
- ½ cup slivered almonds

Preheat oven to 350°F. Grease 13 × 9-inch casserole.

Mix wild rice, soups, broth, mushrooms, chicken, bell peppers and garlic powder in large bowl. Spread in prepared dish. Sprinkle with almonds. Bake, covered, 45 minutes. Uncover and continue baking 15 minutes or until heated through.

Makes 10 to 12 servings

Favorite recipe from **Minnesota Cultivated Wild Rice Council**

Chicken Bourguignonne

POTLUCK POULTRY

CHICKEN FIESTA

- 2½ to 3 pounds chicken pieces
- Salt
- Pepper
- Paprika
- 2 tablespoons butter or margarine
- ¼ pound pork sausage
- ¾ cup sliced celery
- ¾ cup sliced green onions with tops
- 3 cups cooked rice
- 1 can (12 ounces) whole kernel corn with peppers, drained
- 2 teaspoons lemon juice

Preheat oven to 350°F.

Season chicken with salt, pepper and paprika. In large skillet, melt butter. Add chicken to skillet; brown well. Drain chicken on paper towels; set aside. Cook sausage, celery and onions in same skillet over medium-high heat, stirring frequently until vegetables are crisp-tender. Add rice, corn and lemon juice; mix well. Pour into shallow baking dish. Arrange chicken on top of rice mixture, pressing chicken slightly into rice mixture. Cover with foil. Bake 30 to 40 minutes or until chicken is no longer pink in center.

Makes 6 servings

Favorite recipe from USA Rice Council

CHICKEN VEGETABLE SKILLET

- 8 broiler-fryer chicken thighs, skinned, fat trimmed
- ¾ teaspoon salt, divided
- 1 tablespoon vegetable oil
- 3 medium red-skinned potatoes, cut into ¼-inch slices
- 1 medium onion, sliced
- ½ pound fresh mushrooms, sliced
- 1 large tomato, coarsely chopped
- ¼ cup chicken broth
- ¼ cup dry white wine
- ½ teaspoon oregano
- ¼ teaspoon pepper
- 1 tablespoon chopped fresh parsley

Sprinkle chicken with ¼ teaspoon salt. Heat oil in large nonstick saucepan over medium-high heat. Add chicken and cook, turning once, about 8 minutes or until browned on both sides. Remove chicken; set aside. In same pan, layer potatoes, onion, chicken, mushrooms and tomato.

In 1-cup measure, mix together broth and wine; pour over chicken and vegetables. Sprinkle oregano, remaining ½ teaspoon salt and pepper over chicken. Heat to boiling; cover. Reduce heat to medium-low; cook about 20 minutes or until chicken and vegetables are fork-tender. Sprinkle with fresh parsley before serving.

Makes 4 servings

Chicken Fiesta

Fantastic

POTLUCK POULTRY

CORN AND CHICKEN CASSEROLE

- 2 whole chickens (2 to 3 pounds each), each cut into 10 pieces
- 3 tablespoons Chef Paul Prudhomme's POULTRY MAGIC®, divided
- ⅓ cup vegetable oil
- 8 cups fresh corn, cut off cob (about twelve 8-inch ears)
- 3½ cups finely chopped onions
- 1½ cups finely chopped green bell peppers
- 1 pound tomatoes, peeled, chopped
- 3½ cups chicken stock
- 2 cups uncooked rice

Remove excess fat from chicken; season with 2 tablespoons Poultry Magic® and place in plastic bag. Seal and refrigerate overnight.

Heat oil in an 8-quart roasting pan over high heat until oil just starts to smoke, about 6 minutes. Add 10 pieces of chicken (skin side down) and brown, cooking 5 minutes on each side. Remove chicken; brown remaining chicken 5 minutes on each side. Remove and keep warm.

Add half the corn to hot oil; stir well. Cook, without stirring, about 6 minutes. Stir in 1½ teaspoons Poultry Magic®. Cook, without stirring, about 7 minutes. Stir in onions, bell peppers, and remaining 1½ teaspoons Poultry Magic®. Cover with tight-fitting lid and cook 5 minutes. Add remaining corn and tomatoes; mix well.

Cover and cook 10 minutes. Transfer corn mixture to another pan and keep warm. Preheat oven to 400°F.

Add stock and rice to roasting pan. Bring to a boil, stirring occasionally. Layer chicken pieces on top of rice. Cover chicken layer with corn mixture. Cover and bake 25 minutes.

Remove casserole from oven. Let stand 10 minutes.
Makes 8 servings

LAYERED CHICKEN & VEGETABLE BAKE

- 1 package RITZ® Stuffing Mix
- ¾ cup water
- 1 pound chicken tenders
- 1 large tomato, sliced ¼ inch thick
- 1 medium zucchini, sliced ¼ inch thick
- 1 cup shredded mozzarella cheese

In small bowl, toss stuffing crumbs, seasoning packet and water. Place half of mixture in lightly greased 9-inch square baking pan. Place chicken on top; cover with remaining stuffing mixture. Layer tomato and zucchini on top; cover with cheese.

Bake at 375°F 30 to 35 minutes or until top is lightly browned. Cut into squares.
Makes 4 servings

Fantastic

POTLUCK POULTRY

BUFFET CHICKEN MEDLEY

- 4 boneless, skinless chicken breasts, quartered (about 2½ pounds)
- 2 tablespoons butter or margarine
- 1 large onion, cut into ¼-inch pieces
- 1 jar (6 ounces) marinated artichoke hearts, drained and sliced (reserve marinade)
- 4 tomatoes, cut into wedges
- 1 teaspoon salt, divided
- ½ teaspoon pepper, divided
- 1 avocado, halved, peeled, pitted and cut into ½-inch wedges
- 1 cup (4 ounces) crumbled feta cheese

In 10-inch skillet, melt butter over medium-high heat. Add chicken pieces; cook, turning, about 5 minutes or until lightly browned. Remove chicken to warm dish.

Add onion to pan juices; cook over medium heat 3 minutes, stirring frequently. Add artichokes, reserved marinade and tomatoes; cook about 2 minutes. Remove from heat. In 2-quart baking dish, place half of chicken; sprinkle with ½ teaspoon salt and ¼ teaspoon pepper. Spoon half of artichoke mixture over chicken; add half of avocado and half of cheese. Top with remaining chicken; repeat layers. Bake at 350°F about 25 minutes or until chicken is no longer pink in center.

Makes 8 servings

Favorite recipe from **National Broiler Council**

"WILDLY" DELICIOUS CASSEROLE

- 1 package (14 ounces) ground chicken
- 1 package (14 ounces) frozen broccoli with red peppers
- 1½ cups cooked wild rice
- 1 can (10¾ ounces) condensed cream of chicken soup
- ½ cup mayonnaise
- ½ cup plain yogurt
- 1 teaspoon lemon juice
- ½ teaspoon curry powder
- ¼ cup dry bread crumbs
- 3 to 4 slices process American cheese, cut in half diagonally

Preheat oven to 375°F. Grease 8-inch square casserole; set aside. In large skillet, cook chicken until no longer pink. Drain; set aside. Cook broccoli and peppers according to package directions; set aside. In large bowl, combine wild rice, soup, mayonnaise, yogurt, lemon juice and curry. Stir in chicken and broccoli and peppers. Pour into prepared casserole; sprinkle with bread crumbs. Bake 45 to 55 minutes. During last 5 minutes of baking, arrange cheese slices on top of casserole. Remove from oven; let stand 5 minutes.

Makes 6 to 8 servings

Favorite recipe from **Minnesota Cultivated Wild Rice Council**

Spectacular

DEEP SEA DINNERS

HOMESTYLE TUNA POT PIE

- 1 package (15 ounces) refrigerated pie crusts
- 1 can (12 ounces) STARKIST® Solid White or Chunk Light Tuna, drained and chunked
- 1 package (10 ounces) frozen peas and carrots, thawed and drained
- ½ cup chopped onion
- 1 can (10¾ ounces) cream of potato or cream of mushroom soup
- ⅓ cup milk
- ½ teaspoon poultry seasoning or dried thyme
- Salt and pepper to taste

Line 9-inch pie pan with one crust; set aside. Reserve second crust. In medium bowl, combine remaining ingredients; mix well. Pour tuna mixture into pie shell; top with second crust. Crimp edges to seal. Cut slits in top crust to vent. Bake in 375°F oven 45 to 50 minutes or until golden brown.

Makes 6 servings

— *Spectacular* —

BAKED ROCKFISH VERACRUZ

- **1 teaspoon olive oil**
- **½ small onion, chopped**
- **4 cloves garlic, minced**
- **8 to 10 ounces ripe tomatoes, cored and chopped *or* 2 cans (15 ounces each) no-salt-added whole tomatoes, drained, chopped**
- **½ green bell pepper, chopped**
- **½ to 1 jalapeño pepper, seeded, minced (optional)**
- **1 teaspoon dried oregano leaves, crushed**
- **½ teaspoon ground cumin**
- **¼ cup small pimiento-stuffed green olives**
- **2 teaspoons drained capers (optional)**
- **1 pound skinless fillets rockfish, snapper, halibut or cod**

Preheat oven to 375°F. Heat large nonstick skillet over medium-high heat. Add oil, onion and garlic. Cook and stir 3 minutes or until onion is tender. Add tomatoes, bell pepper, jalapeño, oregano and cumin. Cook over high heat, stirring occasionally, 2 to 3 minutes more. Stir in olives and capers, if desired; set aside.

Spray 11 × 7-inch baking pan with nonstick cooking spray. Place fish in single layer in pan, folding thin tail sections under to make fish evenly thick. Pour tomato mixture over fish. Cover with foil; bake 10 minutes or until fish is opaque and flakes easily when tested with fork. Serve with rice and garnish with fresh herbs, if desired.

Makes 4 servings

SEAFOOD GUMBO

- **½ cup sliced celery**
- **½ cup chopped onion**
- **½ cup chopped green bell pepper**
- **1 clove garlic, minced**
- **1 tablespoon vegetable oil**
- **1 can (13¾ ounces) chicken broth**
- **1 can (14 to 16 ounces) whole tomatoes, cut into bite-size pieces**
- **2 cups fresh or frozen sliced okra**
- **¾ cup HEINZ® Chili Sauce**
- **½ teaspoon salt**
- **¼ teaspoon black pepper**
- **¼ teaspoon dried thyme leaves**
- **1 bay leaf**
- **Dash hot pepper sauce**
- **1 pound white fish fillets, cut into 1-inch pieces**
- **Hot cooked rice (about 1⅓ cups)**

In 3-quart saucepan, sauté celery, onion, bell pepper and garlic in oil until crisp-tender. Add broth, tomatoes, okra, chili sauce, salt, black pepper, thyme, bay leaf and hot pepper sauce. Simmer, covered, 20 minutes. Add fish; simmer, covered, 15 to 20 minutes. Remove bay leaf. Place about ⅓ cup rice in each serving bowl; top with gumbo.

Makes 4 servings (about 6 cups)

Baked Rockfish Veracruz

— Spectacular —

Deep Sea Dinners

BISCUIT–TOPPED TUNA BAKE

- 2 tablespoons vegetable oil
- ½ cup chopped onion
- ½ cup chopped celery
- 1 can (12 ounces) STARKIST® Solid White or Chunk Light Tuna, drained and chunked
- 1 can (10¾ ounces) condensed cream of potato soup
- 1 package (10 ounces) frozen peas and carrots, thawed
- ¾ cup milk
- ¼ teaspoon ground black pepper
- ¼ teaspoon garlic powder
- 1 can (7½ ounces) refrigerator flaky biscuits

In large skillet, heat oil over medium-high heat; sauté onion and celery until onion is soft. Add remaining ingredients except biscuits; heat thoroughly. Transfer mixture to 1½-quart casserole. Arrange biscuits around top edge of dish; bake in 400°F oven 10 to 15 minutes or until biscuits are golden brown.

Makes 4 to 6 servings

Prep and Cook Time: 25 minutes

SHRIMP CASSEROLE

- ¾ pound raw medium shrimp, peeled, deveined
- ⅓ cup chopped celery
- ¼ cup chopped green bell pepper
- ¼ cup chopped onion
- 3 tablespoons margarine or butter
- 1 can (10¾ ounces) condensed cream of celery or cream of mushroom soup
- ⅓ cup sliced water chestnuts
- 1 hard-boiled egg, chopped
- 1 tablespoon lemon juice
- ½ cup dry stuffing mix
- ¼ teaspoon salt
- ¼ cup (1 ounce) shredded Cheddar cheese

Cut any large shrimp in half. In 1½-quart shallow casserole, combine shrimp, celery, bell pepper, onion and margarine. Cover and cook on HIGH (100% power) 4 minutes, stirring after 2 minutes. Stir in soup, water chestnuts, egg, lemon juice, stuffing mix and salt. Cover and cook on HIGH 4 minutes, rotating dish once. Sprinkle casserole with cheese; cook, uncovered, on HIGH 1 minute.

Makes 4 servings

Favorite recipe from **Florida Department of Agriculture and Consumer Services, Bureau of Seafood and Aquaculture**

Biscuit-Topped Tuna Bake

Spectacular

DEEP SEA DINNERS

THAI–STYLE TUNA FRIED RICE

- **4 to 5 tablespoons vegetable oil, divided**
- **2 eggs, lightly beaten**
- **⅔ cup uncooked, peeled medium shrimp, chopped into ¾-inch pieces**
- **3 cloves garlic**
- **1 to 2 tablespoons minced fresh serrano chiles**
- **4 to 6 cups cooked rice, chilled overnight**
- **1 tablespoon sugar**
- **1 tablespoon nam pla (fish sauce) (optional)**
- **1 tablespoon soy sauce**
- **1 can (6 ounces) STARKIST® Solid White or Chunk Light Tuna, drained and chunked**
- **½ cup chopped dry-roasted peanuts**
- **¼ cup chopped fresh basil**
- **2 tablespoons chopped fresh cilantro**
- **Lime wedges, for garnish**

In wok, heat 1 tablespoon oil over medium-high heat; add eggs and cook, stirring, until partially cooked but still runny. Return eggs to bowl. Wipe out wok with paper towels. Add 2 tablespoons oil to wok; heat.

Add shrimp, garlic and chiles. Stir-fry until shrimp turn pink, about 3 minutes. Remove shrimp mixture; set aside. Add 1 or 2 tablespoons oil to wok; stir-fry rice, sugar, nam pla, if desired, and soy sauce until rice is heated through. Add tuna and peanuts; heat.

Return shrimp mixture and eggs to pan, chopping eggs into pieces with stir-fry spatula. Add basil and cilantro; toss gently to mix. Serve with lime wedges for garnish; squeeze juice on fried rice, if desired.
Makes 4 to 6 servings

Prep and Cook Time: 15 minutes

SURFER'S SEAFOOD CASSEROLE

- **½ pound fresh crabmeat**
- **½ pound cooked, peeled, deveined shrimp**
- **1⅓ cups chopped celery**
- **½ cup chopped onion**
- **½ cup chopped green bell pepper**
- **½ teaspoon salt**
- **1 cup mayonnaise**
- **1 teaspoon Worcestershire sauce**
- **1 cup crushed potato chips**
- **Paprika**

Preheat oven to 350°F. Grease 1½-quart casserole; set aside.

Mix crabmeat, shrimp, celery, onion, bell pepper, salt, mayonnaise and Worcestershire in large bowl. Pour crab mixture into prepared casserole. Top with crushed potato chips and paprika. Bake 30 to 40 minutes or until knife inserted in center comes out clean.
Makes 6 servings

*Favorite recipe from **Florida Department of Agriculture and Consumer Services, Bureau of Seafood and Aquaculture***

Thai-Style Tuna Fried Rice

— Spectacular —

DEEP SEA DINNERS

LEMON–GARLIC SHRIMP

- 1 package (6.2 ounces) RICE-A-RONI® With ⅓ Less Salt Broccoli Au Gratin
- 1 tablespoon margarine or butter
- 1 pound raw medium shrimp, shelled, deveined or large scallops, halved
- 1 medium red or green bell pepper, cut into short thin strips
- 2 cloves garlic, minced
- ½ teaspoon Italian seasoning
- ½ cup reduced-sodium or regular chicken broth
- 1 tablespoon lemon juice
- 1 tablespoon cornstarch
- 3 medium green onions, cut into ½-inch pieces
- 1 teaspoon grated lemon peel

1. Prepare Rice-A-Roni® Mix as package directs.

2. While Rice-A-Roni® is simmering, heat margarine in second large skillet or wok over medium-high heat. Add shrimp, red pepper, garlic and Italian seasoning. Stir-fry 3 to 4 minutes or until seafood is opaque.

3. Combine chicken broth, lemon juice and cornstarch, mixing until smooth. Add broth mixture and onions to skillet. Stir-fry 2 to 3 minutes or until sauce thickens.

4. Stir ½ teaspoon lemon peel into rice. Serve rice topped with shrimp mixture; sprinkle with remaining ½ teaspoon lemon peel.

Makes 4 servings

EASY THREE CHEESE TUNA SOUFFLÉ

- 4 cups large garlic and herb or ranch-flavored croutons
- 2½ cups milk
- 4 large eggs
- 1 can (10¾ ounces) cream of celery soup
- 3 cups shredded cheese (a combination of Cheddar, Monterey Jack and Swiss)
- 1 can (12 ounces) STARKIST® Solid White or Chunk Light Tuna, drained and flaked
- 1 tablespoon butter or margarine
- ½ cup chopped celery
- ½ cup finely chopped onion
- ¼ pound mushrooms, sliced

In bottom of lightly greased 13 × 9-inch baking dish, arrange croutons. In medium bowl, beat together milk, eggs and soup; stir in cheeses and tuna. In small skillet, melt butter over medium heat. Add celery, onion and mushrooms; sauté until onion is soft.

Spoon sautéed vegetables over croutons; pour egg-tuna mixture over top. Cover; refrigerate overnight. Remove from refrigerator 1 hour before baking; bake in 325°F oven 45 to 50 minutes or until hot and bubbly.

Makes 8 servings

Prep and Cook Time: 60 minutes

Lemon-Garlic Shrimp

— Spectacular —

Deep Sea Dinners

CRAB AND CORN ENCHILADA CASSEROLE

Spicy Tomato Sauce (recipe follows), divided
10 to 12 ounces fresh crabmeat or flaked or chopped imitation crabmeat
1 package (10 ounces) frozen whole kernel corn, thawed, drained
1½ cups (6 ounces) shredded reduced fat Monterey Jack cheese, divided
1 can (4 ounces) diced mild green chilies
12 (6-inch) corn tortillas
1 lime, cut into 6 wedges
Low fat sour cream (optional)

Preheat oven to 350°F. Combine 2 cups Spicy Tomato Sauce, crabmeat, corn, 1 cup cheese and chilies in medium bowl.

Cut each tortilla into 4 wedges. Place one-third of tortilla wedges in bottom of shallow 3- to 4-quart casserole, overlapping to make solid layer. Spread half of crab mixture on top. Repeat with another layer of tortilla wedges, remaining crab mixture and remaining tortillas. Spread remaining 1 cup Spicy Tomato Sauce over top; cover.

Bake 30 to 40 minutes or until heated through. Sprinkle with remaining ½ cup cheese and bake uncovered 5 minutes or until cheese melts. Squeeze lime over individual servings. Serve with low fat sour cream, if desired. *Makes 6 servings*

Spicy Tomato Sauce
2 cans (15 ounces each) no-salt-added stewed tomatoes, undrained *or* 6 medium tomatoes
2 teaspoons olive oil
1 medium onion, chopped
1 tablespoon minced garlic
2 tablespoons chili powder
2 teaspoons ground cumin
2 teaspoons dried oregano leaves, crushed
1 teaspoon ground cinnamon
¼ teaspoon crushed red pepper
¼ teaspoon ground cloves

Combine tomatoes with liquid in food processor or blender; process until finely chopped. Set aside.

Heat oil over medium-high heat in large saucepan or Dutch oven. Add onion and garlic. Cook and stir 5 minutes or until onion is tender. Add chili powder, cumin, oregano, cinnamon, red pepper and cloves. Cook and stir 1 minute.

Add tomatoes; reduce heat to medium-low. Simmer, uncovered, 20 minutes or until sauce is reduced to 3 to 3¼ cups. *Makes about 3 cups*

Crab and Corn Enchilada Casserole

Dazzling PASTA DISHES

COUNTRY CHICKEN DINNER

¼ **cup milk**
2 tablespoons margarine or butter
1 package (4.7 ounces) PASTA RONI®
  Chicken & Broccoli with Linguine
2 cups frozen mixed broccoli, cauliflower
  and carrots vegetable medley
2 cups chopped cooked chicken or turkey
1 teaspoon dried basil

1. In round 3-quart microwaveable glass casserole, combine 1¾ cups water, milk and margarine. Microwave, uncovered, on HIGH 4 to 5 minutes or until boiling.

2. Gradually add pasta while stirring.

3. Stir in contents of seasoning packet, frozen vegetables, chicken and basil.

4. Microwave, uncovered, on HIGH 14 to 15 minutes, stirring gently after 7 minutes. Sauce will be thin, but will thicken upon standing.

5. Let stand 4 to 5 minutes or until desired consistency. Stir before serving.

Makes 4 servings

— Dazzling —

PASTA DISHES

WISCONSIN SWISS LINGUINE TART

- ½ cup butter, divided
- 2 cloves garlic, minced
- 30 thin French bread slices
- 3 tablespoons all-purpose flour
- 1 teaspoon salt
- ¼ teaspoon white pepper
- Dash ground nutmeg
- 2½ cups milk
- ¼ cup grated Wisconsin Parmesan cheese
- 2 eggs, beaten
- 8 ounces fresh linguine, cooked and drained
- 2 cups (8 ounces) shredded Wisconsin Swiss cheese, divided
- ⅓ cup sliced green onions
- 2 tablespoons minced fresh basil *or* 1 teaspoon dried basil leaves, crushed
- 2 plum tomatoes, each cut lengthwise into eighths

Preheat oven to 400°F. Melt ¼ cup butter in small saucepan over medium heat. Add garlic; cook 1 minute. Brush 10-inch pie plate with butter mixture. Line bottom and side of pie plate with bread, allowing bread to extend up to 1 inch over side of dish. Brush bread with remaining butter mixture. Bake 5 minutes or until lightly browned. *Reduce heat to 350°F.*

Melt remaining ¼ cup butter in medium saucepan over low heat. Stir in flour and seasonings. Gradually stir in milk; cook, stirring constantly, until thickened. Add Parmesan cheese. Remove small amount of sauce. Add to eggs; stir until blended. Return egg mixture to saucepan; mix well. Set aside.

Combine linguine, 1¼ cups Swiss cheese, onions and basil in large bowl. Pour sauce over linguine mixture; toss to coat. Pour into crust. Arrange tomatoes on top; sprinkle with remaining ¾ cup Swiss cheese. Bake 25 minutes or until thoroughly heated; let stand 5 minutes. Garnish as desired.
Makes 8 servings

Favorite recipe from **Wisconsin Milk Marketing Board**

Wisconsin Swiss Linguine Tart

Dazzling

Pasta Dishes

Shrimp Noodle Supreme

- 1 package (8 ounces) spinach noodles, cooked and drained
- 1 package (3 ounces) cream cheese, cubed and softened
- 1½ pounds medium shrimp, peeled and deveined
- ½ cup butter, softened
- Salt and pepper to taste
- 1 can (10¾ ounces) condensed cream of mushroom soup
- 1 cup dairy sour cream
- ½ cup half-and-half
- ½ cup mayonnaise
- 1 tablespoon chopped chives
- 1 tablespoon chopped parsley
- ½ teaspoon Dijon mustard
- ¾ cup (6 ounces) shredded sharp Cheddar cheese

Preheat oven to 325°F. Combine noodles and cream cheese in medium bowl. Spread noodle mixture on bottom of greased 13 × 9-inch glass casserole. Cook shrimp in butter in large skillet over medium-high heat until pink and tender, about 5 minutes. Season with salt and pepper. Spread shrimp over noodles.

Combine soup, sour cream, half-and-half, mayonnaise, chives, parsley and mustard in another medium bowl. Spread over shrimp. Sprinkle Cheddar cheese over top. Bake 25 minutes or until hot and cheese is melted. Garnish with lemon slices and paprika, if desired. *Makes 6 servings*

Baked Rigatoni with Sausage

- ½ pound Italian sausage*
- 2 cups low fat milk
- 2 tablespoons all-purpose flour
- ½ pound rigatoni pasta, cooked and drained
- 2½ cups (10 ounces) shredded mozzarella cheese
- ¼ cup grated Parmesan cheese
- 1 teaspoon LAWRY'S® Garlic Salt
- ¾ teaspoon LAWRY'S® Seasoned Pepper
- 2 to 3 tablespoons dry bread crumbs *or*
- ¾ cup croutons

In large skillet, crumble Italian sausage. Brown 5 minutes; drain fat. Stir in mixture of milk and flour; bring to a boil, stirring constantly. Stir in pasta, cheeses, Garlic Salt and Seasoned Pepper. Place in 1½-quart baking dish. Bake in 350°F oven 25 minutes. Sprinkle with bread crumbs; place under broiler to brown. *Makes 6 servings*

*¼ pound cooked, diced ham can replace sausage.

Shrimp Noodle Supreme

— Dazzling —

PASTA DISHES

ENLIGHTENED MACARONI AND CHEESE

- 8 ounces uncooked wagon wheel, bow tie or elbow pasta
- 1 tablespoon all-purpose flour
- 2 teaspoons cornstarch
- ¼ teaspoon dry mustard
- 1 can (12 ounces) evaporated skimmed milk
- 1 cup (4 ounces) shredded reduced fat medium sharp Cheddar cheese
- ½ cup (2 ounces) shredded reduced fat Monterey Jack cheese
- 1 jar (2 ounces) diced pimiento, drained and rinsed
- 1 teaspoon Worcestershire sauce
- ¼ teaspoon ground black pepper
- 1 tablespoon dry bread crumbs
- 1 tablespoon paprika

Preheat oven to 375°F. Cook pasta according to package directions. Drain and set aside.

Combine flour, cornstarch and mustard in medium saucepan; stir in milk until smooth. Cook over medium heat, stirring occasionally, until slightly thickened, about 8 minutes. Remove from heat; stir in cheeses, pimiento, Worcestershire sauce and pepper. Add pasta; mix well.

Spray 1½-quart casserole with nonstick cooking spray. Spoon mixture into casserole; sprinkle with bread crumbs and paprika. Bake 20 minutes or until bubbly and heated through.

Makes 6 (1-cup) servings

POLISH REUBEN CASSEROLE

- 2 cans (10¾ ounces each) condensed cream of mushroom soup
- 1⅓ cups milk
- ½ cup chopped onion
- 1 tablespoon prepared mustard
- 2 cans (16 ounces each) sauerkraut, rinsed and drained
- 1 package (8 ounces) uncooked medium-width noodles
- 1½ pounds Polish sausage, cut into ½-inch pieces
- 2 cups (8 ounces) shredded Swiss cheese
- ¾ cup whole wheat bread crumbs
- 2 tablespoons butter, melted

Combine soup, milk, onion and mustard in medium bowl; blend well. Spread sauerkraut into greased 13 × 9-inch pan. Top with uncooked noodles. Spoon soup mixture evenly over noodles; cover with sausage. Top with cheese. Combine bread crumbs and butter in small bowl; sprinkle over cheese. Cover pan tightly with foil. Bake in preheated 350°F oven 1 hour or until noodles are tender. Garnish as desired.

Makes 8 to 10 servings

Favorite recipe from **North Dakota Wheat Commission**

Enlightened Macaroni and Cheese

Pasta Dishes

Pastitso

- 8 ounces uncooked elbow macaroni
- ½ cup cholesterol free egg substitute
- ¼ teaspoon ground nutmeg
- ¾ pound lean ground lamb, beef or turkey
- ½ cup chopped onion
- 1 clove garlic, minced
- 1 can (8 ounces) tomato sauce
- ¾ teaspoon dried mint leaves
- ½ teaspoon dried oregano leaves
- ½ teaspoon ground black pepper
- ⅛ teaspoon ground cinnamon
- 2 teaspoons reduced calorie margarine
- 3 tablespoons all-purpose flour
- 1½ cups skim milk
- 2 tablespoons grated Parmesan cheese

Cook pasta according to package directions. Drain and transfer to medium bowl; stir in egg substitute and nutmeg. Spray bottom of 9-inch square baking dish with nonstick cooking spray. Spread pasta mixture in baking dish. Set aside.

Preheat oven to 350°F. Cook lamb, onion and garlic in large nonstick skillet over medium heat until lamb is no longer pink. Stir in tomato sauce, mint, oregano, pepper and cinnamon. Reduce heat to low and simmer 10 minutes; spread over pasta.

Melt margarine in small saucepan over medium heat. Add flour. Stir 1 minute. Whisk in milk. Cook, stirring constantly, until thickened, about 6 minutes; spread over meat mixture. Sprinkle with cheese. Bake 30 to 40 minutes or until set.

Makes 6 servings

Chili Wagon Wheel Casserole

- 8 ounces uncooked wagon wheel or other pasta
- Nonstick cooking spray
- 1 pound 95% lean ground beef or ground turkey breast
- ¾ cup chopped green bell pepper
- ¾ cup chopped onion
- 1 can (14½ ounces) no-salt-added stewed tomatoes
- 1 can (8 ounces) no-salt-added tomato sauce
- ½ teaspoon ground black pepper
- ¼ teaspoon ground allspice
- ½ cup (2 ounces) shredded reduced fat Cheddar cheese

Preheat oven to 350°F. Cook pasta according to package directions, omitting salt. Drain and rinse; set aside.

Spray large nonstick skillet with cooking spray. Add ground beef, bell pepper and onion; cook 5 minutes or until meat is no longer pink, stirring frequently. (Drain mixture if using ground beef.) Stir in tomatoes, tomato sauce, black pepper and allspice; cook 2 minutes. Stir in pasta. Spoon mixture into 2½-quart casserole. Sprinkle with cheese. Bake 20 to 25 minutes or until heated through.

Makes 6 servings

Pastitso

— Dazzling —

PASTA DISHES

ANGEL HAIR CARBONARA

- ⅔ cup milk
- 2 tablespoons margarine or butter
- 1 package (4.8 ounces) PASTA RONI® Angel Hair Pasta with Herbs
- 2 cups cubed cooked ham or pork
- 1 package (10 ounces) frozen peas
- ¼ cup sliced green onions

1. In round 3-quart microwaveable glass casserole, combine 1½ cups water, milk and margarine. Microwave, uncovered, on HIGH 4 to 5 minutes or until boiling.

2. Gradually add pasta while stirring. Separate pasta with fork, if needed.

3. Stir in contents of seasoning packet.

4. Microwave, uncovered, on HIGH 4 minutes, stirring gently after 2 minutes. Separate pasta with fork, if needed. Stir in pork, frozen peas and onions. Continue to microwave 2 to 3 minutes. Sauce will be thin, but will thicken upon standing.

5. Let stand 3 minutes or until desired consistency. Stir before serving.   *Makes 4 servings*

CRAZY LASAGNA CASSEROLE

- 1½ pounds ground beef
- 1 teaspoon LAWRY'S® Seasoned Salt
- 1 package (1.5 ounces) LAWRY'S® Original Style Spaghetti Sauce Spices & Seasonings
- 1 can (8 ounces) tomato sauce
- 1 can (6 ounces) tomato paste
- 1½ cups water
- 1 package (10 ounces) medium-size shell macaroni, cooked and drained
- 1 carton (16 ounces) small curd cottage cheese
- 1½ cups (6 ounces) shredded Cheddar cheese

In large skillet, brown ground beef until crumbly; drain fat. Add Seasoned Salt, Spaghetti Sauce Spices & Seasonings, tomato sauce, tomato paste and water; blend well. Bring to a boil; reduce heat and simmer, uncovered, 10 minutes, stirring occasionally. In shallow 2-quart casserole, layer half of macaroni, cottage cheese and meat sauce. Sprinkle ½ cup Cheddar cheese over meat sauce. Repeat layers, ending with remaining meat sauce. Top with remaining 1 cup Cheddar cheese. Bake, uncovered, in 350°F oven 30 to 40 minutes or until bubbly and cheese is melted.   *Makes 8 servings*

Angel Hair Carbonara

— Dazzling —

PASTA DISHES

SKILLET PASTA ROMA

- ½ pound Italian sausage, sliced or crumbled
- 1 large onion, coarsely chopped
- 1 large clove garlic, minced
- 2 cans (14½ ounces each) DEL MONTE® Italian Recipe Stewed Tomatoes, undrained
- 1 can (8 ounces) DEL MONTE® Tomato Sauce
- 1 cup water
- 8 ounces uncooked rotini or other spiral pasta
- 8 sliced mushrooms, optional
- Grated Parmesan cheese and fresh parsley sprigs, optional

In large skillet, brown sausage. Add onion and garlic. Cook until onion is soft; drain. Stir in stewed tomatoes with juice, tomato sauce, water and pasta. Cover and bring to a boil; reduce heat. Simmer, covered, 25 to 30 minutes or until pasta is tender, stirring occasionally. Stir in mushrooms, if desired; simmer 5 minutes. Serve in skillet garnished with cheese and parsley, if desired.

Makes 4 servings

PIZZA PASTA

- 1 medium green bell pepper, chopped
- 1 medium onion, chopped
- 1 cup sliced mushrooms
- ½ teaspoon LAWRY'S® Garlic Powder with Parsley or Garlic Salt
- 1 tablespoon vegetable oil
- ¼ cup sliced ripe olives
- 1 package (1.5 ounces) LAWRY'S® Original Style Spaghetti Sauce Spices & Seasonings
- 1¾ cups water
- 1 can (6 ounces) tomato paste
- 10 ounces mostaccioli, cooked and drained
- 3 ounces thinly sliced pepperoni
- ¾ cup shredded mozzarella cheese

In large skillet, sauté bell pepper, onion, mushrooms and Garlic Powder with Parsley in vegetable oil until vegetables are tender. Stir in olives, Spaghetti Sauce Spices & Seasonings, water and tomato paste; blend well. Bring sauce to a boil; reduce heat. Simmer, uncovered, 10 minutes. Add mostaccioli and pepperoni; blend well. Pour into 12 × 8 × 2-inch casserole; top with cheese. Bake at 350°F 15 minutes or until cheese is melted.

Makes 6 servings

Skillet Pasta Roma

Country VEGETABLES & GRAINS

Tabbouleh

¾ cup bulgur, rinsed, drained
Boiling water
2 cups chopped seeded cucumbers
1 large tomato, seeded, chopped
1 cup snipped parsley
⅓ cup CRISCO® Oil
⅓ cup chopped green onions
2 tablespoons lemon juice
1 teaspoon dried mint leaves, crumbled
2 cloves garlic, minced
½ teaspoon salt
⅛ teaspoon white pepper
⅛ teaspoon ground red pepper

Place bulgur in medium mixing bowl. Add enough boiling water to just cover bulgur. Let stand about 1 hour or until bulgur is rehydrated. Drain.

Combine bulgur, cucumber, tomato and parsley in large serving bowl; set aside. Blend remaining ingredients in small bowl. Pour over bulgur mixture; toss to coat. Cover; refrigerate at least 3 hours. Stir before serving. *Makes 10 to 12 servings*

FRESH VEGETABLE LASAGNA

**8 ounces uncooked lasagna noodles
1 package (10 ounces) frozen chopped spinach, thawed, well drained
1 cup shredded carrots
½ cup sliced green onions
½ cup sliced red bell pepper
¼ cup chopped fresh parsley
½ teaspoon ground black pepper
1½ cups low fat cottage cheese
1 cup buttermilk
½ cup plain nonfat yogurt
2 egg whites
1 cup sliced mushrooms
1 can (14 ounces) artichoke hearts, drained and chopped
2 cups (8 ounces) shredded part-skim mozzarella cheese
¼ cup freshly grated Parmesan cheese**

Cook pasta according to package directions, omitting salt. Drain. Rinse under cold water; drain well. Set aside.

Preheat oven to 375°F. Pat spinach with paper towels to remove excess moisture. Combine spinach, carrots, green onions, bell pepper, parsley and black pepper in large bowl. Set aside. Combine cottage cheese, buttermilk, yogurt and egg whites in food processor or blender; process until smooth.

Spray 13 × 9-inch baking pan with nonstick cooking spray. Arrange half of lasagna noodles in bottom of pan. Spread with half each of cottage cheese mixture, vegetable mixture, mushrooms, artichokes and mozzarella. Repeat layers, ending with noodles. Sprinkle with Parmesan. Cover and bake 30 minutes. Remove cover; continue baking 20 minutes or until bubbly and heated through. Let stand 10 minutes before serving.

Makes 8 servings

DELUXE POTATO BAKE

**2 eggs, beaten
¼ cup unseasoned dry bread crumbs
2 green onions with tops, chopped
2 tablespoons milk
¾ teaspoon LAWRY'S® Seasoned Pepper
½ teaspoon LAWRY'S® Seasoned Salt
2 large potatoes, peeled, grated and held in ice water
1 cup (4 ounces) shredded Cheddar cheese
4 slices cooked and crumbled bacon**

In large bowl, combine eggs, bread crumbs, onions, milk, Seasoned Pepper and Seasoned Salt. Drain potatoes and stir into egg mixture. Add half of Cheddar cheese and half of bacon. Spoon mixture into lightly greased 8-inch square casserole. Bake, uncovered, in 350°F oven for 20 minutes. Sprinkle with remaining cheese and bacon; bake 5 minutes longer.

Makes 4 servings

Fresh Vegetable Lasagna

VEGETABLE RISOTTO

  2 cups broccoli flowerets
  1 cup finely chopped zucchini
  1 cup finely chopped yellow squash
  1 cup finely chopped red bell pepper
2½ cups chicken broth
  1 tablespoon extra virgin olive oil
  2 tablespoons finely chopped onion
  ½ cup Arborio or other short-grain rice
  ¼ cup dry white wine or water
  ⅓ cup freshly grated Parmesan cheese

Steam broccoli, zucchini, yellow squash and bell pepper 3 minutes or just until crisp-tender. Rinse with cold water; drain and set aside.

Bring broth to a simmer in small saucepan; keep hot on low heat. Heat oil in large heavy saucepan over medium-high heat until hot. Add onion; reduce heat to medium. Cook and stir about 5 minutes or until onion is translucent. Add rice, stirring to coat with oil. Add wine; cook and stir until almost dry. Add ½ cup hot broth; cook and stir until broth is absorbed. Continue adding broth, ½ cup at a time, allowing broth to absorb before each addition and stirring frequently. (Total cooking time for broth absorption is about 20 minutes.)

Remove from heat and stir in cheese. Add steamed vegetables and mix well. Serve immediately.

Makes 6 servings

BLAZING BANDITO VEGGIE MEDLEY

1 (12-ounce) package rotini or corkscrew pasta
2 tablespoons olive oil
2 small yellow squash (6 ounces each), sliced
2 small zucchini (6 ounces each), sliced
1 small eggplant (1 pound), cut into ½-inch pieces
1 medium onion, sliced
1 medium green bell pepper, seeded and sliced
1 (8-ounce) package fresh mushrooms, sliced
1 (26-ounce) jar NEWMAN'S OWN® Diavolo Spicy Simmer Sauce
Grated Parmesan cheese (optional)

Prepare pasta according to package directions. Drain; keep warm. Meanwhile, heat olive oil in 12-inch skillet over medium-high heat. Add vegetables; cook until lightly browned and tender, about 15 minutes, stirring often.

Stir in Newman's Own® Diavolo Spicy Simmer Sauce; heat to boiling. Reduce heat to low; cover and simmer 10 minutes to blend flavors. Spoon sauce over pasta on warm large platter; toss to serve. Serve with grated Parmesan cheese.

Makes 4 servings

Vegetable Risotto

ZUCCHINI TOMATO BAKE

- 1 pound eggplant, coarsely chopped
- 2 cups thinly sliced zucchini
- 2 cups sliced fresh mushrooms
- 2 teaspoons olive oil
- ½ cup chopped onion
- ½ cup chopped fresh fennel
- 2 cloves garlic, minced
- 1 can (14½ ounces) no-salt-added whole tomatoes, undrained
- 1 tablespoon no-salt-added tomato paste
- 2 teaspoons dried basil leaves
- 1 teaspoon sugar

Preheat oven to 350°F. Arrange eggplant, zucchini and mushrooms in 9-inch square baking dish.

Heat oil in small skillet over medium heat. Cook and stir onion, fennel and garlic 3 to 4 minutes or until onion is tender. Add tomatoes, tomato paste, basil and sugar. Cook and stir about 4 minutes or until sauce thickens.

Pour sauce over eggplant mixture. Cover and bake 30 minutes. Cool slightly before serving. Garnish as desired. *Makes 6 servings*

CHILI BEAN RAGOÛT

- 1 cup chopped onions
- 1 cup sliced celery
- 1 cup cubed green peppers
- 2 cloves garlic, minced
- 3 to 4 teaspoons chili powder
- 1 teaspoon dried oregano leaves
- 1 teaspoon dried basil leaves
- ½ teaspoon dried thyme leaves
- 1 can (17 ounces) lima beans, drained
- 1 can (16 ounces) no-salt-added whole tomatoes, undrained, coarsely chopped
- 1 can (15½ ounces) kidney beans, drained
- 1 can (16 ounces) ½-less-salt whole kernel corn, drained
- 1 can (15 ounces) black-eyed peas, drained
- Hot cooked rice or cornbread

Spray bottom of large saucepan with nonstick cooking spray; heat over high heat. Cook and stir onions, celery, green peppers and garlic until tender. Stir in chili powder, oregano, basil and thyme; cook 1 minute. Stir in lima beans, tomatoes with juice, kidney beans, corn and black-eyed peas; heat to boiling. Reduce heat and simmer, uncovered, 10 minutes. Serve over rice or cornbread. *Makes 8 servings*

Favorite recipe from **Canned Food Information Council**

Zucchini Tomato Bake

VEGETABLES & GRAINS

HARVEST VEGETABLE SCALLOP

- 4 medium carrots, thinly sliced
- 1 package (10 ounces) frozen chopped broccoli, thawed and drained
- 1⅓ cups (2.8-ounce can) FRENCH'S® French Fried Onions, divided
- 5 small red potatoes, sliced ⅛ inch thick
- 1 jar (8 ounces) pasteurized processed cheese spread
- ¼ cup milk
- Freshly ground black pepper
- Seasoned salt

Preheat oven to 375°F. In 8×12-inch baking dish, combine carrots, broccoli and ⅔ cup French Fried Onions. Tuck potato slices into vegetable mixture at an angle. Dot vegetables evenly with cheese spread. Pour milk over vegetables; sprinkle with seasonings as desired. Bake, covered, at 375°F for 30 minutes or until vegetables are tender. Top with remaining ⅔ cup onions; bake, uncovered, 3 minutes or until onions are golden brown.

Makes 6 servings

MICROWAVE DIRECTIONS: In 8×12-inch microwave-safe dish, prepare vegetables as above. Top with cheese spread, milk and seasonings as above. Cook, covered, on HIGH 12 to 14 minutes or until vegetables are tender, rotating dish halfway through cooking time. Top with remaining onions; cook, uncovered, 1 minute. Let stand 5 minutes.

POTATO GORGONZOLA GRATIN

- 1 pound (2 medium-large) Colorado baking potatoes, unpeeled, very thinly sliced, divided
- Salt
- Pepper
- Ground nutmeg
- ½ medium onion, thinly sliced
- 1 medium tart green apple, such as pippin or Granny Smith, or 1 medium pear, unpeeled, cored, very thinly sliced
- 1 cup low-fat milk or half-and-half
- ¾ cup (3 ounces) Gorgonzola or other blue cheese, crumbled
- 2 tablespoons freshly grated Parmesan cheese

Preheat oven to 400°F. In 8- or 9-inch square baking dish, arrange half the potatoes. Season generously with salt and pepper; sprinkle lightly with nutmeg. Top with onion and apple. Arrange remaining potatoes on top. Season again with salt and pepper; add milk. Cover dish with aluminum foil. Bake 30 to 40 minutes or until potatoes are tender. Remove foil; top with both cheeses. Bake, uncovered, 10 to 15 minutes or until top is lightly browned.

Makes 4 to 6 servings

Favorite recipe from Colorado Potato Administrative Committee

VEGETABLES & GRAINS

CARIBBEAN VEGETARIAN CURRY

    3 firm, medium DOLE® Bananas, peeled
    3 teaspoons margarine, divided
    1 onion, halved, thinly sliced
    2 large cloves garlic, pressed
    1 tart apple, peeled, cored, chopped
  1½ teaspoons curry powder
  1½ teaspoons grated lemon peel
    1 teaspoon *each:* ground ginger, ground coriander
    ⅛ teaspoon *each:* turmeric, ground red pepper
    1 can (15 ounces) black-eyed peas, drained
    1 can (15 ounces) kidney beans, undrained
    ⅓ cup DOLE® Raisins
    1 cup plain nonfat yogurt
    3 warm hard-cooked eggs, halved
    3 cups hot cooked rice (about 1 cup uncooked)
    6 DOLE® Radishes, thinly sliced
    3 DOLE® Green Onions, thinly sliced
    ½ cup chopped fresh cilantro
    ¼ cup chopped peanuts

• Cut bananas in half crosswise, then lengthwise in half to make 12 pieces. Cook and stir in nonstick skillet with 2 teaspoons margarine until lightly browned. Remove to plate.

• Add remaining 1 teaspoon margarine to skillet. Cook and stir onion, garlic and apple until soft.

• Combine curry powder, lemon peel, ginger, coriander, turmeric and red pepper. Stir into onion mixture.

• Add black-eyed peas, undrained kidney beans and raisins. Cover; simmer 5 minutes. Remove from heat; stir in yogurt.

• On individual serving plates, place egg halves on rice. Surround with cooked bananas. Spoon curry-vegetable mixture over rice. Top with radishes, green onions, cilantro and peanuts.

Makes 6 servings

"WILD" BLACK BEANS

    2 cups cooked wild rice
    1 can (15 ounces) black beans, undrained
    1 cup canned or thawed frozen corn, drained
    ½ cup chopped red bell pepper
    1 small jalapeño pepper, seeded and chopped
    1 tablespoon red wine vinegar
    1 cup (4 ounces) shredded Monterey Jack cheese
    ¼ cup chopped fresh cilantro

Preheat oven to 350°F. In 1½-quart baking dish, combine wild rice, beans, corn, bell pepper, jalapeño and vinegar. Cover; bake 20 minutes. Top with cheese; bake, uncovered, 10 minutes. Garnish with cilantro.

Makes 6 to 8 servings

Favorite recipe from **Minnesota Cultivated Wild Rice Council**

DOUBLE SPINACH BAKE

- 1 cup fresh mushroom slices
- 1 green onion with top, finely chopped
- 1 clove garlic, minced
- 4 to 5 cups fresh spinach, coarsely chopped *or* 1 package (10 ounces) frozen spinach, thawed and drained
- 1 tablespoon water
- 1 container (15 ounces) nonfat ricotta cheese
- ¼ cup skim milk
- 1 egg
- ½ teaspoon ground nutmeg
- ½ teaspoon ground black pepper
- 8 ounces spinach fettuccine, cooked and drained
- ¼ cup (1 ounce) shredded reduced fat Swiss cheese

Preheat oven to 350°F. Spray medium skillet with nonstick cooking spray. Add mushrooms, green onion and garlic. Cook and stir over medium heat until mushrooms are softened. Add spinach and water. Cover; cook until spinach is wilted, about 3 minutes.

Combine ricotta cheese, milk, egg, nutmeg and black pepper in large bowl. Gently stir in noodles and vegetables; toss to coat evenly. Lightly coat shallow 1½-quart casserole with nonstick cooking spray. Spread noodle mixture in casserole. Sprinkle with Swiss cheese. Bake 25 to 30 minutes or until knife inserted halfway to center comes out clean.

Makes 6 (1-cup) servings

BROCCOLI CASSEROLE WITH CRUMB TOPPING

- 2 slices day-old white bread, coarsely crumbled (about 1¼ cups)
- ½ cup (2 ounces) shredded mozzarella cheese
- 2 tablespoons chopped fresh parsley (optional)
- 2 tablespoons olive or vegetable oil
- 1 small clove garlic, finely chopped
- 6 cups broccoli florets and/or cauliflowerets
- 1 envelope LIPTON® Recipe Secrets® Onion Soup Mix
- 1 cup water
- 1 large tomato, diced

In small bowl, combine bread crumbs, cheese, parsley, 1 tablespoon oil and garlic; set aside.

In 12-inch skillet, heat remaining 1 tablespoon oil over medium heat and cook broccoli, stirring frequently, 2 minutes. Stir in Onion Soup Mix blended with water. Bring to a boil over high heat. Reduce heat to low and simmer uncovered, stirring occasionally, 8 minutes or until broccoli is almost tender. Add tomato; simmer an additional 2 minutes. Spoon vegetable mixture into 2-quart ovenproof baking dish; top with bread crumb mixture. Broil 1½ minutes or until crumbs are golden and cheese is melted.

Makes about 6 servings

Double Spinach Bake

ORIGINAL GREEN BEAN CASSEROLE

- 2 cans (16 ounces each) cut green beans, drained or 2 packages (9 ounces each) frozen cut green beans, cooked and drained
- ¾ cup milk
- 1 can (10¾ ounces) condensed cream of mushroom soup
- ⅛ teaspoon freshly ground black pepper
- 1⅓ cups (2.8-ounce can) FRENCH'S® French Fried Onions, divided

Preheat oven to 350°F. In medium bowl, combine beans, milk, soup, pepper and *⅔ cup* French Fried Onions; pour into 1½-quart casserole. Bake, uncovered, at 350°F for 30 minutes or until heated through. Top with remaining *⅔ cup* onions; bake, uncovered, 5 minutes or until onions are golden brown. *Makes 6 servings*

MICROWAVE DIRECTIONS: Prepare green bean mixture as above; pour into 1½-quart microwave-safe casserole. Cook, covered, on HIGH 8 to 10 minutes or until heated through, stirring beans halfway through cooking time. Top with remaining onions; cook, uncovered, 1 minute. Let stand 5 minutes.

SWISS VEGETABLE MEDLEY

- 1 package (16 ounces) frozen vegetable combination (broccoli, carrots, cauliflower), thawed and drained
- 1 can (10¾ ounces) condensed cream of mushroom soup
- 1 cup (4 ounces) shredded Swiss cheese
- ⅓ cup sour cream
- ¼ teaspoon freshly ground black pepper
- 1 jar (4 ounces) diced pimiento, drained (optional)
- 1⅓ cups (2.8-ounce can) FRENCH'S® French Fried Onions, divided

Preheat oven to 350°F. In large bowl, combine vegetables, soup, *½ cup* cheese, sour cream, pepper, pimiento and *⅔ cup* French Fried Onions. Pour into shallow 1-quart casserole. Bake, covered, at 350°F for 30 minutes or until vegetables are tender. Sprinkle remaining cheese and *⅔ cup* onions in diagonal rows across top; bake, uncovered, 5 minutes or until onions are golden brown. *Makes 6 servings*

MICROWAVE DIRECTIONS: Prepare vegetable mixture as above; pour into shallow 1-quart microwave-safe casserole. Cook, covered, on HIGH 8 to 10 minutes or until vegetables are tender, stirring vegetables halfway through cooking time. Top with remaining cheese and onions; cook, uncovered, 1 minute or until cheese is melted. Let stand 5 minutes.

Top to bottom: Original Green Bean Casserole; Swiss Vegetable Medley

Hearty INTERNATIONAL FARE

FRENCH BEEF STEW

1½ pounds stew beef, cut into 1-inch cubes
¼ cup all-purpose flour
2 tablespoons vegetable oil
Salt and pepper (optional)
2 cans (14½ ounces each) DEL MONTE® Original Recipe Stewed Tomatoes
1 can (14 ounces) beef broth
4 medium carrots, pared, cut into 1-inch chunks
2 medium potatoes, pared, cut into 1-inch chunks
¾ teaspoon dried thyme
2 tablespoons Dijon mustard (optional)
Chopped parsley (optional)

Combine meat and flour in plastic bag; toss to coat evenly. In 6-quart saucepan, brown meat in oil. Season with salt and pepper, if desired. Add remaining ingredients, except mustard and parsley. Bring to boil; reduce heat. Cover and simmer 1 hour or until beef is tender. Blend in mustard, if desired. Garnish with chopped parsley, if desired.

Makes 6 to 8 servings

— Hearty —

INTERNATIONAL FARE

MEXICAN CHEESE–RICE PIE

- 4 eggs, divided
- 2 cups cooked instant brown rice
- 1 cup (4 ounces) shredded Cheddar cheese, divided
- 1 can (4 ounces) chopped green chilies, drained
- 1 can (12 ounces) evaporated milk
- 2 tablespoons chopped green onion
- ½ teaspoon ground cumin
- ¼ teaspoon salt
- 1 cup shredded iceberg lettuce
- ¼ cup prepared chunky salsa
- ¼ cup sliced ripe olives

In medium bowl beat 1 egg; add rice and mix well. In 9-inch glass pie plate, press rice mixture firmly on bottom and up side. Microwave on MEDIUM (50% power) about 3 to 4 minutes or until set. Sprinkle with ¾ cup Cheddar cheese and chilies; set aside.

In 1-quart glass measure or microwavable bowl combine remaining 3 eggs, milk, green onion, cumin and salt. Microwave on MEDIUM-HIGH (75% power) about 4 minutes or until hot, stirring occasionally. Pour into prepared crust; cover loosely with waxed paper.

Microwave on MEDIUM-HIGH 10 to 12 minutes or until center is almost set, rotating ½ turn after 5 minutes. Uncover; let stand 10 minutes. Remove pie from pie plate to serving platter. Arrange lettuce around edge of pie; top with salsa, olives and remaining Cheddar cheese.

Makes 6 servings

Favorite recipe from **National Dairy Board**

ORIENTAL BEEF AND BROCCOLI

- ½ cup HEINZ® Chili Sauce
- ½ teaspoon Oriental sesame oil
- ¼ to ½ teaspoon crushed red pepper
- 1 (1-pound) flank steak
- 2 tablespoons soy sauce
- 2 teaspoons cornstarch
- 2 cups broccoli flowerets
- 1 medium red bell pepper, cut into strips
- 1 medium onion, cut into thin wedges
- 1 tablespoon vegetable oil
- 1 can (8 ounces) sliced water chestnuts, drained

Combine chili sauce, sesame oil and crushed red pepper; set aside. Cut flank steak lengthwise in half, then cut across the grain into thin slices. Combine soy sauce and cornstarch; pour over steak and toss to coat. In large skillet or wok, cook broccoli, bell pepper and onion in vegetable oil until tender-crisp; remove. In same skillet, quickly cook steak over high heat in 2 batches. Return steak and vegetables to skillet; stir in reserved chili sauce mixture and water chestnuts.

Makes 4 servings

Mexican Cheese-Rice Pie

— Hearty —

INTERNATIONAL FARE

Orzo Casserole

- 2 tablespoons margarine or butter
- 1 clove garlic, finely chopped
- 1½ cups uncooked orzo pasta
- 1 envelope LIPTON® Recipe Secrets® Onion or Onion-Mushroom Soup Mix
- 3¼ cups water
- 6 ounces shiitake or white mushrooms, sliced
- ¼ cup chopped fresh parsley

In 3-quart heavy saucepan, melt margarine over medium heat and cook garlic with orzo, stirring constantly, 2½ minutes or until golden. Stir in onion soup mix blended with water. Bring to a boil over high heat. Reduce heat to low and simmer, covered, 10 minutes. Add mushrooms; do not stir. Simmer, covered, 10 minutes. Stir in parsley. Turn into serving bowl. (Liquid will not be totally absorbed.) Let stand 10 minutes or until liquid is absorbed. *Makes about 10 (½-cup) servings*

Savory Orzo Casserole: Increase water to 4 cups and use LIPTON® Recipe Secrets® Savory Herb with Garlic Soup Mix.

Beef Tamale Pie

- 12 ounces cooked beef, cut into ½-inch pieces (about 2½ cups)
- 1 can (15¾ ounces) chili beans in mild chili sauce
- 1 can (4 ounces) chopped green chilies, undrained
- ¼ cup sliced green onion
- ¼ teaspoon *each:* ground cumin and ground black pepper
- 1 package (8½ ounces) corn muffin mix
- 1 cup cold water
- ½ cup (2 ounces) shredded sharp Cheddar cheese

Preheat oven to 425°F. Combine beef, chili beans, chilies, green onion, cumin and pepper; mix well. Set aside. Combine corn muffin mix and water (mixture will be very thin). Grease bottom and sides of 9-inch square baking pan or 10-inch metal skillet. Pour corn muffin batter into pan. Spoon beef mixture into center of corn muffin mixture, leaving 1-inch border. Bake 30 minutes or until corn muffin mixture is slightly browned and begins to pull away from edge of pan. Sprinkle with cheese; let stand 5 minutes before serving.
Makes 4 servings

Favorite recipe from **National Cattlemen's Beef Association**

Orzo Casserole

— Hearty —

INTERNATIONAL FARE

ENCHILADAS SUISSE

- 1 package (1.62 ounces) LAWRY'S® Spices & Seasonings for Enchilada Sauce
- 1 can (6 ounces) tomato paste
- 3 cups water
- 2 tablespoons vegetable oil
- 1 onion, finely chopped
- ⅛ teaspoon LAWRY'S® Garlic Powder with Parsley
- 3 cups shredded cooked chicken
- 2 tablespoons diced green chiles (optional)
- LAWRY'S® Seasoned Salt to taste
- LAWRY'S® Seasoned Pepper to taste
- 3 chicken bouillon cubes
- 2 cups whipping cream
- 12 corn tortillas
- Vegetable oil for frying
- 8 ounces shredded Monterey Jack cheese

Prepare Spices & Seasonings for Enchilada Sauce with tomato paste and water according to package directions. In large skillet, heat oil and sauté onion and Garlic Powder with Parsley until onion is tender. Add 2 cups enchilada sauce, chicken, chiles, Seasoned Salt and Seasoned Pepper; simmer, uncovered, 5 minutes. Pour remaining enchilada sauce in bottom of 13 × 9 × 2-inch baking dish; set aside. Meanwhile, in medium saucepan, combine bouillon cubes and cream; heat until bouillon dissolves. Keep warm. To assemble enchiladas, soften each tortilla in hot oil and dip in hot cream mixture. Place ¼ cup chicken mixture on each tortilla and roll up. Place, seam side down, on sauce in baking dish. Pour remaining cream mixture over enchiladas and top with cheese. Bake, uncovered, in 350°F oven 20 to 25 minutes.

Makes 6 to 8 servings

BASQUE BEAN CASSEROLE

- 1 pound dried beans (Great Northern, yellow eye or pinto)
- 4½ cups cold water
- ¼ pound unsliced bacon or salt pork
- 2 medium leeks, thinly sliced
- 2 cups chopped onions
- 1 medium onion
- 6 whole cloves
- 1 can (13¾ ounces) chicken broth
- 5 carrots, cut into 1-inch slices
- 3 cloves garlic, minced
- 2 teaspoons TABASCO® pepper sauce
- 1 teaspoon dried thyme leaves
- 1 teaspoon dried marjoram leaves
- 1 teaspoon dried sage leaves
- 2 bay leaves
- 6 whole black peppercorns
- 1 can (16 ounces) whole tomatoes, crushed
- 1 pound Polish sausage, cut into 1-inch slices

In 6-quart Dutch oven or saucepan, combine beans and water. Let soak 2 hours. Do *not* drain beans. Meanwhile, in skillet over medium heat, brown bacon on both sides. Remove. Add leeks and chopped onions. Cook 10 minutes. Add to

Hearty

INTERNATIONAL FARE

soaked beans. Stud whole onion with cloves. Add onion, chicken broth, carrots, garlic, TABASCO® sauce, thyme, marjoram, sage, bay leaves and peppercorns. Bring to boil. Reduce heat and simmer, covered, 1 hour. Stir in tomatoes and sausage. Cover; bake in preheated 350°F oven 1 hour or until almost all liquid is absorbed.

Makes 6 to 8 servings

CHILAQUILES

- 1 medium onion, chopped
- 2 tablespoons vegetable oil
- 1 can (28 ounces) whole tomatoes, cut up
- 1 package (1 ounce) LAWRY'S® Taco Spices & Seasonings
- 1 can (4 ounces) diced green chiles (optional)
- 6 ounces tortilla chips
- 4 cups (16 ounces) grated Monterey Jack cheese
- 1 cup dairy sour cream
- ½ cup (2 ounces) grated Cheddar cheese

In large skillet, sauté onion in oil. Add tomatoes, Taco Spices & Seasonings and chiles; blend well. Simmer, uncovered, 10 to 15 minutes. In lightly greased 2-quart casserole, layer ½ of tortilla chips, sauce and Monterey Jack cheese. Repeat layers; top with sour cream. Bake in 350°F oven 30 minutes. Sprinkle with Cheddar cheese and bake 10 minutes longer. Let stand 15 minutes before cutting into squares.

Makes 6 to 8 servings

BRAZILIAN CORN AND SHRIMP MOQUECA CASSEROLE

- 2 tablespoons olive oil
- ½ cup chopped onion
- ¼ cup chopped green bell pepper
- ¼ cup tomato sauce
- 2 tablespoons chopped parsley
- ½ teaspoon TABASCO® pepper sauce
- 1 pound medium cooked shrimp
- Salt to taste
- 2 tablespoons all-purpose flour
- 1 cup milk
- 1 can (16 ounces) cream-style corn
- Grated Parmesan cheese

In large oven-proof skillet over medium-high heat, heat oil. Add onion, bell pepper, tomato sauce, parsley and TABASCO® sauce and cook, stirring occasionally, for 5 minutes. Add shrimp and salt. Cover and reduce heat to low, and simmer for 2 to 3 minutes. Preheat oven to 375°F. Sprinkle flour over shrimp mixture; stir. Add milk gradually, stirring after each addition. Cook over medium heat until mixture thickens. Remove from heat. Pour corn over mixture; do not stir. Sprinkle with Parmesan cheese. Bake for 30 minutes or until browned.

Makes 4 servings

Hearty

INTERNATIONAL FARE

CHICKEN MILANO

- 2 cloves garlic, minced
- 2 boneless skinless chicken breasts, halved (about 1¼ pounds)
- ½ teaspoon dried basil leaves, crushed
- ⅛ teaspoon crushed red pepper flakes
- Salt and black pepper
- 1 tablespoon olive oil
- 1 can (14½ ounces) DEL MONTE® Italian Recipe Stewed Tomatoes
- 1 can (14½ ounces) DEL MONTE® FreshCut™ Green Italian Beans, drained
- ¼ cup whipping cream

Rub garlic over chicken. Sprinkle with basil and red pepper. Season with salt and black pepper. In skillet, brown chicken in oil over medium-high heat. Stir in tomatoes. Cover; simmer 5 minutes. Uncover; reduce heat to medium and cook 8 to 10 minutes or until liquid is slightly thickened and chicken is tender. Stir in green beans and cream; heat through. *Do not boil.* *Makes 4 servings*

Prep and Cook Time: 25 minutes

ORIENTAL BEEF & NOODLE TOSS

- 1 pound lean ground beef
- 2 packages (3 ounces each) Oriental flavor instant ramen noodles, divided
- 2 cups water
- 2 cups frozen Oriental vegetable mixture
- ⅛ teaspoon ground ginger
- 2 tablespoons thinly sliced green onion

1. In large nonstick skillet, brown ground beef over medium heat 8 to 10 minutes or until beef is no longer pink. Remove with slotted spoon; pour off drippings. Season beef with one seasoning packet from noodles; set aside.

2. In same skillet, combine water, vegetables, noodles, ginger and remaining seasoning packet. Bring to a boil; reduce heat. Cover; simmer 3 minutes or until noodles are tender, stirring occasionally.

3. Return beef to skillet; heat through. Stir in green onion before serving. *Makes 4 servings*

Favorite recipe from **National Cattlemen's Beef Association**

Chicken Milano

Hearty

INTERNATIONAL FARE

SAUSAGE & PASTA PRIMAVERA

  4 ounces uncooked spaghetti
12 ounces beef knockwurst or beef polish sausage links, cut diagonally into ½-inch-thick slices
  ½ pound fresh asparagus,* trimmed, cut diagonally into 1-inch pieces
  1 medium onion, cut lengthwise into thin wedges
  ¼ cup water
  1 clove garlic, minced
  2 medium tomatoes, coarsely chopped
  2 tablespoons thinly sliced fresh basil**
  2 tablespoons grated Parmesan cheese (optional)

1. Cook spaghetti according to package directions; keep warm.

2. Meanwhile in large skillet, combine beef sausage, asparagus, onion, water and garlic. Cook over medium-high heat 5 to 7 minutes or until asparagus is crisp-tender, stirring occasionally. Add spaghetti, tomatoes and basil; toss lightly. Cook 2 minutes or until heated through.

3. Serve with Parmesan cheese, if desired.

Makes 4 servings

*One package (10 ounces) thawed frozen cut asparagus may be substituted for fresh asparagus.

**1½ teaspoons dried basil leaves may be substituted for 2 tablespoons fresh basil.

Favorite recipe from **National Cattlemen's Beef Association**

CHICKEN RISOTTO

  ¾ pound boneless skinless chicken breast, thinly sliced
  ¾ cup onion, chopped
  1 tablespoon vegetable oil
  2 cups uncooked instant brown rice
  1 tablespoon plus 1 teaspoon sugar
  1 tablespoon prepared horseradish
  4 cups chicken broth
  1 medium green bell pepper, sliced
  1 medium red bell pepper, sliced
  1 can (14 ounces) black beans, rinsed and drained
  ¼ cup grated Parmesan cheese

In large skillet, cook and stir chicken and onion in oil over high heat 5 minutes. Add rice, sugar, horseradish and broth. Reduce heat to medium. Simmer, covered, 15 minutes or until rice is tender. Add both peppers and beans. Simmer 5 minutes. Sprinkle with Parmesan cheese before serving.

Makes 4 servings

Sausage & Pasta Primavera

— Hearty —

INTERNATIONAL FARE

PAELLA A LA ESPAÑOLA

- 2 tablespoons margarine or butter
- 1¼ to 1½ pounds chicken thighs, skinned
- 1 package (7.2 ounces) RICE-A-RONI® Rice Pilaf
- 1 can (14½ or 16 ounces) tomatoes or stewed tomatoes, undrained
- ½ teaspoon turmeric (optional)
- ⅛ teaspoon hot pepper sauce or black pepper
- 8 ounces cooked, deveined, shelled medium shrimp
- 1 cup frozen peas
- Lemon wedges

1. In large skillet, melt margarine over medium heat. Add chicken; cook 2 minutes on each side or until browned. Remove from skillet; set aside, reserving drippings. Keep warm.

2. In same skillet, sauté rice pilaf mix in reserved drippings over medium heat until pasta is lightly browned. Stir in 1½ cups water, tomatoes, turmeric, hot pepper sauce and contents of seasoning packet. Bring to a boil over high heat; stir in chicken.

3. Cover; reduce heat. Simmer 20 minutes. Stir in shrimp and peas.

4. Cover; continue to simmer 5 to 10 minutes or until liquid is absorbed and rice is tender. Serve with lemon wedges.
Makes 4 servings

CHINA CHOY QUICHE

- 1 unbaked (9-inch) pie shell
- 3 eggs
- ⅔ cup milk
- 1 (8-ounce) can LA CHOY® Sliced Water Chestnuts, drained and coarsely chopped
- 1 cup (4 ounces) shredded Monterey Jack cheese
- ¾ cup *each:* finely chopped red bell pepper and sliced fresh mushrooms
- ⅓ cup sliced green onions
- 1 tablespoon LA CHOY® Soy Sauce
- ½ teaspoon *each:* garlic powder and dry mustard
- ¼ teaspoon *each:* black pepper and Oriental sesame oil

Preheat oven to 425°F. Bake pie shell 5 minutes; set aside. *Reduce oven temperature to 350°F.* In large bowl, beat together eggs and milk; stir in remaining ingredients. Pour into partially baked shell. Bake 50 to 55 minutes or until knife inserted 1 inch from edge comes out clean. Let stand 10 minutes before serving. Garnish, if desired.
Makes 1 (9-inch) quiche

Paella a la Española

COUNTRY

BAKING

CONTENTS

Sensational Morning Glories • 184

Tasty Team-Ups • 204

Terrific Light Delights • 224

Sweet Snackin' Treats • 244

Clockwise from top left: Marble Swirl Bread (page 214), Cinnamon-Date Scones (page 192), Gingerbread Pear Muffins (page 246), Dinner Rolls (page 216) and Cherry Coconut Cheese Coffee Cake (page 198)

— *Sensational* —
MORNING GLORIES

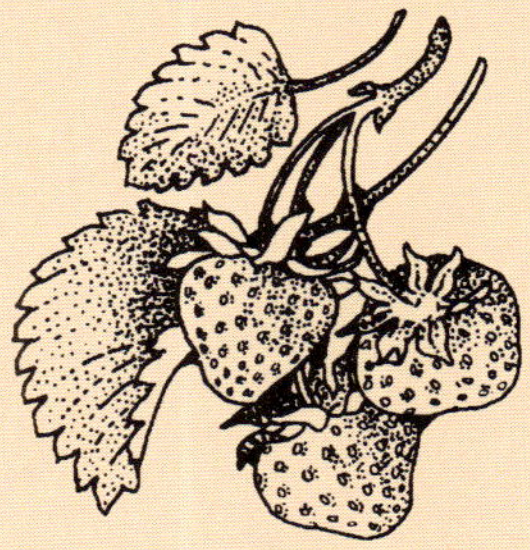

COUNTRY BISCUITS

2 cups all-purpose flour
1 tablespoon baking powder
1 teaspoon salt
⅓ CRISCO® Stick or ⅓ cup CRISCO all-vegetable shortening
¾ cup milk

1. **Preheat** oven to 425°F. **Combine** flour, baking powder and salt in medium bowl. **Cut** in shortening using pastry blender (or two knives) to form coarse crumbs. **Add** milk. **Mix** with fork until dry mixture is moistened. **Form** dough into a ball.

2. **Transfer** dough to lightly floured surface. **Knead** gently 8 to 10 times. **Roll** dough ½ inch thick. **Cut** with floured 2-inch round cutter. **Place** on ungreased baking sheet.

3. **Bake** at 425°F. 12 to 14 minutes or until golden. Serve warm.

Makes 12 to 16 biscuits

— Sensational —

MORNING GLORIES

APPLE BUTTER SPICE MUFFINS

- ½ cup sugar
- 1 teaspoon ground cinnamon
- ¼ teaspoon ground nutmeg
- ⅛ teaspoon ground allspice
- ½ cup pecans or walnuts, chopped
- 2 cups all-purpose flour
- 2 teaspoons baking powder
- ¼ teaspoon salt
- 1 cup milk
- ¼ cup vegetable oil
- 1 egg
- ¼ cup apple butter

Preheat oven to 400°F. Grease or paper-line 12 (2½-inch) muffin cups; set aside.

Combine sugar, cinnamon, nutmeg and allspice in large bowl. Toss 2 tablespoons sugar mixture with pecans in small bowl; set aside. Add flour, baking powder and salt to remaining sugar mixture. Combine milk, oil and egg in medium bowl until well blended; stir into flour mixture just until moistened. Spoon 1 tablespoon batter into each prepared muffin cup. Spoon 1 teaspoon apple butter into each cup. Spoon remaining batter over apple butter. Sprinkle reserved pecan mixture over top of each muffin.

Bake 20 to 25 minutes or until golden brown and wooden pick inserted in center comes out clean. Remove from pan. Cool on wire rack 10 minutes.

Makes 12 muffins

BUTTERMILK OATMEAL SCONES

- 2 cups all-purpose flour, sifted
- 1 cup uncooked rolled oats
- ⅓ cup granulated sugar
- 1 tablespoon baking powder
- ½ teaspoon baking soda
- ⅛ teaspoon salt
- 6 tablespoons cold unsalted margarine, cut into small pieces
- 1 cup buttermilk

Preheat oven to 375°F. Grease baking sheets; set aside.

Combine flour, oats, sugar, baking powder, baking soda and salt in large bowl. Cut in margarine with pastry blender or process in food processor until mixture resembles coarse crumbs. Add buttermilk; stir with fork until soft dough forms. Turn out dough onto lightly floured surface; knead 10 to 12 times. Roll out dough to ½-inch-thick rectangle with lightly floured rolling pin. Cut dough into circles with lightly floured 1½-inch biscuit cutter. Place on prepared baking sheets. Brush tops with buttermilk and sprinkle with sugar. Bake 18 to 20 minutes or until golden brown and wooden pick inserted in center comes out clean. Remove from baking sheets. Cool on wire racks 10 minutes. Serve warm or cool completely.

Makes about 30 scones

Favorite recipe from **The Sugar Association, Inc.**

Apple Butter Spice Muffins

— Sensational —

MORNING GLORIES

CINNAMON BUNS

- 1 recipe Sweet Yeast Dough (page 190)
- ½ cup granulated sugar
- 2 teaspoons ground cinnamon
- 2 tablespoons butter or margarine, melted
- ½ cup raisins, divided (optional)
- 2 cups sifted powdered sugar
- 2 tablespoons milk
- ½ teaspoon vanilla

Prepare Sweet Yeast Dough; let rise as directed.

Combine granulated sugar and cinnamon in small bowl; set aside. Grease two 9-inch round cake pans. Divide dough in half. Roll half of dough into 12×8-inch rectangle on lightly floured surface with lightly floured rolling pin. Brush rectangle with half of melted butter; sprinkle with half of sugar mixture and half of raisins, if desired. Starting with 1 (12-inch) side, roll up jelly-roll fashion. (Do not roll dough too tightly because centers of rolls will pop up as they rise.) Repeat with remaining dough, butter, sugar mixture and raisins.

Cut each roll into 12 (1-inch) slices with floured sharp knife or dental floss. (To use dental floss, position under roll; bring up ends, cross over center and gently pull floss to cut each slice.)

Place slices ½ inch apart in prepared pans. Rolls will spread as they rise. Cover with towel; let rise in warm place about 1 hour or until doubled in bulk.

Preheat oven to 350°F. Bake 20 to 25 minutes or until rolls are golden brown. Cool in pans on wire racks 10 minutes.

Combine powdered sugar, milk and vanilla in small bowl until smooth. Spread mixture over rolls. Serve warm.
Makes 24 buns

ORANGE–ALMOND MUFFINS

- 2 tablespoons butter or margarine
- ¼ cup packed brown sugar
- ½ cup BLUE DIAMOND® Blanched Slivered Almonds, toasted
- ½ package (14 ounces) orange muffin mix
- ¼ cup orange juice

Beat butter and sugar in small bowl until creamy; gently stir in almonds. Spoon evenly into 6 to 8 well-greased muffin cups, filling each about two-thirds full. Prepare muffin mix as package directs, substituting orange juice for water. Spoon evenly into muffin cups.

Bake as package directs. Remove from pan. Cool on wire rack 10 minutes. Serve warm or cool completely.
Makes 6 to 8 muffins

ALMOND BLUEBERRY MUFFINS: Substitute blueberry muffin mix for orange muffin mix. Continue as directed.

Cinnamon Buns

—Sensational—

MORNING GLORIES

SWEET YEAST DOUGH

- 4 to 4¼ cups all-purpose flour, divided
- ½ cup sugar
- 2 packages active dry yeast
- 1 teaspoon salt
- ¾ cup milk
- 4 tablespoons butter or margarine
- 2 eggs
- 1 teaspoon vanilla

Combine 1 cup flour, sugar, yeast and salt in large bowl; set aside.

Combine milk and butter in 1-quart saucepan. Heat over low heat until mixture is 120° to 130°F. (Butter does not need to completely melt.) Gradually beat milk mixture into flour mixture with electric mixer at low speed. Increase speed to medium; beat 2 minutes. Reduce speed to low. Beat in eggs, vanilla and 1 cup flour. Increase speed to medium; beat 2 minutes. Stir in enough additional flour, about 2 cups, with wooden spoon to make soft dough.

Turn out dough onto lightly floured surface; flatten slightly. Knead dough about 5 minutes or until smooth and elastic, adding ¼ cup more flour to prevent sticking if necessary. Shape dough into a ball; place in large greased bowl. Turn dough over so that top is greased. Cover with towel; let rise in warm place 1½ to 2 hours or until doubled in bulk.

Punch down dough. Knead dough on lightly floured surface 1 minute. Cover with towel; let rest 10 minutes.

NOTE: This dough is used to make Cinnamon Buns (page 188) and Maple Nut Twist (page 196).

REFRIGERATOR SWEET YEAST DOUGH: Prepare Sweet Yeast Dough. Shape dough into a ball; place in large greased bowl. Turn dough over so that top is greased. Cover with plastic wrap; refrigerate 3 to 24 hours. Punch down dough. Knead dough on lightly floured surface 1 to 2 minutes. Cover with towel; let dough rest 20 minutes before shaping and second rising. (Second rising may take up to 1½ hours.)

GOLDEN APPLE CHEESE MUFFINS

- 1 or 2 (about 6 ounces each) Washington Golden Delicious apples, cored and sliced
- 2 tablespoons butter or margarine
- ½ cup creamed cottage cheese
- 2 tablespoons sugar
- 1 teaspoon instant minced onion
- 1 egg
- 2 cups buttermilk baking mix

FOOD PROCESSOR METHOD: Place apples in bowl of food processor; chop with steel blade to measure 1½ cups. Combine apples and butter; cook, covered, several minutes or until tender. Cool

slightly. With steel blade in bowl of food processor, process cottage cheese, sugar and onion. Add egg; process until smooth. Add apple mixture to cheese mixture and process thoroughly. Add baking mix; process only to mix. *Do not over process.* Spoon into well-greased muffin pan.* Bake at 400°F. 25 to 30 minutes. *Makes 12 muffins*

*Muffin pan will be very full.

CONVENTIONAL METHOD: Finely chop apples by hand to measure 1½ cups. Combine apples and butter; cook, covered, several minutes or until tender. Cream cottage cheese, sugar and onion in small bowl of electric mixer. Add egg; mix well. Add apple mixture to cheese mixture and beat thoroughly. Stir in baking mix with spoon; stir only until mixed. Bake as above.

FREEZER TIP: Muffins can be frozen. Wrap securely in foil or freezer wrap. Best if used within 2 weeks.

Favorite recipe from **Washington Apple Commission**

WHEAT GERM SCONES

 ½ **cup wheat germ, divided**
1½ **cups all-purpose flour**
 2 **tablespoons packed brown sugar**
 1 **tablespoon baking powder**
 ½ **teaspoon salt**
 6 **tablespoons butter or margarine**
 ⅓ **cup golden raisins, coarsely chopped**
 2 **eggs**
 ¼ **cup milk**

Preheat oven to 425°F.

Reserve 1 tablespoon wheat germ. Combine remaining wheat germ, flour, brown sugar, baking powder and salt in large bowl. Cut in butter with pastry blender or 2 knives until mixture resembles coarse crumbs. Stir in raisins. Beat eggs in small bowl. Add milk; beat until well blended. Reserve 2 tablespoons milk mixture. Add remaining milk mixture to flour mixture; stir until mixture forms soft dough that pulls away from side of bowl.

Turn out dough onto well-floured surface. Knead dough 10 times.* Roll out dough with lightly floured rolling pin into 9×6-inch rectangle. Cut dough into 6 (3-inch) squares with lightly floured knife. Cut each square diagonally in half, making 12 triangles. Place triangles 2 inches apart on *ungreased* baking sheets. Brush triangles with reserved milk mixture; sprinkle with reserved wheat germ.

Bake 10 to 12 minutes or until golden brown. Cool on wire racks 10 minutes. Serve warm or cool completely. *Makes 12 scones*

*To knead dough, fold dough in half toward you and press dough away from you with heels of hands. Give dough a quarter turn and continue folding, pressing and turning.

Sensational

CINNAMON–DATE SCONES

- ¼ cup sugar, divided
- ¼ teaspoon ground cinnamon
- 2 cups all-purpose flour
- 2½ teaspoons baking powder
- ½ teaspoon salt
- 5 tablespoons cold butter or margarine
- ½ cup chopped pitted dates
- 2 eggs
- ⅓ cup half-and-half or milk

1. Preheat oven to 425°F.

2. Combine 2 tablespoons sugar and cinnamon in small bowl; set aside. Combine flour, baking powder, salt and remaining 2 tablespoons sugar in medium bowl. Cut in butter with pastry blender or 2 knives until mixture resembles coarse crumbs. Stir in dates.

3. Beat eggs in separate small bowl with fork. Add half-and-half; beat until well blended. Reserve 1 tablespoon egg mixture in small cup; set aside. Stir remaining egg mixture into flour mixture until soft dough forms.

4. Turn out dough onto well-floured surface. Knead dough gently 10 to 12 times.

5. Roll out dough with lightly floured rolling pin into 9×6-inch rectangle.

6. Cut dough into 6 (3-inch) squares with lightly floured knife. Cut each square diagonally in half, making 12 triangles.

7. Place triangles 2 inches apart on *ungreased* baking sheets. Brush triangles with reserved egg mixture; sprinkle with reserved sugar mixture.

8. Bake 10 to 12 minutes or until golden brown. Immediately remove from baking sheets. Cool on wire racks 10 minutes. Serve warm or cool completely.
Makes 12 scones

BANANA–HONEY MUFFINS

- 1½ cups oat bran flakes cereal
- 1 cup mashed ripe bananas (about 2 medium)
- ¾ cup milk
- ¼ cup butter, melted
- 1 egg, beaten
- 2 tablespoons honey
- 1¼ cups all-purpose flour
- 1 tablespoon baking powder
- ¼ teaspoon salt

Preheat oven to 400°F. Grease or paper-line 12 (2½-inch) muffin cups; set aside. Combine cereal, bananas, milk, butter, egg and honey in medium bowl. Let stand 5 minutes. Combine flour, baking powder and salt in large bowl. Add cereal mixture to flour mixture, stirring just until moistened. Spoon evenly into prepared muffin cups.

Bake 20 to 25 minutes or until wooden pick inserted in center comes out clean. Remove from pan. Cool on wire rack 10 minutes. Serve warm or cool completely.
Makes 12 muffins

Cinnamon-Date Scones

— Sensational —

Morning Glories

PINEAPPLE–RAISIN MUFFINS

- ¼ cup finely chopped pecans
- ¼ cup packed light brown sugar
- 2 cups all-purpose flour
- ¼ cup granulated sugar
- 2½ teaspoons baking powder
- ¾ teaspoon salt
- ½ teaspoon ground cinnamon
- 6 tablespoons cold butter or margarine
- ½ cup raisins
- 1 can (8 ounces) crushed pineapple in juice, undrained
- ⅓ cup unsweetened pineapple juice
- 1 egg

1. Preheat oven to 400°F. Grease or paper-line 12 (2½-inch) muffin cups; set aside.

2. Combine pecans and brown sugar in small bowl; set aside.

3. Combine flour, granulated sugar, baking powder, salt and cinnamon in large bowl. Cut in butter with pastry blender or 2 knives until mixture resembles fine crumbs. Stir in raisins.

4. Combine undrained pineapple, pineapple juice and egg in small bowl until blended; stir into flour mixture just until moistened.

5. Spoon evenly into prepared muffin cups, filling two-thirds full. Sprinkle with reserved pecan mixture.

6. Bake 20 to 25 minutes or until golden brown and wooden pick inserted in center comes out clean. Remove from pan. Cool on wire rack 10 minutes. Serve warm or cool completely.

Makes 12 muffins

FIVE–FRUIT GRANOLA SCONES

- 2 cups all-purpose flour
- ⅓ cup sugar, divided
- 1 tablespoon baking powder
- ½ teaspoon salt
- ¼ cup butter or margarine
- 1 cup granola
- 1 can (16 ounces) California fruit cocktail in juice or extra light syrup, drained
- 2 eggs, beaten

Preheat oven to 375°F. Grease baking sheet; set aside. Combine flour, ¼ cup sugar, baking powder and salt in large bowl. Cut in butter with pastry blender or 2 knives until mixture resembles coarse crumbs; stir in granola. Stir in fruit cocktail and eggs; blend just until moistened. Place dough on lightly floured surface. Roll out dough into 7-inch circle with lightly floured rolling pin; place on prepared baking sheet. Sprinkle remaining sugar over top of dough. Bake 45 minutes or until wooden pick inserted in center comes out clean. Cut into 6 wedges. Remove from baking sheet. Cool on wire rack 10 minutes. *Makes 6 scones*

Favorite recipe from **Canned Fruit Promotion Service**

Pineapple-Raisin Muffins

— Sensational —

MAPLE NUT TWIST

- 1 recipe Sweet Yeast Dough (page 190)
- 2 tablespoons butter or margarine, melted
- 2 tablespoons honey
- ½ cup chopped pecans
- ¼ cup granulated sugar
- 2½ teaspoons maple extract, divided
- ½ teaspoon ground cinnamon
- 1 cup sifted powdered sugar
- 5 teaspoons milk

Prepare Sweet Yeast Dough; let rise as directed. Combine butter and honey in custard cup; set aside. Combine pecans, granulated sugar, 2 teaspoons maple extract and cinnamon in small bowl. Toss to coat; set aside.

Grease 2 baking sheets; set aside. Cut dough in half; cut half of dough into 2 pieces. Roll out 1 piece dough into 9-inch circle on lightly floured surface with lightly floured rolling pin. (Keep remaining dough covered with towel.) Place on prepared baking sheet. Brush half of butter mixture over dough. Sprinkle half of pecan mixture over butter.

Roll remaining piece dough into 9-inch circle. Place rolling pin on one side of dough. Gently roll dough over rolling pin once. Carefully lift rolling pin and dough, unrolling dough over pecan filling, stretching dough as necessary to cover. Pinch edges to seal. Place 1-inch biscuit cutter* in center of circle as cutting guide, being careful not to cut through dough. Cut dough into 12 wedges with scissors or sharp knife, from edge of circle to edge of biscuit cutter, cutting through all layers. Pick up wide edge of 1 wedge, twist several times and lay back down on prepared sheet. Repeat twisting procedure with remaining 11 wedges. Repeat with remaining half of dough, butter mixture and pecan mixture. Cover coffee cakes with towel. Let rise in warm place about 1 hour or until doubled in bulk.

Preheat oven to 350°F. Bake on 2 racks in oven 20 to 25 minutes or until coffee cakes are golden brown and sound hollow when tapped. (Rotate baking sheets top to bottom halfway through baking.) Immediately remove from baking sheets; cool on wire racks about 30 minutes.

Combine powdered sugar, milk and remaining ½ teaspoon maple extract in small bowl until smooth. Drizzle over warm coffee cakes.

Makes 24 servings (2 coffee cakes)

*Or, use the lid of an herb jar if biscuit cutter is not available.

Maple Nut Twist

— Sensational —

Morning Glories

CHERRY COCONUT CHEESE COFFEE CAKE

- 2½ cups all-purpose flour
- ¾ cup sugar
- ½ teaspoon baking powder
- ½ teaspoon baking soda
- 2 packages (3 ounces each) cream cheese, softened, divided
- ¾ cup milk
- 2 tablespoons vegetable oil
- 2 eggs, divided
- 1 teaspoon vanilla
- ½ cup flaked coconut
- ¾ cup cherry preserves
- 2 tablespoons butter or margarine

Preheat oven to 350°F. Grease and flour 9-inch springform pan.

Combine flour and sugar in large bowl. Reserve ½ cup flour mixture. Stir baking powder and baking soda into flour mixture in large bowl. Cut in 1 package cream cheese with pastry blender or 2 knives until mixture resembles coarse crumbs; set aside.

Combine milk, oil and 1 egg in medium bowl. Add to flour-cream cheese mixture; stir just until moistened. Spread batter on bottom and 1 inch up side of prepared pan. (Batter should be about ¼ inch thick on sides.) Combine remaining package cream cheese, remaining egg and vanilla in small bowl; stir until smooth. Pour over batter, spreading to within 1 inch of edge. Sprinkle coconut over cheese mixture. Spoon preserves evenly over coconut.

Cut butter into reserved flour mixture with pastry blender or 2 knives until mixture resembles coarse crumbs. Sprinkle over preserves.

Bake 55 to 60 minutes or until browned and toothpick inserted in coffee cake crust comes out clean. Cool in pan on wire rack 15 minutes. Remove side of pan. Serve warm or cool completely.
Makes 10 servings

GRAHAM MUFFINS

- 2 Stay Fresh Packs HONEY MAID® Grahams, finely rolled (about 3 cups crumbs)
- ¼ cup sugar
- 1 tablespoon DAVIS® Baking Powder
- 2 eggs, well beaten
- 1½ cups milk
- ⅓ cup margarine, melted

In medium bowl, combine crumbs, sugar and baking powder; set aside.

In small bowl, combine eggs, milk and margarine; stir into crumb mixture just until moistened. Spoon batter into 12 greased 2½-inch muffin-pan cups.

Bake at 400°F for 18 to 20 minutes or until toothpick inserted in center comes out clean. Serve warm.
Makes 1 dozen muffins

Cherry Coconut Cheese Coffee Cake

— Sensational —

MORNING GLORIES

APPLE RING COFFEE CAKE

- 3 cups all-purpose flour
- 1 teaspoon baking soda
- 1 teaspoon salt
- 1 teaspoon ground cinnamon
- 1 cup chopped walnuts
- 1½ cups granulated sugar
- 1 cup vegetable oil
- 2 teaspoons vanilla
- 2 eggs
- 2 cups peeled chopped tart apples
- Powdered sugar for garnish

Preheat oven to 325°F. Grease 10-inch tube pan; set aside.

Sift together flour, baking soda, salt and cinnamon into large bowl. Stir in walnuts; set aside. Combine granulated sugar, oil, vanilla and eggs in medium bowl. Stir in apples. Stir into flour mixture just until moistened. Spoon batter into prepared pan, spreading evenly.

Bake 1 hour or until wooden toothpick inserted in center of cake comes out clean. Cool cake in pan on wire rack 10 minutes. Remove from pan; cool completely on wire rack. Sprinkle powdered sugar over cake. *Makes 12 servings*

BANANA BREAKFAST MUFFINS

- 1½ cups NABISCO® 100% Bran™
- 1 cup milk
- ¼ cup FLEISCHMANN'S® Margarine, melted
- 1 egg, slightly beaten
- 1 cup all-purpose flour
- ⅓ cup firmly packed light brown sugar
- 2 teaspoons DAVIS® Baking Powder
- 1 teaspoon ground cinnamon
- ½ cup mashed banana
- ½ cup seedless raisins

Mix bran, milk, margarine and egg; let stand 5 minutes.

In bowl, blend flour, brown sugar, baking powder and cinnamon; stir in bran mixture just until blended. (Batter will be lumpy.)

Stir in banana and raisins. Spoon batter into 12 greased 2½-inch muffin-pan cups.

Bake at 400°F for 20 to 25 minutes or until toothpick inserted in center comes out clean. Serve warm. *Makes 1 dozen muffins*

MICROWAVE DIRECTIONS: Prepare batter as directed. In each of 6 microwavable muffin-pan cups, place 2 paper liners. Spoon batter into cups, filling ⅔ full. Microwave on HIGH (100% power) for 3 to 3½ minutes or until toothpick inserted in center comes out clean, rotating pan ½ turn after 2 minutes. Let stand in pan 5 minutes. Repeat with remaining batter. Serve warm.

Apple Ring Coffee Cake

— Sensational —

HONEY CURRANT SCONES

  2½ cups all-purpose flour
   2 teaspoons grated orange peel
   1 teaspoon baking powder
  ½ teaspoon baking soda
  ½ teaspoon salt
  ½ cup butter or margarine
  ½ cup currants
  ½ cup sour cream
  ⅓ cup honey
   1 egg, slightly beaten

Preheat oven to 375°F. Grease baking sheet; set aside.

Combine flour, orange peel, baking powder, baking soda and salt in large bowl. Cut in butter with pastry blender or 2 knives until mixture resembles coarse crumbs. Stir in currants. Combine sour cream, honey and egg in medium bowl until well blended. Stir into flour mixture until soft dough forms. Turn out dough onto lightly floured surface. Knead dough 10 times. Shape dough into 8-inch square. Cut into 4 squares; cut each square diagonally in half, making 8 triangles. Place triangles 1 inch apart on prepared baking sheet.

Bake 15 to 20 minutes or until golden brown and wooden pick inserted in center comes out clean. Remove from baking sheet. Cool on wire rack 10 minutes. Serve warm or cool completely.

Makes 8 scones

Favorite recipe from **National Honey Board**

HEALTHY BANANA–WALNUT MUFFINS

   2 cups oat bran flakes cereal
  1½ cups mashed ripe bananas (about 3 medium)
  ½ cup buttermilk
  ¼ cup butter, melted
   1 egg
  1½ cups all-purpose flour
  ¼ cup packed brown sugar
   1 tablespoon baking powder
  ½ teaspoon ground cinnamon
  ¼ teaspoon baking soda
  ¼ cup chopped walnuts

Preheat oven to 400°F. Grease or paper-line 12 (2½-inch) muffin cups; set aside.

Combine cereal, bananas, buttermilk, butter and egg in medium bowl. Let stand 5 minutes. Combine flour, brown sugar, baking powder, cinnamon and baking soda in large bowl. Add cereal mixture to flour mixture, stirring just until moistened. Spoon evenly into prepared muffin cups. Sprinkle with walnuts.

Bake 20 to 22 minutes or until wooden pick inserted in center comes out clean. Remove from pan. Cool on wire rack 10 minutes. Serve warm or cool completely. *Makes 12 muffins*

NOTE: To freeze muffins, wrap tightly with foil or place in airtight container.

Honey Currant Scones

Tasty
TEAM-UPS

WHOLE WHEAT POPOVERS

2 eggs
1 cup milk
2 tablespoons butter or margarine, melted
½ cup all-purpose flour
½ cup whole wheat flour
¼ teaspoon salt

Position rack in lower third of oven. Preheat oven to 450°F. Grease 6 (6-ounce) custard cups. Set custard cups in jelly-roll pan for easier handling; set aside.

Beat eggs in large bowl with electric mixer at low speed 1 minute. Beat in milk and butter until blended. Beat in flours and salt until batter is smooth. Pour evenly into prepared custard cups.

Bake 20 minutes. *Reduce oven temperature to 350°F.* Bake 15 minutes more; quickly make small slit in top of each popover to let out steam. Bake 5 to 10 minutes more or until browned. Remove from cups. Cool on wire rack 10 minutes. Serve warm or cool completely.

Makes 6 popovers

TEAM-UPS

THYME-CHEESE BUBBLE LOAF

- 1 package active dry yeast
- 1 teaspoon sugar
- 1 cup warm water (105° to 115°F)
- 3 cups all-purpose flour
- 1 teaspoon salt
- 2 tablespoons vegetable oil
- 1 cup (4 ounces) shredded Monterey Jack cheese
- 4 tablespoons butter or margarine, melted
- ¼ cup chopped fresh parsley
- 3 teaspoons finely chopped fresh thyme *or* ¾ teaspoon dried thyme leaves, crushed

To proof yeast, sprinkle yeast and sugar over warm water in small bowl; stir until yeast is dissolved. Let stand 5 minutes or until mixture is bubbly. Combine flour and salt in food processor.* With food processor running, add yeast mixture and oil through feed tube. Process until mixture forms dough that leaves side of food processor. If dough is too dry, add 1 to 2 tablespoons water. If dough is too wet, add 1 to 2 tablespoons additional flour until dough leaves side of bowl. Dough will be sticky. Place dough in large greased bowl. Turn dough over so that top is greased. Cover with towel; let rise in warm place about 1 hour or until doubled in bulk.

Punch down dough. Flour hands lightly. Knead cheese into dough on lightly floured surface until evenly distributed. Cover with towel; let rest 10 minutes.

Grease 8½×4½-inch loaf pan; set aside. Combine butter, parsley and thyme in small bowl. Roll out dough into 8×6-inch rectangle with lightly floured rolling pin. Cut dough into 48 squares with pizza cutter. Shape each square into a ball. Dip into parsley mixture. Place balls in prepared pan. Cover with towel; let rise in warm place about 45 minutes or until doubled in bulk.

Preheat oven to 375°F. Bake 35 to 40 minutes or until top is golden and loaf sounds hollow when tapped. Immediately remove from pan; cool on wire rack 30 minutes. Serve warm. Store leftover bread in refrigerator.

Makes 1 loaf

*TO PREPARE WITH ELECTRIC MIXER: Proof yeast as directed. Beat yeast mixture, 1½ cups flour, salt and oil in large bowl with electric mixer at low speed until blended, scraping down side of bowl once. Increase speed to medium; beat 2 minutes. Stir in enough additional flour, about 1 cup, to make soft dough. Turn out dough onto lightly floured surface; flatten slightly. Knead dough about 5 minutes or until smooth and elastic, adding ½ cup more flour to prevent sticking if necessary. Shape dough into a ball. Proceed as directed.

Thyme-Cheese Bubble Loaf

Tasty

TEAM-UPS

SALSA MUFFINS

- 1 cup all-purpose flour
- 1 cup yellow cornmeal
- 3 tablespoons sugar
- 1 tablespoon baking powder
- ½ teaspoon salt
- 6 tablespoons butter or margarine, softened
- ¾ cup bottled chunky salsa
- ½ cup milk
- 1 egg

Preheat oven to 400°F. Grease or paper-line 12 (2½-inch) muffin cups; set aside.

Combine flour, cornmeal, sugar, baking powder and salt in large bowl. Cut in butter with pastry blender or 2 knives until mixture resembles fine crumbs. Combine salsa, milk and egg in small bowl until blended. Stir into flour mixture just until moistened. Spoon evenly into prepared muffin cups.

Bake 25 to 30 minutes or until golden brown and wooden pick inserted in center comes out clean. Remove from pan. Cool on wire rack 10 minutes. Serve warm or cool completely.

Makes 12 muffins

CORNMEAL STICKS

- 2 cups cold water
- 1½ cups yellow cornmeal
- ¾ teaspoon salt
- 6 ounces sharp Cheddar cheese, finely shredded (1½ cups)
- CRISCO® all-vegetable shortening for deep frying

1. Combine water, cornmeal and salt in a heavy saucepan. **Mix** until smooth. **Cook** over medium heat, stirring constantly, until mixture is very stiff, thick and pulls away from sides of pan. (This takes 6 to 9 minutes.)

2. Remove from heat. **Add** cheese. **Stir** until melted.

3. Pat mixture evenly into ungreased 13×9×2-inch baking dish. **Let** stand uncovered 30 minutes at room temperature. Do not chill dough.

4. Cut into 3 lengthwise sections and 18 crosswise strips.

5. Heat shortening to 365°F. in a deep saucepan or deep fryer.

6. Add sticks to hot shortening, 1 at a time, frying 3 sticks at a time for 3 minutes or until golden brown. (If sticks run together, cut apart after frying.) **Remove** with slotted spatula. **Drain** on paper towels. **Serve** warm.

Makes 4½ dozen cornmeal sticks

Salsa Muffins

— Tasty —

TEAM-UPS

SCONES

    2 cups all-purpose flour
    1 tablespoon baking powder
    1 tablespoon sugar
    ½ teaspoon salt
    ¼ BUTTER FLAVOR* CRISCO® Stick or ¼ cup BUTTER FLAVOR CRISCO all-vegetable shortening
    2 eggs (1 whole, 1 separated)
    ½ cup heavy cream**

*Butter Flavor Crisco is artificially flavored.
**Use milk in place of cream for lighter scones.

1. Heat oven to 400°F.

2. Combine flour, baking powder, sugar and salt in large bowl. **Cut** in shortening with pastry blender (or two knives).

3. Combine whole egg, egg yolk and cream in medium bowl. **Beat** until well blended. **Add** to flour mixture. **Stir** until flour is moistened. **Work** with hands to form a ball. *Do not overwork.*

4. Roll dough to ½-inch thickness on lightly floured surface. **Cut** out rounds using 2-inch cutter. **Place** on *ungreased* baking sheet.

5. Beat egg white lightly. Brush on top of scones. Sprinkle with sugar.

6. Bake at 400°F. for 9 to 11 minutes or until lightly browned.
Makes 20 scones

RAISIN SCONES: Add 2 *additional* teaspoons sugar, ¾ cup golden raisins and ¼ cup diced candied orange peel to flour mixture.

CHEESE AND NUT SCONES: *Decrease* sugar to 2 teaspoons. Add ½ cup crumbled blue or grated Parmesan cheese and ½ cup chopped walnuts or pecans to flour mixture.

HERB AND CHEDDAR SCONES: *Decrease* sugar to 2 teaspoons. Add ¾ cup shredded sharp Cheddar cheese and ¼ cup chopped fresh herbs, such as dill *or* 1 teaspoon dried herbs to flour mixture.

PESTO SURPRISE MUFFINS

    2 cups all-purpose flour
    2 tablespoons grated Parmesan cheese
    1 tablespoon baking powder
    ½ teaspoon salt
    1 cup milk
    ¼ cup vegetable oil
    1 egg
    ¼ cup prepared pesto sauce
    Additional grated Parmesan cheese (optional)

Preheat oven to 400°F. Grease 12 (2½-inch) muffin cups; set aside.

Combine flour, 2 tablespoons Parmesan cheese, baking powder and salt in large bowl. Combine milk, oil and egg in small bowl until blended. Stir

— Tasty —

TEAM-UPS

into flour mixture just until moistened. Spoon into prepared muffin cups, filling one-third full. Stir pesto sauce to blend; spoon 1 teaspoon pesto sauce into each muffin cup. Spoon remaining batter evenly over pesto sauce. Sprinkle additional Parmesan cheese over tops of muffins, if desired.

Bake 25 to 30 minutes or until golden brown and wooden pick inserted in center comes out clean. Remove from pan. Cool on wire rack 10 minutes. Serve warm or cool completely.   *Makes 12 muffins*

PARMESAN GARLIC TWISTS

  1 cup all-purpose flour
  ½ teaspoon baking powder
  ½ teaspoon salt
  ½ teaspoon Italian seasoning*
  ¾ cup grated Parmesan cheese, divided
  ⅓ BUTTER FLAVOR** CRISCO® Stick or
     ⅓ cup BUTTER FLAVOR CRISCO
     all-vegetable shortening
  3 egg yolks
  4 garlic cloves, minced or crushed *or*
     ½ teaspoon garlic powder
  2 teaspoons water
  1 egg white
    Paprika

*Or, substitute ½ teaspoon of oregano, basil, rosemary or marjoram or some combination of these dried herbs.
**Butter Flavor Crisco in artificially flavored.

1. Heat oven to 400°F. **Grease** baking sheets with shortening.

2. Combine flour, baking powder, salt and Italian seasoning in large bowl. **Reserve** 1 tablespoon Parmesan cheese. **Add** remaining cheese. **Cut** in shortening with pastry blender (or two knives) until mixture resembles coarse crumbs. **Beat** egg yolks, garlic and water lightly. **Sprinkle** over flour mixture. **Toss** lightly with fork until dough forms a ball. **Flour** lightly.

3. Roll dough out on floured surface or between two sheets of waxed paper to form a 13×9-inch rectangle. **Trim** edges to straighten.

4. Cut in half crosswise. **Cut** strips ¼ inch wide (they will be 6½ inches long). **Twist** two strips together, overlapping each strip over the other. **Place** 2 inches apart on prepared baking sheets. **Repeat** until all strips are twists. **Brush** with egg white. **Sprinkle** with reserved Parmesan cheese.

5. Bake at 400°F. for 8 to 10 minutes or until lightly browned. **Cool** 1 minute before removing to cooling rack. **Cool** completely. **Sprinkle** with paprika.   *Makes 3 dozen twists*

Tasty Team-Ups

Herb-Cheese Biscuit Loaf

- 1½ cups all-purpose flour
- ¼ cup grated Parmesan cheese
- 2 tablespoons yellow cornmeal
- 2 teaspoons baking powder
- ½ teaspoon salt
- ¼ cup butter or margarine
- 2 eggs
- ½ cup heavy cream
- ¾ teaspoon dried basil leaves, crushed
- ¾ teaspoon dried oregano leaves, crushed
- ⅛ teaspoon garlic powder
- Additional Parmesan cheese (optional)

Preheat oven to 425°F. Grease large baking sheet; set aside.

Combine flour, ¼ cup cheese, cornmeal, baking powder and salt in large bowl. Cut in butter with pastry blender or 2 knives until mixture resembles coarse crumbs. Beat eggs in medium bowl. Add cream, basil, oregano and garlic powder; beat until well blended. Add cream mixture to flour mixture; stir until mixture forms soft dough that clings together and forms a ball. Turn out dough onto well-floured surface. Knead dough gently 10 to 12 times. Place dough on prepared baking sheet. Roll or pat dough into 7-inch round, about 1 inch thick. Starting from center, score top of dough into 8 wedges with tip of sharp knife, taking care not to cut completely through dough. Sprinkle with additional cheese, if desired.

Bake 20 to 25 minutes or until toothpick inserted in center comes out clean. Cool on baking sheet on wire rack 10 minutes. Serve warm.

Makes 8 servings

Feta-Dill Muffins

- 2 cups all-purpose flour
- 2 tablespoons sugar
- 1 tablespoon baking powder
- 1 cup milk
- ½ cup (4 ounces) crumbled feta cheese
- ⅓ cup vegetable oil
- 1 tablespoon chopped fresh dill *or* 1 teaspoon dried dill weed
- 1 egg

Preheat oven to 400°F. Grease or paper-line 12 (2½-inch) muffin cups; set aside.

Combine flour, sugar and baking powder in large bowl. Combine milk, cheese, oil, dill and egg in small bowl until blended. Stir into flour mixture just until moistened. Spoon evenly into prepared muffin cups.

Bake 25 to 30 minutes or until golden brown and wooden pick inserted in center comes out clean. Remove from pan. Cool on wire rack 10 minutes. Serve warm or cool completely.

Makes 12 muffins

Herb-Cheese Biscuit Loaf

MARBLE SWIRL BREAD

- 2¾ to 3¼ cups all-purpose flour, divided
- ¼ cup sugar
- 1 package active dry yeast
- 1 teaspoon salt
- 1⅓ cups plus 1 tablespoon water, divided
- ¼ cup butter or margarine
- 1 whole egg
- 2 tablespoons molasses
- 2 teaspoons unsweetened cocoa powder
- 1 teaspoon instant coffee powder
- 1 to 1¼ cups rye flour
- 1 egg yolk

Combine 1½ cups all-purpose flour, sugar, yeast and salt in large bowl; set aside. Combine 1⅓ cups water and butter in 1-quart saucepan. Heat over low heat until mixture is 120° to 130°F. (Butter does not need to completely melt.) Gradually beat water mixture into flour mixture with electric mixer at low speed. Increase speed to medium; beat 2 minutes. Reduce speed to low; beat in 1 egg and ½ cup all-purpose flour. Increase speed to medium; beat 2 minutes.

Reserve half of batter (about 1⅓ cups) in another bowl. Stir ¾ cup all-purpose flour into remaining batter to make stiff dough, adding remaining ½ cup all-purpose flour if necessary; set aside. To make darker dough, stir molasses, cocoa, coffee and enough rye flour, about 1¼ cups, into reserved batter to make stiff dough. Cover doughs with towels. Let rise in warm place about 1 hour or until doubled in bulk.

Punch down doughs. Knead doughs on lightly floured surface 1 minute. Cover with towel; let rest 10 minutes. Grease large baking sheet.

Roll out lighter dough to 12×9-inch rectangle with lightly floured rolling pin; set aside. Roll darker dough into 12×8-inch rectangle; place on top of lighter dough. Starting with 1 (12-inch) side, roll up doughs together jelly-roll fashion. Pinch seam and ends to seal. Place loaf, seam side down, on prepared baking sheet, tucking ends under. Cover with towel; let rise in warm place about 45 minutes or until doubled in bulk.

Preheat oven to 350°F. For egg wash, add remaining 1 tablespoon water to egg yolk; beat until just combined. Make 3 (½-inch-deep) slashes across top of loaf with tip of sharp knife. Brush with egg yolk mixture.

Bake 35 to 40 minutes or until loaf is browned and sounds hollow when tapped. Immediately remove from baking sheet; cool completely on wire rack.

Makes 1 loaf

Marble Swirl Bread

DINNER ROLLS

- 3¾ to 4¼ **cups all-purpose flour, divided**
- ¼ **cup sugar**
- 2 **packages active dry yeast**
- 1 **teaspoon salt**
- 1¼ **cups milk**
- ½ **cup vegetable shortening**
- 2 **eggs**

Combine 1½ cups flour, sugar, yeast and salt in large bowl; set aside. Combine milk and shortening in 1-quart saucepan. Heat over low heat until mixture is 120° to 130°F. (Shortening does not need to completely melt.) Gradually beat milk mixture into flour mixture with electric mixer at low speed. Increase speed to medium; beat well. Reduce speed to low. Beat in eggs and 1 cup flour. Increase speed to medium; beat 2 minutes.

Stir in enough additional all-purpose flour, about 1¼ cups, with wooden spoon to make soft dough. Turn out dough onto lightly floured surface; flatten slightly. Knead dough about 5 minutes or until smooth and elastic, adding ½ cup more all-purpose flour to prevent sticking if necessary. Shape dough into a ball. Place in large greased bowl. Turn dough over so that top is greased. Cover with towel. Let rise in warm place about 1 hour or until doubled in bulk.

Punch down dough. Knead dough on lightly floured surface 1 minute. Cut dough in half. Cover with towel; let rest 10 minutes.

Shape rolls as desired: see Crescents, Cloverleaf and Fan-Tans. Cover rolls with towel; let rise in warm place about 30 minutes or until doubled in bulk.

Preheat oven to 375°F. Bake on 2 racks in oven 15 to 20 minutes or until rolls are golden brown and sound hollow when tapped. (Rotate baking sheets halfway through baking.) Immediately remove from pans or baking sheets; cool on wire racks 10 minutes. Serve warm.

CRESCENTS: Grease 2 large baking sheets. Melt 2 tablespoons butter or margarine; set aside. Cut dough in half. Roll out half of dough into 16-inch circle with lightly floured rolling pin; keep remaining half covered with towel. Brush circle with 1 tablespoon melted butter; cut into 12 wedges. Roll up each wedge, starting at wide end and rolling toward point. Place rolled wedges, point end down, about 2 inches apart on prepared baking sheets; curve ends to form crescents. Repeat with remaining dough and butter. Makes 24 rolls.

CLOVERLEAF: Grease 24 (2½-inch) muffin pan cups. Cut dough in half. Cut half of dough into 36 pieces, keeping remaining half covered with towel. Shape each piece into a ball, pulling down edges and tucking them under to make tops smooth. Arrange 3 balls in each prepared muffin cup. Repeat with remaining dough. Makes 24 rolls.

Tasty Team-Ups

FAN-TANS: Grease 24 (2½-inch) muffin pan cups. Melt 2 tablespoons butter or margarine; set aside. Cut dough in half. Roll out half of dough into 15×12-inch rectangle on lightly floured surface with lightly floured rolling pin, keeping remaining half covered with towel. Brush with 1 tablespoon melted butter. Cut rectangle lengthwise into 5 strips; stack strips evenly on top of each other, buttered side up. Cut stack into 12 squares. Place squares, cut side up, in prepared muffin pans. Repeat with remaining dough and butter. Makes 24 rolls.

TABASCO® CORN BREAD WEDGES

- 1 package corn bread mix
- 1 cup (4 ounces) finely shredded sharp Cheddar cheese
- ¼ cup butter or margarine
- ¼ teaspoon Worcestershire sauce
- ¼ teaspoon TABASCO® pepper sauce
- 1 egg white, stiffly beaten
- Paprika

Prepare corn bread according to package directions; bake in 9-inch pie plate. Remove corn bread when done. Cool in pan on wire rack 10 minutes. Cut into 8 wedges.

Meanwhile, combine cheese, butter, Worcestershire sauce and TABASCO® sauce in small bowl, beating until smooth. Fold in egg white. Spread cheese mixture evenly over wedges. Sprinkle with paprika.

Preheat broiler to 400°F; broil corn bread about 4 minutes or until cheese topping is puffy and golden brown. Serve warm. *Makes 8 wedges*

SAVORY PUMPKIN BACON MUFFINS

- 1¾ cups all-purpose flour
- ¼ cup sugar
- 2 teaspoons baking powder
- ¾ teaspoon ground nutmeg
- ½ teaspoon salt
- ⅔ cup solid pack pumpkin
- ⅔ cup milk
- ¼ cup vegetable oil
- 1 egg, beaten
- ½ cup cooked crumbled bacon

Preheat oven to 425°F. Grease or paper-line 24 (1¾-inch) mini-muffin cups; set aside.

Combine flour, sugar, baking powder, nutmeg and salt in large bowl. Combine pumpkin, milk, oil and egg in small bowl until blended. Stir into flour mixture just until moistened. Fold in bacon. Spoon into prepared muffin cups, filling almost full.

Bake 16 to 18 minutes or until wooden pick inserted in center comes out clean. Remove from pans. Cool on wire racks 10 minutes. Serve warm or cool completely. *Makes 24 mini-muffins*

— Tasty —

TEAM-UPS

CARAWAY CHEESE MUFFINS

- 1¼ cups all-purpose flour
- ½ cup rye flour
- 2 tablespoons sugar
- 2½ teaspoons baking powder
- ½ teaspoon salt
- 1 cup (4 ounces) shredded sharp Cheddar or Swiss cheese
- 1½ teaspoons caraway seeds
- 1 cup milk
- ¼ cup vegetable oil
- 1 egg

Preheat oven to 400°F. Grease or paper-line 12 (2½-inch) muffin cups; set aside.

Combine flours, sugar, baking powder and salt in large bowl. Add cheese and caraway seeds; toss to coat. Combine milk, oil and egg in small bowl until well blended. Stir into flour mixture just until moistened. Spoon evenly into prepared muffin cups.

Bake 20 to 25 minutes or until golden brown and wooden pick inserted in center comes out clean. Remove from pan. Cool on wire rack 10 minutes. Serve warm or cool completely.

Makes 12 muffins

SQUASH MUFFINS

- 1 cup all-purpose flour
- 1 cup whole wheat flour
- ⅓ cup packed brown sugar
- 2 teaspoons baking powder
- 1½ teaspoons ground cinnamon
- ½ teaspoon baking soda
- ½ teaspoon salt
- ½ teaspoon ground cloves
- ¼ teaspoon ground nutmeg
- 6 tablespoons butter or margarine
- ½ cup golden raisins
- ¾ cup milk
- ½ of 12-ounce package frozen cooked squash, thawed and well drained (½ cup)
- 1 egg

Preheat oven to 400°F. Grease or paper-line 12 (2½-inch) muffin cups; set aside.

Combine flours, sugar, baking powder, cinnamon, baking soda, salt, cloves and nutmeg in large bowl. Cut in butter with pastry blender or 2 knives until mixture resembles fine crumbs. Stir in raisins. Combine milk, squash and egg in small bowl until blended. Stir into flour mixture just until moistened. Spoon evenly into prepared muffin cups.

Bake 25 to 30 minutes or until golden brown and wooden pick inserted in center comes out clean. Remove from pan. Cool on wire rack 10 minutes. Serve warm or cool completely. *Makes 12 muffins*

Caraway Cheese Muffins

— Tasty —

TEAM-UPS

TOMATO–CARROT MUFFIN TOPS

- 1 large (about 8 ounces) fresh Florida tomato, ripened at room temperature until bright red
- ⅓ cup low fat milk
- 1 egg
- 2 tablespoons vegetable oil
- 2 cups buttermilk baking mix
- ½ cup packed brown sugar
- 1 teaspoon ground cinnamon
- ¼ cup shredded carrot

1. Preheat oven to 400°F. Spray 2 large baking sheets with nonstick cooking spray; set aside.

2. Core tomato; chop. Measure 1¼ cups tomato; set aside.

3. In small bowl combine milk, egg and oil until well blended; set aside.

4. In large bowl combine baking mix, sugar and cinnamon. Stir into milk mixture just until moistened. Stir in carrot and reserved tomato.

5. Drop ¼-cupfuls of batter 1 inch apart onto prepared baking sheets. Bake 10 minutes or until golden brown and wooden pick inserted in center comes out clean. Cool on baking sheets 1 minute; remove. Cool on wire racks 10 minutes. Serve warm or cool completely. *Makes 12 muffin tops*

Favorite recipe from **Florida Tomato Committee**

APPLE CHEDDAR SCONES

- 1½ cups unsifted all-purpose flour
- ½ cup toasted wheat germ
- 3 tablespoons sugar
- 2 teaspoons baking powder
- ½ teaspoon salt
- 2 tablespoons butter
- 1 small Rome Beauty apple, cored and chopped
- ¼ cup shredded Cheddar cheese
- 1 large egg white
- ½ cup low fat (1%) milk

1. Heat oven to 400°F. Grease 8-inch round cake pan. In medium bowl, combine flour, wheat germ, sugar, baking powder and salt. With two knives or pastry blender, cut in butter until the size of coarse crumbs. Toss chopped apple and cheese in flour mixture.

2. Beat together egg white and milk until well combined. Add to flour mixture, mixing with fork until dough forms. Turn dough out onto lightly floured surface and knead 6 times.

3. Spread dough evenly in cake pan and score deeply with knife into 6 wedges. Bake 25 to 30 minutes or until top springs back when gently pressed. Let stand 5 minutes; remove from pan and cool before serving. *Makes 6 scones*

Favorite recipe from **Washington Apple Commission**

Tomato–Carrot Muffin Top

— Tasty —

TEAM-UPS

PUMPKIN-GINGER SCONES

- ½ cup sugar, divided
- 2 cups all-purpose flour
- 2 teaspoons baking powder
- 1 teaspoon ground cinnamon
- ½ teaspoon baking soda
- ½ teaspoon salt
- 5 tablespoons butter or margarine, divided
- 1 egg
- ½ cup solid pack pumpkin
- ¼ cup sour cream
- ½ teaspoon grated fresh ginger *or* 2 tablespoons finely chopped crystallized ginger

Preheat oven to 425°F. Reserve 1 tablespoon sugar. Combine remaining sugar, flour, baking powder, cinnamon, baking soda and salt in large bowl. Cut in 4 tablespoons butter with pastry blender or 2 knives until mixture resembles coarse crumbs. Beat egg in small bowl; add pumpkin, sour cream and ginger. Beat until well blended. Add pumpkin mixture to flour mixture; stir until soft dough forms.

Turn out dough onto well-floured surface; knead 10 times. Roll out dough into 9×6-inch rectangle with lightly floured rolling pin. Cut dough into 6 (3-inch) squares with lightly floured knife. Cut each square diagonally in half, making 12 triangles. Place triangles 2 inches apart on *ungreased* baking sheet. Melt remaining 1 tablespoon butter. Brush triangles with butter; sprinkle with reserved sugar.

Bake 10 to 12 minutes or until golden brown and wooden pick inserted in center comes out clean. Cool on wire rack 10 minutes. Serve warm or cool completely.
Makes 12 scones

INDIAN CORN MUFFINS

- 1 cup all-purpose flour
- 1 cup cornmeal
- ⅓ cup granulated sugar
- 1 tablespoon baking powder
- ½ teaspoon salt
- 2 eggs, lightly beaten
- 1 cup LIBBY'S® Solid Pack Pumpkin
- ¼ cup vegetable oil
- ¼ cup water

In large bowl, combine flour, cornmeal, sugar, baking powder and salt. Mix well; set aside. In small mixer bowl, combine eggs, pumpkin, oil and water; beat well. Add wet ingredients to dry ingredients; mix thoroughly. Spoon batter into 10 greased or paper-lined muffin cups.

Bake in preheated 375°F. oven for 25 to 30 minutes or until toothpick comes out clean. Serve warm.
Makes 10 muffins

Pumpkin-Ginger Scones

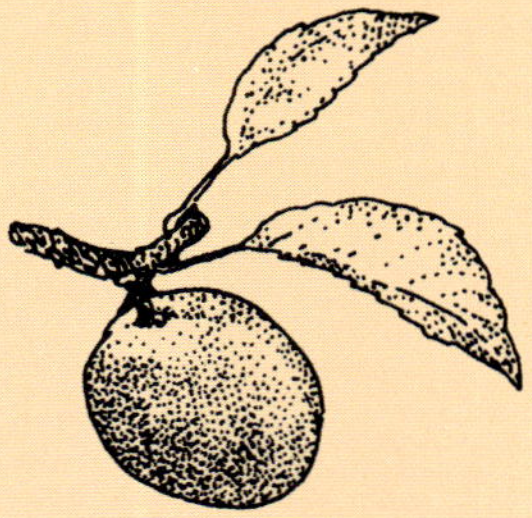

Terrific
LIGHT DELIGHTS

BLUEBERRY YOGURT MUFFINS

- 2 cups QUAKER® Oat Bran hot cereal, uncooked
- ¼ cup firmly packed brown sugar
- 2 teaspoons baking powder
- 1 carton (8 ounces) plain low fat yogurt
- 2 egg whites, slightly beaten
- ¼ cup skim milk
- ¼ cup honey
- 2 tablespoons vegetable oil
- 1 teaspoon grated lemon peel
- ½ cup fresh or frozen blueberries

Heat oven to 425°F. Line 12 medium muffin cups with paper baking cups. Combine oat bran, brown sugar and baking powder. Add combined yogurt, egg whites, skim milk, honey, oil and lemon peel, mixing just until moistened. Fold in blueberries. Fill muffin cups almost full. Bake 18 to 20 minutes or until golden brown.

Makes 12 muffins

NUTRIENTS PER MUFFIN:

Calories	130
% of Calories from Fat	25
Total Fat	4 g

Terrific

LIGHT DELIGHTS

WHOLE WHEAT HERB BREAD

- ⅔ cup water
- ⅔ cup skim milk
- 2 teaspoons sugar
- 2 envelopes active dry yeast
- 3 egg whites, lightly beaten
- 3 tablespoons olive oil
- 1 teaspoon salt
- ½ teaspoon dried basil
- ½ teaspoon dried oregano leaves
- 4 to 4½ cups whole wheat flour

1. Bring water to a boil in small saucepan. Remove from heat; stir in milk and sugar. When mixture is warm (110° to 115°F), add yeast. Mix well; let stand 10 minutes or until bubbly.

2. Combine egg whites, oil, salt, basil and oregano in large bowl until well blended. Add yeast mixture; mix well. Add 4 cups flour, ½ cup at a time, mixing well after each addition, until dough is no longer sticky. Knead about 5 minutes or until smooth and elastic, adding more flour if dough is sticky. Form into a ball. Cover and let rise in warm place about 1 hour or until doubled in bulk.

3. Preheat oven to 350°F. Punch dough down and place on lightly floured surface. Divide into 4 pieces and roll each piece into a ball. Place on baking sheet sprayed with nonstick cooking spray. Bake 30 to 35 minutes until golden brown.

Makes 24 servings

NUTRIENTS PER SERVING:

Calories	99
% of Calories from Fat	18
Total Fat	2 g

MOTT'S® BEST EVER STRAWBERRY MUFFINS

- 2 cups all-purpose flour
- 1 cup sugar
- 1 teaspoon baking soda
- 1 teaspoon ground cinnamon
- ½ teaspoon salt
- ½ teaspoon ground nutmeg
- ½ cup nonfat buttermilk
- ½ cup MOTT'S® Natural Apple Sauce
- 3 egg whites
- ½ cup strawberry jam

1. Preheat oven to 350°F. Spray 12-cup muffin pan with nonstick cooking spray or paper-line; set aside.

2. In large bowl, combine flour, sugar, baking soda, cinnamon, salt and nutmeg.

3. In medium bowl, combine buttermilk, apple sauce and egg whites until well blended.

4. Stir apple sauce mixture into flour mixture just until moistened. Fold in strawberry jam.

5. Fill prepared muffin cups ¾ full.

6. Bake 18 to 20 minutes or until golden brown and wooden pick inserted in center comes out clean. Remove from pan. Cool on wire rack 10 minutes. Serve warm or cool completely.

Makes 12 muffins

NUTRIENTS PER MUFFIN:

Calories	190
% of Calories from Fat	2
Total Fat	<1 g

Whole Wheat Herb Bread

APPLE SAUCE CINNAMON ROLLS

ROLLS
- 4 cups all-purpose flour, divided
- 1 package active dry yeast
- 1 cup MOTT'S® Natural Apple Sauce, divided
- ½ cup skim milk
- ⅓ cup plus 2 tablespoons granulated sugar, divided
- 2 tablespoons margarine
- ½ teaspoon salt
- 1 egg, beaten lightly
- 2 teaspoons ground cinnamon

ICING
- 1 cup sifted powdered sugar
- 1 tablespoon skim milk
- ½ teaspoon vanilla extract

1. To prepare rolls, in large bowl, combine 1½ cups flour and yeast. In small saucepan, combine ¾ cup applesauce, ½ cup milk, 2 tablespoons granulated sugar, margarine and salt. Cook over medium heat, stirring frequently, until mixture reaches 120° to 130°F and margarine is almost melted. (Milk will appear curdled.) Add to flour mixture along with egg. Beat with electric mixer on low speed 30 seconds, scraping bowl frequently. Beat on high speed 3 minutes. Stir in 2¼ cups flour until soft dough forms.

2. Turn out dough onto lightly floured surface; flatten slightly. Knead 3 to 5 minutes or until smooth and elastic, adding remaining ¼ cup flour to prevent sticking if necessary. Shape dough into ball; place in large bowl sprayed with nonstick cooking spray. Turn dough over so that top is greased. Cover with towel; let rise in warm place about 1 hour or until doubled in bulk.

3. Punch down dough; turn out onto lightly floured surface. Cover with towel; let rise 10 minutes. Roll out dough into 12-inch square. Spread remaining ¼ cup apple sauce over dough, to within ½ inch of edges. Combine remaining ⅓ cup granulated sugar and cinnamon; sprinkle over apple sauce. Roll up dough jelly-roll style. Moisten edge with water; pinch to seal. Cut roll into 12 (1-inch) slices. Spray two 8- or 9-inch round baking pans with nonstick cooking spray. Arrange 6 rolls ½ inch apart in each prepared pan. Cover with towel; let rise in warm place about 20 minutes or until nearly doubled.

4. Preheat oven to 375°F. Bake 20 to 25 minutes or until lightly browned. Cool on wire rack 5 minutes. Invert each pan onto serving plate.

5. To prepare icing, combine powdered sugar, 1 tablespoon milk and vanilla. Drizzle over tops of rolls. Serve warm.

Makes 12 servings

NUTRIENTS PER ROLL:	
Calories	260
% of Calories from Fat	10
Total Fat	3 g

Apple Sauce Cinnamon Rolls

SESAME CRUNCH BANANA MUFFINS

       Sesame Crunch Topping (recipe follows)
1½ cups uncooked rolled oats
½ cup all-purpose flour
½ cup whole wheat flour
2 tablespoons granulated sugar
1 tablespoon baking powder
½ teaspoon salt
2 medium, ripe bananas, mashed
1 cup low fat milk
2 egg whites
2 tablespoons vegetable oil
1 teaspoon vanilla

Prepare Sesame Crunch Topping; set aside. Preheat oven to 400°F. Spray muffin cups with nonstick cooking spray or paper-line; set aside.

Combine oats, flours, sugar, baking powder and salt in large bowl. Combine bananas, milk, egg whites, oil and vanilla in medium bowl until well blended. Stir into oat mixture just until moistened. (Batter will be lumpy.) Spoon evenly into prepared muffin cups, filling three-fourths full. Sprinkle 2 teaspoons Sesame Crunch over top of each muffin.

Bake 20 to 25 minutes or until golden brown and wooden pick inserted in center comes out clean. Cool in pan 5 minutes; remove. Cool on wire rack 10 minutes. Serve warm or cool completely.

Makes 17 muffins

Sesame Crunch Topping

4 tablespoons packed brown sugar
2 tablespoons chopped walnuts
2 tablespoons whole wheat flour
1 tablespoon sesame seeds
1 tablespoon margarine
¼ teaspoon ground nutmeg
¼ teaspoon ground cinnamon

Combine all ingredients in small bowl until well blended.

Makes about ¾ cup

NUTRIENTS PER MUFFIN:

Calories	124
% of Calories from Fat	28
Total Fat	4 g

Sesame Crunch Banana Muffins

Terrific

LIGHT DELIGHTS

PEAR SCONES

- 1 pear, cored
- 2½ cups all-purpose flour
- 1 cup granulated sugar
- ½ cup whole wheat flour
- 1 tablespoon baking powder
- ½ teaspoon baking soda
- ½ teaspoon ground ginger
- 2 tablespoons cold margarine
- 2 tablespoons cold butter
- ½ cup buttermilk
- 1 tablespoon granulated sugar

Preheat oven to 400°F. Spray baking sheets with nonstick cooking spray; set aside. In food processor shred pear. Remove from work bowl; set aside. In food processor combine all-purpose flour, 1 cup sugar, whole wheat flour, baking powder, baking soda and ginger; process until blended. Add margarine and butter; process until mixture resembles coarse crumbs. Transfer to large bowl. Stir in reserved pear and buttermilk until soft dough forms.

Knead dough on lightly floured surface 8 to 10 times. Roll out to ½-inch thickness; cut into rounds with biscuit cutter. Sprinkle remaining 1 tablespoon sugar over tops of scones. Bake 10 to 15 minutes or until golden brown.

Makes about 30 scones

NUTRIENTS PER SCONE:
Calories	89
% of Calories from Fat	17
Total Fat	2 g

Favorite recipe from **The Sugar Association, Inc.**

CARROT ZUCCHINI MUFFINS

MUFFINS
- 2 tablespoons CRISCO® all-vegetable shortening
- ½ cup firmly packed brown sugar
- 2 egg whites, lightly beaten
- ⅔ cup skim milk
- 1¾ cups QUAKER® Oats (quick or old fashioned, uncooked)
- 1 cup all-purpose flour
- 1 tablespoon baking powder
- ¼ teaspoon nutmeg
- 1 cup shredded carrot (about 1 large)
- ½ cup shredded zucchini (about 1 small)

TOPPING
- ¼ cup QUAKER® Oats (quick or old fashioned, uncooked)
- 1 tablespoon chopped almonds
- 1 tablespoon CRISCO® all-vegetable shortening, melted

1. Heat oven to 400°F. **Line** 12 medium (about 2½-inch) muffin cups with foil or paper liners.

2. *For muffins,* combine 2 tablespoons shortening and brown sugar in large bowl. **Beat** at medium speed of electric mixer or **stir** with fork until well blended. **Stir** in egg whites and milk gradually.

3. Combine 1¾ cups oats, flour, baking powder and nutmeg. **Stir** into liquid ingredients. **Add** carrot and zucchini. **Stir** until just blended. **Fill** muffin cups almost full.

Terrific

LIGHT DELIGHTS

4. *For topping,* **combine** ¼ cup oats, nuts and 1 tablespoon shortening. **Sprinkle** over each muffin. **Press** into batter lightly.

5. Bake at 400°F. for 20 to 25 minutes or until golden brown. Serve warm. *Makes 12 muffins*

NOTE: Baked muffins can be frozen. To reheat, microwave on HIGH about 30 seconds per muffin.

NUTRIENTS PER MUFFIN:	
Calories	177
% of Calories from Fat	27
Total Fat	5 g

MOTT'S® LUSCIOUS LEMON LITE MUFFINS

MUFFINS
- 1 cup all-purpose flour
- 1 cup uncooked rolled oats
- ⅔ cup golden raisins
- ½ cup granulated sugar
- ¼ cup wheat germ
- 1½ teaspoons baking soda
- 1 teaspoon baking powder
- 1 cup MOTT'S® Natural Apple Sauce
- ½ cup frozen lemonade concentrate, thawed
- ⅓ cup nonfat buttermilk
- 1 egg
- 1 egg white, lightly beaten
- 2 tablespoons vegetable oil
- ½ teaspoon lemon extract

GLAZE
- ½ cup confectioners' sugar
- 2 to 3 tablespoons frozen lemonade concentrate, thawed

1. Preheat oven to 375°F. Spray 12-cup muffin pan with nonstick cooking spray or paper-line; set aside.

2. In large bowl, combine flour, oats, raisins, granulated sugar, wheat germ, baking soda and baking powder.

3. In medium bowl, combine apple sauce, ½ cup lemonade concentrate, buttermilk, egg, egg white, oil and lemon extract until well blended.

4. Stir apple sauce mixture into flour mixture just until moistened.

5. Fill muffin cups ¾ full.

6. Bake 17 to 20 minutes or until golden brown and wooden pick inserted in center comes out clean. Remove from pan. Cool on wire rack 10 minutes. Meanwhile, combine confectioners' sugar and 2 tablespoons lemonade concentrate; drizzle over top of each muffin. Serve warm or cool completely. *Makes 12 muffins*

NUTRIENTS PER MUFFIN:	
Calories	230
% of Calories from Fat	16
Total Fat	4 g

Terrific

LIGHT DELIGHTS

OATMEAL APPLE CRANBERRY SCONES

- 2 cups all-purpose flour
- 1 cup uncooked rolled oats
- ⅓ cup sugar
- 2 teaspoons baking powder
- ½ teaspoon salt
- ½ teaspoon baking soda
- ½ teaspoon ground cinnamon
- ¾ cup MOTT'S® Natural Apple Sauce, divided
- 2 tablespoons margarine
- ½ cup coarsely chopped cranberries
- ½ cup peeled, chopped apple
- ¼ cup skim milk
- ¼ cup plus 2 tablespoons honey, divided

1. Preheat oven to 425°F. Spray baking sheet with nonstick cooking spray.

2. In large bowl, combine flour, oats, sugar, baking powder, salt, baking soda and cinnamon. Add ½ cup apple sauce and margarine; cut in with pastry blender or fork until mixture resembles coarse crumbs. Stir in cranberries and apple.

3. In small bowl, combine milk and ¼ cup honey. Add milk mixture to flour mixture; stir together until dough forms a ball.

4. Turn out dough onto well-floured surface; knead 10 to 12 times. Pat dough into 8-inch circle. Place on prepared baking sheet. Use tip of knife to score dough into 12 wedges.

5. In another small bowl, combine remaining ¼ cup apple sauce and 2 tablespoons honey. Brush mixture over top of dough.

6. Bake 12 to 15 minutes or until lightly browned. Immediately remove from baking sheet; cool on wire rack 10 minutes. Cut into 12 wedges. Serve warm or cool completely. *Makes 12 servings*

NUTRIENTS PER SCONE:	
Calories	170
% of Calories from Fat	13
Total Fat	3 g

Oatmeal Apple Cranberry Scones

BLUEBERRY MUFFINS

- 1 cup fresh or thawed, frozen blueberries
- 1¾ cups plus 1 tablespoon all-purpose flour, divided
- 2 teaspoons baking powder
- 1 teaspoon grated lemon peel
- ½ teaspoon salt
- ½ cup MOTT'S® Apple Sauce
- ½ cup sugar
- 1 whole egg
- 1 egg white
- 2 tablespoons vegetable oil
- ¼ cup skim milk

Preheat oven to 375°F. Line 12 (2½-inch) muffin cups with paper liners or spray with nonstick cooking spray.

Toss blueberries with 1 tablespoon flour; set aside. In large bowl, combine remaining 1¾ cups flour, baking powder, lemon peel and salt. Combine apple sauce, sugar, whole egg, egg white and oil; stir into flour mixture alternately with milk. Mix just until moistened. Fold in blueberry mixture. Spoon evenly into prepared muffin cups.

Bake 20 minutes or until toothpick inserted in center comes out clean. Immediately remove from pan; cool on wire rack. *Makes 12 servings*

NUTRIENTS PER MUFFIN:

Calories	150
% of Calories from Fat	18
Total Fat	3 g

BANANA NUT BREAD

- ½ cup granulated sugar
- 2 tablespoons brown sugar
- 5 tablespoons margarine
- 1⅓ cups mashed ripe bananas
- 1 egg
- 2 egg whites
- 2½ cups all-purpose flour
- 1 teaspoon baking soda
- ½ teaspoon salt
- ⅓ cup walnuts

Preheat oven to 375°F. Spray large loaf pan with nonstick cooking spray; set aside. Beat sugars and margarine in large bowl with electric mixer until light and fluffy. Add bananas, egg and egg whites. Sift together flour, baking soda and salt in medium bowl; add to banana mixture. Stir in walnuts. Pour into prepared loaf pan. Bake 1 hour or until wooden pick inserted in center comes out clean. Remove from pan. Cool on wire rack 10 minutes. Serve warm or cool completely.

Makes 1 loaf (16 servings)

NUTRIENTS PER SERVING:

Calories	174
% of Calories from Fat	28
Total Fat	6 g

Favorite recipe from **The Sugar Association, Inc.**

Blueberry Muffins

— Terrific —

LIGHT DELIGHTS

SPICE–PRUNE LOAF

- 1 cup chopped pitted prunes
- ½ cup prune juice
- 1 cup all-purpose flour
- 1 cup whole wheat flour
- 1 teaspoon baking powder
- ¾ teaspoon ground cinnamon
- ½ teaspoon baking soda
- ¼ teaspoon ground ginger
- ⅛ teaspoon salt
- 2 egg whites
- ⅓ cup molasses
- 3 tablespoons vegetable oil
- ¼ teaspoon vanilla

Preheat oven to 350°F. Spray 8×4-inch loaf pan with nonstick cooking spray; set aside. Bring prunes and prune juice to a boil over medium-high heat. Remove from heat; let stand 5 minutes.

Combine flours, baking powder, cinnamon, baking soda, ginger and salt. Stir remaining ingredients into flour mixture just until moistened. Stir in prune mixture.

Pour batter into prepared pan. Bake 55 to 60 minutes or until wooden pick inserted in center comes out clean. Cool completely. Wrap and store overnight at room temperature before slicing.

Makes 16 servings

NUTRIENTS PER SERVING:

Calories	124
% of Calories from Fat	20
Total Fat	3 g

WILD RICE BLUEBERRY MUFFINS

- 1½ cups all-purpose flour
- ½ cup sugar
- 2 teaspoons baking powder
- 1 teaspoon ground cinnamon
- ½ teaspoon salt
- 1 cup fresh blueberries
- ½ cup skim milk
- ¼ cup applesauce
- 4 egg whites
- 1 cup cooked wild rice

Preheat oven to 400°F. Spray muffin cups with nonstick cooking spray or paper-line. Combine flour, sugar, baking powder, cinnamon and salt in large bowl. Sprinkle 1 tablespoon flour mixture over blueberries; toss to coat. Combine milk, applesauce and egg whites in medium bowl. Fold into batter with blueberries and wild rice. (Batter will be stiff.) Spoon evenly into prepared muffin cups, filling two-thirds full. Bake 15 to 20 minutes or until wooden pick inserted in center comes out clean. Remove from pan. Cool on wire rack 10 minutes. Serve warm or cool completely.

Makes 12 muffins

NUTRIENTS PER MUFFIN:

Calories	120
% of Calories from Fat	2
Total Fat	<1 g

Spice-Prune Loaf

— Terrific —

CRANBERRY OAT BRAN MUFFINS

　2 cups flour
　1 cup oat bran
　½ cup packed brown sugar
　2 teaspoons baking powder
　½ teaspoon baking soda
　½ teaspoon salt (optional)
　½ cup MIRACLE WHIP® LIGHT Reduced Calorie Salad Dressing
　3 egg whites, slightly beaten
　½ cup skim milk
　⅓ cup orange juice
　1 teaspoon grated orange peel
　1 cup coarsely chopped cranberries

Preheat oven to 375°F. Line 12 medium muffin cups with paper baking cups or spray with nonstick cooking spray. Mix together dry ingredients. Add combined dressing, egg whites, milk, juice and peel; mix just until moistened. Fold in cranberries. Fill prepared muffin cups almost full. Bake 15 to 17 minutes or until golden brown.

Makes 12 muffins

NUTRIENTS PER MUFFIN:
Calories	183
% of Calories from Fat	20
Total Fat	4 g

APPLE OAT BRAN MUFFINS

　¾ cup unsifted all-purpose flour
　¾ cup whole wheat flour
　1½ teaspoons ground cinnamon
　1 teaspoon baking powder
　½ teaspoon baking soda
　¼ teaspoon salt
　1 cup buttermilk
　½ cup oat bran
　¼ cup packed brown sugar
　2 tablespoons vegetable oil
　1 large egg
　1½ cups Golden Delicious apples, peeled, cored and finely diced

1. Heat oven to 400°F. Grease 12 muffin cups or fill with paper muffin-cup liners. In large bowl, combine flours, cinnamon, baking powder, baking soda and salt. In medium-size bowl, beat together buttermilk, oat bran, sugar, oil and egg. Add buttermilk mixture to flour mixture, stirring until just combined; fold in apples.

2. Divide batter among prepared muffin cups. Bake 18 to 20 minutes or until wooden pick inserted in centers comes out clean. Cool muffins 5 minutes in pan; remove from pan and cool on wire rack.

Makes 12 muffins

NUTRIENTS PER MUFFIN:
Calories	121
% of Calories from Fat	22
Total Fat	3 g

Favorite recipe from **Washington Apple Commission**

Cranberry Oat Bran Muffins

Terrific

LIGHT DELIGHTS

CHIVE WHOLE WHEAT DROP BISCUITS

- 1¼ cups whole wheat flour
- ¾ cup all-purpose flour
- 3 tablespoons toasted wheat germ, divided
- 1 tablespoon baking powder
- 1 tablespoon chopped fresh chives *or* 1 teaspoon dried chives
- 2 teaspoons sugar
- 3 tablespoons margarine
- 1 cup skim milk
- ½ cup shredded low fat process American cheese

Preheat oven to 450°F. Spray baking sheet with nonstick cooking spray; set aside. Combine flours, 2 tablespoons wheat germ, baking powder, chives and sugar in medium bowl. Cut in margarine with pastry blender until mixture resembles coarse crumbs. Add milk and cheese; stir just until moistened.

Drop rounded teaspoonfuls of dough 1 inch apart onto prepared baking sheet. Sprinkle remaining 1 tablespoon wheat germ over tops of biscuits. Bake 10 to 12 minutes or until golden brown and wooden pick inserted in center comes out clean. Remove immediately from baking sheet.

Makes 12 servings

NUTRIENTS PER BISCUIT:	
Calories	125
% of Calories from Fat	28
Total Fat	4 g

BLUEBERRY CRUNCH MUFFINS

- ¾ cup skim milk
- 3 tablespoons vegetable oil
- 1 egg
- 1¼ cups all-purpose flour
- ½ cup whole wheat flour
- ½ cup packed brown sugar
- ¼ cup uncooked rolled oats
- ¼ cup granulated sugar
- 2 teaspoons baking powder
- ¼ teaspoon salt
- ⅛ teaspoon ground cinnamon
- 1 cup fresh or frozen blueberries, thawed, drained
- **Crunch Topping (recipe follows)**

Preheat oven to 400°F. Spray muffin cups or loaf pan with nonstick cooking spray; set aside. In food processor or large bowl combine milk, oil and egg; process until smooth. Combine flours, brown sugar, oats, granulated sugar, baking powder, salt and cinnamon in medium bowl. Stir into milk mixture just until moistened. Fold in blueberries. Spoon evenly into prepared muffin cups. Sprinkle Crunch Topping over top of each muffin. Bake muffins 15 to 18 minutes (25 to 30 minutes for loaf) or until golden brown and wooden pick inserted in center comes out clean. Remove from pan. Cool on wire rack 10 minutes. Serve warm or cool completely.

Makes about 18 small muffins or 1 loaf

— Terrific —

LIGHT DELIGHTS

CRUNCH TOPPING: Blend ¼ cup whole wheat breakfast cereal flakes, 1 tablespoon flour, 2 tablespoons granulated sugar and 1 teaspoon butter in food processor.

NUTRIENTS PER MUFFIN:	
Calories	114
% of Calories from Fat	22
Total Fat	3 g

PUMPKIN VARIATION: Omit blueberries. *Decrease* milk to ½ cup. Fold ¾ cup canned pumpkin, ⅛ teaspoon nutmeg, 2 tablespoons walnut pieces into batter.

Favorite recipe from **The Sugar Association, Inc.**

MINI MUFFINS

- 2 ripe bananas *or* 8 ounces solid pack pumpkin
- 1 cup packed brown sugar
- 2 egg whites
- 2 tablespoons vegetable oil
- 1¼ cups all-purpose flour
- ¾ cup whole wheat flour
- 2 teaspoons baking powder
- ½ teaspoon baking soda
- ½ teaspoon ground cinnamon
- 1 tablespoon granulated sugar
- Peach Spread (recipe follows)

Preheat oven to 400°F. Spray mini-muffin cups with cooking spray; set aside. In large bowl mash bananas. Combine brown sugar, egg whites and oil until well blended; add to bananas. Combine flours, baking powder, baking soda, cinnamon and granulated sugar in medium bowl. Stir into banana mixture just until moistened. Let stand 5 minutes. Spoon evenly into prepared muffin cups, filling half full. Sprinkle additional granulated sugar over top of each muffin. Bake 15 to 18 minutes or until golden brown and wooden pick inserted in center comes out clean. Remove from pans. Cool on wire racks 10 minutes. Serve with Peach Spread.

Makes about 48 mini muffins

Peach Spread
- ½ cup frozen peaches, thawed, drained
- ¼ cup part-skim ricotta cheese
- 2 tablespoons powdered sugar

In food processor combine all ingredients; process until smooth.

Makes 30 servings

NUTRIENTS PER MINI MUFFIN:	
Calories	55
% of Calories from Fat	13
Fat	<1 g

Favorite recipe from **The Sugar Association, Inc.**

Sweet SNACKIN' TREATS

NEWTON MUFFINS

1¾ cups all-purpose flour
¼ cup sugar
1 tablespoon DAVIS® Baking Powder
⅓ cup FLEISCHMANN'S® Margarine, melted
1 egg, slightly beaten
¾ cup apple juice
10 Fat Free FIG or APPLE NEWTONS® Fruit Chewy Cookies, coarsely chopped

In medium bowl, combine flour, sugar and baking powder. Stir in margarine, egg and apple juice just until blended. (Batter will be lumpy.) Stir in cookies. Fill 12 greased 2½-inch muffin-pan cups.

Bake at 400°F for 15 to 20 minutes or until toothpick inserted in center comes out clean. Serve warm or cold.

Makes 1 dozen muffins

Sweet

SNACKIN' TREATS

GINGERBREAD PEAR MUFFINS

- 1¾ cups all-purpose flour
- ⅓ cup sugar
- 2 teaspoons baking powder
- ¾ teaspoon ground ginger
- ¼ teaspoon baking soda
- ¼ teaspoon salt
- ¼ teaspoon ground cinnamon
- 1 medium pear
- ⅓ cup milk
- ¼ cup vegetable oil
- ¼ cup light molasses
- 1 egg

1. Preheat oven to 375°F. Grease or paper-line 12 (2½-inch) muffin cups; set aside.

2. Sift flour, sugar, baking powder, ginger, baking soda, salt and cinnamon into large bowl.

3. Peel pear with vegetable peeler. Cut pear lengthwise into halves, then into quarters with utility knife; remove core and seeds.

4. Finely chop pear with chef's knife to measure 1 cup.

5. Combine milk, oil, molasses and egg in medium bowl until well blended; stir in pear. Stir into flour mixture just until moistened.

6. Spoon evenly into prepared muffin cups, filling two-thirds full.

7. Bake 20 minutes or until wooden pick inserted in center comes out clean. Remove from pan. Cool on wire rack 10 minutes. Serve warm or cool completely.

Makes 12 muffins

QUICK NECTARINE OAT MUFFINS

- 2 cups whole wheat flour
- 3 fresh California nectarines, finely chopped (2 cups)
- 1½ cups buttermilk
- 1 cup uncooked rolled oats
- ½ cup unprocessed bran
- ½ cup packed brown sugar
- ¼ cup vegetable oil
- 2 eggs
- 1 tablespoon grated orange peel
- 1½ teaspoons baking soda
- 1½ teaspoons ground cinnamon
- 1 teaspoon salt

Preheat oven to 400°F. Grease 20 (2½-inch) muffin cups; set aside. Combine all ingredients in mixing bowl just until moistened. Spoon evenly into prepared muffin cups. Bake 20 minutes or until wooden pick inserted in center comes out clean. Remove from pans. Cool on wire racks 10 minutes. Serve warm or cool completely.

Makes 20 muffins

Favorite recipe from **California Tree Fruit Agreement**

Gingerbread Pear Muffins

Sweet

SNACKIN' TREATS

STREUSEL-TOPPED BLUEBERRY MUFFINS

- 1½ cups plus ⅓ cup all-purpose flour, divided
- ½ cup plus ⅓ cup sugar, divided
- 1 teaspoon ground cinnamon
- 3 tablespoons butter or margarine, cut into small pieces
- 2 teaspoons baking powder
- ½ teaspoon salt
- 1 cup milk
- ¼ cup butter or margarine, melted and slightly cooled
- 1 egg, beaten
- 1 teaspoon vanilla
- 1 cup fresh blueberries

Preheat oven to 375°F. Grease or paper-line 12 (2½-inch) muffin cups; set aside.

Combine ⅓ cup flour, ⅓ cup sugar and cinnamon in small bowl; mix well. Cut in 3 tablespoons butter with pastry blender or 2 knives until mixture resembles coarse crumbs; set aside for topping.

Combine remaining 1½ cups flour, ½ cup sugar, baking powder and salt in large bowl. Combine milk, ¼ cup melted butter, egg and vanilla in small bowl until well blended. Stir into flour mixture just until moistened. (Do not overmix.) Fold in blueberries. Spoon evenly into prepared muffin cups. Sprinkle reserved topping over top of each muffin.

Bake 20 to 25 minutes or until wooden pick inserted in center comes out clean. Remove from pan. Cool on wire rack 10 minutes. Serve warm or cool completely.
Makes 12 muffins

MINT CHOCOLATE CHIP MUFFINS

- 2⅓ cups all-purpose flour
- 1¼ cups sugar
- ⅓ cup unsweetened cocoa powder
- 2 teaspoons baking powder
- 1 teaspoon baking soda
- ½ teaspoon salt
- 1 cup sour cream
- ⅓ cup butter or margarine, melted
- ¼ cup milk
- 2 eggs, beaten
- 1 cup mint flavored semi-sweet chocolate chips

Preheat oven to 400°F. Grease 12 (3½-inch) large muffin cups; set aside. Combine flour, sugar, cocoa, baking powder, baking soda and salt in large bowl. Combine sour cream, butter, milk and eggs in small bowl until blended. Stir into flour mixture just until moistened. Fold in mint chips. Spoon into prepared muffin cups, filling half full. Bake 25 to 30 minutes or until wooden pick inserted in center comes out clean. Cool in pan 5 minutes. Remove from pan. Cool on wire rack 10 minutes. Serve warm or cool completely.
Makes 12 jumbo muffins

Streusel-Topped Blueberry Muffins

— Sweet —

BAKED DOUGHNUTS WITH CINNAMON GLAZE

- 5 to 5½ cups all-purpose flour, divided
- ⅔ cup granulated sugar
- 2 packages active dry yeast
- 1 teaspoon salt
- 1 teaspoon grated lemon peel
- ½ teaspoon ground nutmeg
- 2 cups milk, divided
- ½ cup butter or margarine
- 2 eggs
- 2 cups sifted powdered sugar
- ½ teaspoon ground cinnamon

Combine 2 cups flour, granulated sugar, yeast, salt, lemon peel and nutmeg in large bowl. Combine 1¾ cups milk and butter in 1-quart saucepan. Heat over low heat until mixture is 120° to 130°F. (Butter does not need to completely melt.) Gradually beat milk mixture into flour mixture with electric mixer at low speed. Increase speed to medium; beat 2 minutes. Beat in eggs and 1 cup flour at low speed. Increase speed to medium; beat 2 minutes. Stir in enough additional flour, about 2 cups, to make soft dough. Cover with plastic wrap; refrigerate at least 2 hours or up to 24 hours.

Punch down dough. Turn out dough onto lightly floured surface. Knead dough about 1 minute or until dough is no longer sticky, adding ½ cup flour to prevent sticking if necessary. Grease 2 large baking sheets. Roll out dough to ½-inch thickness with lightly floured rolling pin. Cut dough with floured 2¾-inch doughnut cutter. Reroll scraps, reserving doughnut holes. Place doughnuts and holes 2 inches apart on prepared baking sheets. Cover with towel and let rise in warm place about 30 minutes or until doubled in bulk.

Preheat oven to 400°F. To prepare glaze, combine powdered sugar and cinnamon in small bowl. Stir in enough remaining milk, about ¼ cup, to thin glaze to desired consistency. Cover; set aside.

Bake doughnuts and holes 8 to 10 minutes or until golden brown. Remove from pan with spatula; cool on wire racks 5 minutes. Dip tops of warm doughnuts into glaze. Place right side up on racks, allowing glaze to drip down sides. Best when served warm.

Makes 2 dozen doughnuts and holes

Baked Doughnuts with Cinnamon Glaze

— Sweet —

SNACKIN' TREATS

CHOCOLATE PUMPKIN MUFFINS

- 1½ cups all-purpose flour
- ½ cup granulated sugar
- 2 teaspoons baking powder
- ½ teaspoon ground cinnamon
- ½ teaspoon salt
- 1 cup milk
- ½ cup LIBBY'S® Solid Pack Pumpkin
- ¼ cup margarine or butter, melted
- 1 egg
- 1 cup (6-ounce package) NESTLÉ® TOLL HOUSE® Semi-Sweet Chocolate Morsels
- ⅓ cup finely chopped nuts

Preheat oven to 400°F. Grease 12 (2½-inch) muffin cups.

In large bowl, combine flour, sugar, baking powder, cinnamon and salt; make well in center. In small bowl, combine milk, pumpkin, margarine and egg; add to well in flour mixture. Add morsels; stir just until dry ingredients are moistened. Spoon into prepared muffin cups, filling each ¾ full. Sprinkle 1 teaspoon nuts over each muffin.

Bake 18 to 20 minutes or until wooden pick inserted into center comes out clean. Cool 5 minutes; remove from pans. Cool completely on wire racks.

Makes 12 muffins

HONEY MUFFINS

- 2 cups all-purpose flour
- ¼ cup sugar
- 2 teaspoons baking powder
- 1 teaspoon baking soda
- ½ teaspoon salt
- ½ cup honey
- ½ cup orange juice
- ⅓ cup butter or margarine, melted
- 2 eggs, beaten
- 1 teaspoon vanilla

Preheat oven to 375°F. Grease 12 muffin cups; set aside.

Combine flour, sugar, baking powder, baking soda and salt in large bowl. Combine honey, orange juice, butter, eggs and vanilla in medium bowl until well blended. Stir into flour mixture just until blended. Spoon evenly into prepared muffin cups, filling two-thirds full. Bake 15 to 20 minutes or until golden brown and wooden pick inserted in center comes out clean. Remove from pan. Cool on wire rack 10 minutes. Serve warm or cool completely.

Makes 12 muffins

TIP: To make giant muffins, spoon batter equally into 5 giant muffin tins. Bake at 350°F 25 to 30 minutes or until golden.

Favorite recipe from **National Honey Board**

Chocolate Pumpkin Muffins

— Sweet —

SNACKIN' TREATS

GLAZED STRAWBERRY LEMON STREUSEL MUFFINS

      Lemon Streusel Topping (recipe follows)
      Lemony Glaze (recipe follows)
1½ cups all-purpose flour
 ½ cup sugar
 2 teaspoons baking powder
 1 teaspoon ground cinnamon
 ¼ teaspoon salt
 ½ cup milk
 ½ cup butter or margarine, melted
 1 egg
1½ cups fresh strawberries, chopped
 1 teaspoon grated lemon peel

Preheat oven to 375°F. Paper-line 12 (2½-inch) muffin cups. Prepare Lemon Streusel Topping and Lemony Glaze; set aside.

Combine flour, sugar, baking powder, cinnamon and salt in large bowl. Combine milk, butter and egg in small bowl until well blended. Stir into flour mixture just until moistened. Fold in strawberries and lemon peel. Spoon evenly into prepared muffin cups. Sprinkle Lemon Streusel Topping evenly over tops of muffins.

Bake 20 to 25 minutes or until wooden pick inserted in center comes out clean. Remove from pan. Cool on wire rack 10 minutes. Drizzle Lemony Glaze over tops of warm muffins. Serve warm or cool completely. *Makes 12 muffins*

LEMON STREUSEL TOPPING: Combine ¼ cup chopped pecans, ¼ cup packed brown sugar, 2 tablespoons all-purpose flour, ½ teaspoon ground cinnamon and ½ teaspoon grated lemon peel in medium bowl. Add 1 tablespoon melted butter or margarine, stirring until crumbly.

LEMONY GLAZE: Combine ½ cup powdered sugar and 1 tablespoon fresh lemon juice in small bowl, stirring until smooth.

GOLDEN APPLE SOUR CREAM MUFFINS

 1 cup dairy sour cream
 1 egg, beaten
 3 tablespoons sugar
 2 tablespoons vegetable oil
1½ cups flour
 1 teaspoon baking powder
 ½ teaspoon salt
 ¼ teaspoon baking soda
 ⅛ teaspoon ground allspice
 ½ cup currants or raisins
 1 cup chopped Golden Delicious apple

Combine sour cream, egg, sugar and oil. Combine flour, baking powder, salt, baking soda and allspice; stir into sour cream mixture. Fold in currants and apple. Spoon evenly into 12 greased muffin cups. Bake at 400°F 20 to 25 minutes or until wooden pick inserted near center comes out clean.
Makes 12 muffins

Favorite recipe from **Washington Apple Commission**

Glazed Strawberry Lemon Streusel Muffins

Sweet

SNACKIN' TREATS

Cinnamon–Raisin Bread

- 1 package active dry yeast
- ½ cup plus 1 teaspoon sugar, divided
- ¼ cup warm water (105° to 115°F)
- 2 eggs, divided
- 3 to 3½ cups all-purpose flour, divided
- 1 teaspoon salt
- ⅔ cup warm milk (105° to 115°F)
- 3 tablespoons butter or margarine, softened
- 1 teaspoon vanilla
- ¾ cup raisins
- 1 tablespoon ground cinnamon
- 1 tablespoon butter or margarine, melted
- 1 tablespoon water

To proof yeast, sprinkle yeast and 1 teaspoon sugar over warm water in small bowl; stir until yeast is dissolved. Let stand 5 minutes or until mixture is bubbly. Separate 1 egg. Place yolk in another bowl; set aside. Cover white with plastic wrap; store in refrigerator until needed.

Combine 1½ cups flour, ¼ cup sugar and salt in large bowl. Gradually beat yeast mixture, warm milk and softened butter into flour mixture with electric mixer at low speed. Increase speed to medium; beat 2 minutes. Reduce speed to low. Beat in remaining whole egg, reserved egg yolk and vanilla. Increase speed to medium; beat 2 minutes, scraping down side of bowl once. Stir in raisins and enough additional flour, about 1½ cups, with wooden spoon to make soft dough. Turn out dough onto lightly floured surface; flatten slightly. Knead dough about 5 minutes or until smooth and elastic, adding ½ cup more flour to prevent sticking, if necessary. Dough will be soft and slightly sticky.

Shape dough into a ball; place in large greased bowl. Turn dough over so that top is greased. Cover with towel; let rise in warm place 1 to 1½ hours or until doubled in bulk. Punch down dough. Knead dough on lightly floured surface 1 minute. Cover with towel; let rest 10 minutes. Grease 9×5-inch loaf pan; set aside. Combine remaining ¼ cup sugar and cinnamon. Place 1 tablespoon mixture in small cup; set aside.

Roll dough into 20×9-inch rectangle with lightly floured rolling pin. Brush with 1 tablespoon melted butter. Sprinkle ¼ cup cinnamon mixture evenly over butter. Starting with 1 (9-inch) side, roll up dough jelly-roll fashion. Pinch ends and seam to seal. Place loaf, seam side down, in prepared pan, tucking ends under. Cover with towel; let rise in warm place about 1¼ hours or until doubled in bulk. (Dough should rise to top of pan.)

Preheat oven to 350°F. Combine reserved egg white and 1 tablespoon water in small bowl. Brush loaf with egg white mixture; sprinkle with reserved 1 tablespoon cinnamon mixture.

Bake 40 to 45 minutes or until loaf sounds hollow when tapped. Immediately remove from pan; cool completely on wire rack. *Makes 1 loaf*

Cinnamon–Raisin Bread

Sweet

SNACKIN' TREATS

LEMON POPPY SEED MUFFINS

- 3 cups all-purpose flour
- 1 cup sugar
- 3 tablespoons poppy seeds
- 1 tablespoon grated lemon peel
- 2 teaspoons baking powder
- 1 teaspoon baking soda
- ½ teaspoon salt
- 1 container (16 ounces) low fat plain yogurt
- ½ cup fresh lemon juice
- ¼ cup vegetable oil
- 2 eggs, beaten
- 1½ teaspoons vanilla

Preheat oven to 400°F. Grease 12 (3½-inch) large muffin cups; set aside.

Combine flour, sugar, poppy seeds, lemon peel, baking powder, baking soda and salt in large bowl. Combine yogurt, lemon juice, oil, eggs and vanilla in small bowl until well blended. Stir into flour mixture just until moistened. Spoon into prepared muffin cups, filling two-thirds full.

Bake 25 to 30 minutes or until wooden pick inserted in center comes out clean. Cool in pans on wire racks 5 minutes. Remove from pans. Cool on wire racks 10 minutes. Serve warm or cool completely.   *Makes 12 jumbo muffins*

MINI CRUMBCAKES

- 2 cups (12-ounce package) NESTLÉ® TOLL HOUSE® Semi-Sweet Chocolate Mini Morsels, divided
- 2 cups all-purpose flour
- 3 tablespoons granulated sugar
- 1 tablespoon baking powder
- ¼ teaspoon salt
- ½ cup (1 stick) butter, melted
- ⅔ cup milk
- 2 eggs
- 1 teaspoon vanilla extract
- Topping (recipe follows)

Combine 1½ cups morsels, flour, sugar, baking powder and salt in large bowl. Combine butter, milk, eggs and vanilla in small bowl; add to flour mixture and stir just until moistened.

Spoon batter into greased or paper-lined muffin cups, filling about ¾ full. Sprinkle with Topping.

Bake in preheated 400°F. oven for 18 to 20 minutes or until wooden pick inserted in center comes out clean. Let stand for 5 minutes on wire racks. Remove from pans to wire racks to cool completely.   *Makes 18 crumbcakes*

Topping: Combine ½ cup chopped walnuts, ⅓ cup packed brown sugar, 2 tablespoons butter, melted and 1 tablespoon all-purpose flour in small bowl; stir in remaining morsels.

Lemon Poppy Seed Muffins

— Sweet —

SNACKIN' TREATS

PEANUT BUTTER MINI CHIP LOAVES

　3 cups all-purpose flour
1½ teaspoons baking powder
　1 teaspoon baking soda
　1 teaspoon salt
　1 cup creamy peanut butter
　½ cup butter or margarine, softened
　½ cup granulated sugar
　½ cup light brown sugar
　2 eggs
1½ cups buttermilk*
　2 teaspoons vanilla
　1 cup mini semisweet chocolate chips

*Or, substitute soured fresh milk. To sour milk, place 1½ tablespoons lemon juice *plus* enough milk to equal 1½ cups in 2-cup measure. Stir; let stand 5 minutes before using.

Preheat oven to 350°F. Grease 2 (8½×4½-inch) loaf pans. Sift flour, baking powder, baking soda and salt into large bowl; set aside.

Beat peanut butter, butter, granulated sugar and brown sugar in large bowl with electric mixer at medium speed until light and fluffy. Beat in eggs, one at a time, scraping down side of bowl after each addition. Beat in buttermilk and vanilla. Gradually add flour mixture. Beat at low speed. Stir in chips with wooden spoon. Spoon into prepared pans.

Bake 45 minutes or until wooden toothpick inserted in center comes out clean. Cool in pans on wire rack 10 minutes. Remove from pans; cool completely on rack. *Makes 2 loaves*

OREO® MUFFINS

1¾ cups all-purpose flour
　½ cup sugar
　1 tablespoon DAVIS® Baking Powder
　½ teaspoon salt
　¾ cup milk
　⅓ cup sour cream
　1 egg
　¼ cup margarine, melted
　20 OREO® Chocolate Sandwich Cookies, coarsely chopped

In medium bowl, combine flour, sugar, baking powder and salt; set aside.

In small bowl, combine milk, sour cream and egg; stir into flour mixture with margarine until just blended. Gently stir in cookies. Spoon batter into 12 greased 2½-inch muffin-pan cups.

Bake at 400°F for 20 to 25 minutes or until toothpick inserted in center comes out clean. Remove from pan; cool on wire rack. Serve warm or cold. *Makes 1 dozen muffins*

Peanut Butter Mini Chip Loaves

Sweet

SNACKIN' TREATS

WHITE CHOCOLATE CHUNK MUFFINS

- 2½ cups all-purpose flour
- 1 cup packed brown sugar
- ⅓ cup unsweetened cocoa powder
- 2 teaspoons baking soda
- ½ teaspoon salt
- 1⅓ cups buttermilk
- 6 tablespoons butter or margarine, melted
- 2 eggs, beaten
- 1½ teaspoons vanilla
- 1½ cups chopped white chocolate

Preheat oven to 400°F. Grease 12 (3½-inch) large muffin cups; set aside.

Combine flour, sugar, cocoa, baking soda and salt in large bowl. Combine buttermilk, butter, eggs and vanilla in small bowl until blended. Stir into flour mixture just until moistened. Fold in white chocolate. Spoon into prepared muffin cups, filling half full.

Bake 25 to 30 minutes or until wooden pick inserted in center comes out clean. Cool in pan on wire rack 5 minutes. Remove from pan. Cool on wire rack 10 minutes. Serve warm or cool completely. *Makes 12 jumbo muffins*

TOFFEE CRUNCH MUFFINS

- 1½ cups all-purpose flour
- ⅓ cup packed brown sugar
- 2 teaspoons baking powder
- ½ teaspoon baking soda
- ½ teaspoon salt
- ½ cup milk
- ½ cup sour cream
- 3 tablespoons butter or margarine, melted
- 1 egg, beaten
- 1 teaspoon vanilla
- 3 bars (1.4 ounces each) chocolate-covered toffee, chopped and divided

Preheat oven to 400°F. Grease or paper-line 36 (1¾-inch) mini-muffin cups; set aside.

Combine flour, sugar, baking powder, baking soda and salt in large bowl. Combine milk, sour cream, butter, egg and vanilla in small bowl until well blended. Stir into flour mixture just until moistened. Fold in two-thirds of toffee. Spoon into prepared muffin cups, filling almost full. Sprinkle remaining toffee evenly over tops of muffins.

Bake 16 to 18 minutes or until wooden pick inserted in center comes out clean. Remove from pans. Cool on wire racks 10 minutes. Serve warm or cool completely. *Makes 36 mini muffins*

White Chocolate Chunk Muffins

OLD-FASHIONED

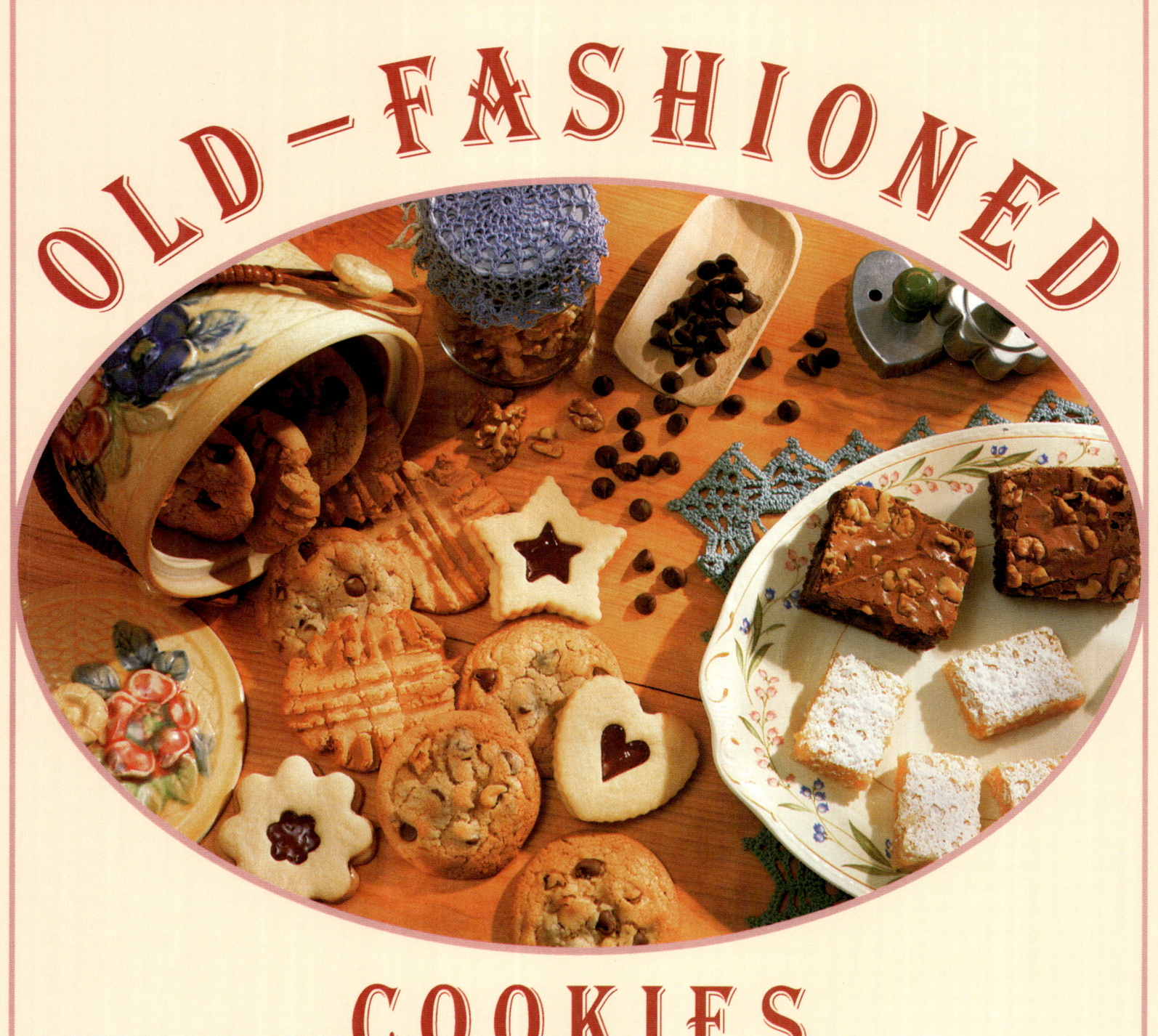

COOKIES

CONTENTS

Traditional Cookie-Jar Favorites • 266

Classic Chips & Chunks • 284

Keepsake Bar Cookies • 298

Time-Honored Brownies • 312

Grandkids' Delights • 324

Old-World Holiday Treats • 334

Clockwise from right: Caramel-Layered Brownies (page 318), Luscious Lemon Bars (page 308), Original Nestlé® Toll House® Chocolate Chip Cookies (page 292), Linzer Sandwich Cookies (page 346) and Peanut Butter Sensations (page 268)

— *Traditional* —

COOKIE-JAR FAVORITES

CHOCOLATE-DIPPED ALMOND HORNS

 1½ cups powdered sugar
  1 cup butter or margarine, softened
  2 egg yolks
 1½ teaspoons vanilla
  2 cups all-purpose flour
  ½ cup ground almonds
  1 teaspoon cream of tartar
  1 teaspoon baking soda
  1 cup semisweet chocolate chips, melted
  Powdered sugar

Preheat oven to 325°F. In large bowl, combine powdered sugar and butter. Beat at medium speed until creamy. Add egg yolks and vanilla; continue beating until well blended. Reduce speed to low. Add flour, almonds, cream of tartar and baking soda. Continue beating until well mixed. Shape into 1-inch balls. Roll balls into 2-inch ropes; shape into crescents. Place 2 inches apart on cookie sheets. Flatten slightly with bottom of glass covered in waxed paper. Bake for 8 to 10 minutes or until set. (Cookies do not brown.) Cool completely. Dip half of each cookie into chocolate; sprinkle remaining half with powdered sugar. Refrigerate until set.

Makes about 3 dozen cookies

—Traditional—

COOKIE-JAR FAVORITES

OATMEAL APPLE COOKIES

¾ CRISCO® Stick or ¾ cup CRISCO all-vegetable shortening
1¼ cups firmly packed brown sugar
1 egg
¼ cup milk
1½ teaspoons vanilla
1 cup all-purpose flour
1¼ teaspoons ground cinnamon
½ teaspoon salt
¼ teaspoon baking soda
¼ teaspoon ground nutmeg
3 cups quick oats (not instant or old-fashioned)
1 cup peeled, diced apples
¾ cup raisins (optional)
¾ cup coarsely chopped walnuts (optional)

1. Preheat oven to 375°F. Grease cookie sheet with shortening.

2. Combine shortening, sugar, egg, milk and vanilla in large bowl. Beat at medium speed of electric mixer until well blended.

3. Combine flour, cinnamon, salt, baking soda and nutmeg in small bowl. Mix into creamed mixture at low speed until just blended. Stir in, one at a time, oats, apples, raisins and nuts with spoon.

4. Drop rounded tablespoonfuls of dough 2 inches apart onto cookie sheet.

5. Bake at 375°F for 13 minutes or until set. Cool 2 minutes on cookie sheet. Remove to wire rack. Cool completely. *Makes about 2½ dozen cookies*

PEANUT BUTTER SENSATIONS

½ CRISCO® Stick or ½ cup CRISCO all-vegetable shortening
1 cup JIF® Creamy Peanut Butter
¾ cup granulated sugar
½ cup firmly packed brown sugar
1 tablespoon milk
1 teaspoon vanilla
1 egg
1¼ cups all-purpose flour
¾ teaspoon baking soda
½ teaspoon baking powder
¼ teaspoon salt

1. Preheat oven to 375°F.

2. Combine shortening, peanut butter, granulated sugar, brown sugar, milk and vanilla in large bowl. Beat at medium speed of electric mixer until well blended. Beat in egg.

3. Combine flour, baking soda, baking powder and salt in small bowl. Mix into creamed mixture at low speed until just blended. Drop rounded tablespoonfuls of dough 2 inches apart onto ungreased cookie sheet. Make crisscross pattern on dough with floured fork.

4. Bake at 375°F for 8 to 10 minutes. Cool 2 minutes on cookie sheet. Remove to wire rack. Cool completely. *Makes about 2 dozen cookies*

Oatmeal Apple Cookies

– *Traditional* –

CHOCOLATE SUGAR COOKIES

- 3 squares BAKER'S® Unsweetened Chocolate
- 1 cup (2 sticks) margarine or butter
- 1 cup sugar
- 1 egg
- 1 teaspoon vanilla
- 2 cups all-purpose flour
- 1 teaspoon baking soda
- ¼ teaspoon salt
- Additional sugar

MICROWAVE chocolate and margarine in large microwavable bowl on HIGH 2 minutes or until margarine is melted. **Stir until chocolate is completely melted.**

STIR 1 cup sugar into melted chocolate mixture until well blended. Stir in egg and vanilla until completely mixed. Mix in flour, baking soda and salt. Refrigerate 30 minutes.

HEAT oven to 375°F. Shape dough into 1-inch balls; roll in additional sugar. Place on ungreased cookie sheets. (If a flatter, crisper cookie is desired, flatten ball with bottom of drinking glass.)

BAKE for 8 to 10 minutes or until set. Remove from cookie sheets to cool on wire racks.

Makes about 3½ dozen cookies

Prep Time: 15 minutes
Chill Time: 30 minutes
Baking Time: 8 to 10 minutes

JAM-FILLED CHOCOLATE SUGAR COOKIES: PREPARE Chocolate Sugar Cookie dough as directed. Roll in finely chopped nuts in place of sugar. Make indentation in each ball; fill center with your favorite jam. Bake as directed.

CHOCOLATE-CARAMEL SUGAR COOKIES: PREPARE Chocolate Sugar Cookie dough as directed. Roll in finely chopped nuts in place of sugar. Make indentation in each ball; bake as directed. Microwave 1 package (14 ounces) KRAFT® Caramels with 2 tablespoons milk in microwavable bowl on HIGH 3 minutes or until melted, stirring after 2 minutes. Fill centers of cookies with caramel mixture. Drizzle with melted BAKER'S® Semi-Sweet Chocolate.

Top to bottom: Chocolate Sugar Cookies, Jam-Filled Chocolate Sugar Cookies, Chocolate-Caramel Sugar Cookies

– Traditional –

COCOA SNICKERDOODLES

    1 cup butter or margarine, softened
    ¾ cup firmly packed brown sugar
    ¾ cup plus 2 tablespoons granulated sugar, divided
    2 eggs
    2 cups uncooked rolled oats
 1½ cups all-purpose flour
    ¼ cup plus 2 tablespoons unsweetened cocoa powder, divided
    1 teaspoon baking soda
    2 tablespoons ground cinnamon

Preheat oven to 375°F. Lightly grease cookie sheets or line with parchment paper. Beat butter, brown sugar and ¾ cup granulated sugar in large bowl until light and fluffy. Add eggs; mix well. Combine oats, flour, ¼ cup cocoa and baking soda in medium bowl. Stir into butter mixture until blended. Mix remaining 2 tablespoons granulated sugar, cinnamon and remaining 2 tablespoons cocoa in small bowl. Drop dough by rounded teaspoonfuls into cinnamon mixture; toss to coat. Place 2 inches apart on prepared cookie sheets. Bake 8 to 10 minutes or until firm in center. *Do not overbake.* Remove to wire racks to cool.

Makes about 4½ dozen cookies

SPICY PUMPKIN COOKIES

  2 CRISCO® Sticks or 2 cups CRISCO all-vegetable shortening
  2 cups sugar
  1 can (16 ounces) solid pack pumpkin
  2 eggs
  2 teaspoons vanilla
  4 cups all-purpose flour
  2 teaspoons baking powder
  2 teaspoons ground cinnamon
  1 teaspoon salt
  1 teaspoon baking soda
  1 teaspoon ground nutmeg
 ½ teaspoon ground allspice
  2 cups raisins
  1 cup chopped nuts

1. Preheat oven to 350°F.

2. Combine shortening, sugar, pumpkin, eggs and vanilla in large bowl; beat well.

3. Combine flour, baking powder, cinnamon, salt, baking soda, nutmeg and allspice in medium bowl. Add to pumpkin mixture; mix well. Stir in raisins and nuts. Drop rounded teaspoonfuls of dough, 2 inches apart, onto greased cookie sheet.

4. Bake at 350°F for 12 to 15 minutes. Cool on wire rack. If desired, frost with vanilla frosting.

Makes about 7 dozen cookies

*Chocolate-Peanut Cookies (page 286),
Cocoa Snickerdoodles*

— Traditional —

RASPBERRY ALMOND SANDWICH COOKIES

- 1 package DUNCAN HINES® Golden Sugar Cookie Mix
- 1 egg
- ¼ cup CRISCO® Oil
- 1 tablespoon water
- ¾ teaspoon almond extract
- 1⅓ cups sliced natural almonds, broken
- Seedless red raspberry jam

1. Preheat oven to 375°F.

2. Combine cookie mix, egg, oil, water and almond extract in large bowl. Stir until thoroughly blended. Drop half the dough by level measuring teaspoons 2 inches apart onto ungreased cookie sheets. (It is a small amount of dough but will spread during baking to 1½ to 1¾ inches.)

3. Place almonds on waxed paper. Drop other half of dough by level measuring teaspoons onto nuts. Place almond side up 2 inches apart on cookie sheets.

4. Bake both plain and almond cookies at 375°F for 6 minutes or until set but not browned. Cool 1 minute on cookie sheets. Remove to wire racks. Cool completely.

5. Spread bottoms of plain cookies with jam; top with almond cookies. Press together to make sandwiches. Store in airtight containers.

Makes 6 dozen sandwich cookies

OLD-FASHIONED OATMEAL COOKIES

- ¾ CRISCO® Stick or ¾ cup CRISCO all-vegetable shortening
- 1¼ cups firmly packed brown sugar
- 1 egg
- ⅓ cup milk
- 1½ teaspoons vanilla
- 1 cup all-purpose flour
- ½ teaspoon baking soda
- ½ teaspoon salt
- ¼ teaspoon ground cinnamon
- 3 cups quick oats (not instant or old-fashioned)
- 1 cup raisins
- 1 cup coarsely chopped walnuts

1. Preheat oven to 375°F. Grease cookie sheet.

2. Combine shortening, sugar, egg, milk and vanilla in large bowl. Beat at medium speed of electric mixer until well blended.

3. Combine flour, baking soda, salt and cinnamon in small bowl. Mix into creamed mixture at low speed until just blended. Stir in oats, raisins and nuts with spoon.

4. Drop rounded tablespoonfuls of dough 2 inches apart onto cookie sheet.

5. Bake at 375°F for 10 to 12 minutes or until lightly browned. Cool 2 minutes on cookie sheet. Remove to wire rack. Cool completely.

Makes about 2½ dozen cookies

Raspberry Almond Sandwich Cookies

— Traditional —

SWISS MOCHA TREATS

- 2 ounces imported Swiss bittersweet chocolate candy bar, broken
- ½ cup plus 2 tablespoons butter, softened, divided
- 1 tablespoon instant espresso powder
- 1 teaspoon vanilla
- 1¾ cups all-purpose flour
- ½ teaspoon baking soda
- ½ teaspoon salt
- ¾ cup sugar
- 1 large egg
- 3 ounces imported Swiss white chocolate candy bar, broken

1. Melt bittersweet chocolate and 2 tablespoons butter in small, heavy saucepan over low heat, stirring often. Add espresso powder; stir until dissolved. Remove from heat; stir in vanilla. Let cool to room temperature.

2. Combine flour, baking soda and salt in medium bowl.

3. Beat remaining ½ cup butter and sugar in large bowl with mixer at medium speed until fluffy. Beat in bittersweet chocolate mixture and egg. Gradually add flour mixture. Beat at low speed until well blended. Cover; refrigerate 30 minutes or until firm.

4. Preheat oven to 375°F. Roll tablespoonfuls of dough into 1-inch balls; place 3 inches apart on *ungreased* cookie sheets. Flatten each ball into ½-inch-thick round with fork dipped in sugar.

5. Bake 9 to 10 minutes or until set (do not overbake or cookies will become dry). Immediately remove cookies to wire racks; cool completely.

6. Place white chocolate in small resealable plastic freezer bag; seal bag. Microwave at MEDIUM (50% power) 1 minute. Turn bag over; microwave at MEDIUM 1 minute or until melted. Knead until chocolate is smooth. Cut off tiny corner of bag; pipe or drizzle white chocolate onto cooled cookies. Let stand 30 minutes or until set. Store tightly covered at room temperature or freeze up to 3 months. *Makes about 4 dozen cookies*

WALNUT MACAROONS

- 2⅔ cups flaked coconut
- 1¼ cups coarsely chopped California walnuts
- ⅓ cup all-purpose flour
- ½ teaspoon ground cinnamon
- ¼ teaspoon salt
- 4 egg whites
- 1 teaspoon grated lemon peel
- 2 (1-ounce) squares semisweet chocolate, melted

Combine coconut, walnuts, flour, cinnamon and salt in large bowl. Mix in egg whites and lemon peel. Drop by teaspoonfuls onto lightly greased cookie sheets. Bake at 325°F for 20 minutes or until golden brown. Dip macaroon bottoms in melted chocolate. Place on waxed paper to set.

Makes about 3 dozen cookies

Favorite recipe from **Walnut Marketing Board**

Swiss Mocha Treats

— Traditional —

ULTIMATE SUGAR COOKIES

- 1¼ cups granulated sugar
- 1 CRISCO® Stick or 1 cup CRISCO all-vegetable shortening
- 2 eggs
- ¼ cup light corn syrup or regular pancake syrup
- 1 tablespoon vanilla
- 3 cups all-purpose flour (plus 4 tablespoons), divided
- ¾ teaspoon baking powder
- ½ teaspoon baking soda
- ½ teaspoon salt
- Granulated sugar or colored sugar crystals

1. Place sugar and shortening in large bowl. Beat at medium speed of electric mixer until well blended. Add eggs, syrup and vanilla; beat until well blended and fluffy.

2. Combine 3 cups flour, baking powder, baking soda and salt in medium bowl. Add gradually to shortening mixture, beating at low speed until well blended.

3. Divide dough into 4 equal pieces; shape each piece into disk. Wrap with plastic wrap. Refrigerate 1 hour or until firm.

4. Preheat oven to 375°F. Place sheets of foil on countertop for cooling cookies.

5. Sprinkle about 1 tablespoon flour on large sheet of waxed paper. Place disk of dough on floured paper; flatten slightly with hands. Turn dough over; cover with another large sheet of waxed paper. Roll dough to ¼-inch thickness. Remove top sheet of waxed paper. Cut into desired shapes with floured cookie cutters. Place 2 inches apart on ungreased cookie sheet. Repeat with remaining dough.

6. Sprinkle with granulated sugar.

7. Bake one cookie sheet at a time at 375°F for 5 to 7 minutes or until edges of cookies are lightly browned. *Do not overbake.* Cool 2 minutes on cookie sheet. Remove cookies to foil to cool completely.   *Makes about 3½ dozen cookies*

Ultimate Sugar Cookies

— Traditional —

COOKIE-JAR FAVORITES

MAPLE WALNUT COOKIES

- 1¼ cups firmly packed light brown sugar
- ¾ CRISCO® Stick or ¾ cup CRISCO all-vegetable shortening
- 2 tablespoons maple syrup
- 1 teaspoon vanilla
- 1 teaspoon maple extract
- 1 egg
- 1¾ cups all-purpose flour
- 1 teaspoon salt
- ¾ teaspoon baking soda
- ½ teaspoon ground cinnamon
- 1½ cups chopped walnuts
- 30 to 40 walnut halves

1. Preheat oven to 375°F. Place sheets of foil on countertop for cooling cookies.

2. Place brown sugar, shortening, maple syrup, vanilla and maple extract in large bowl. Beat at medium speed of electric mixer until well blended. Add egg; beat well.

3. Combine flour, salt, baking soda and cinnamon in small bowl. Add to shortening mixture; beat at low speed just until blended. Stir in chopped walnuts.

4. Drop dough by rounded measuring tablespoonfuls 3 inches apart onto ungreased cookie sheets. Press walnut half into center of each cookie.

5. Bake one cookie sheet at a time at 375°F for 8 to 10 minutes for chewy cookies, or 11 to 13 minutes for crisp cookies. *Do not overbake.* Cool 2 minutes on cookie sheet. Remove cookies to foil to cool completely. *Makes about 3 dozen cookies*

COCOA PECAN CRESCENTS

- 1 cup (2 sticks) butter or margarine, softened
- ⅔ cup granulated sugar
- 1½ teaspoons vanilla extract
- 1¾ cups all-purpose flour
- ⅓ cup HERSHEY®S Cocoa
- ⅛ teaspoon salt
- 1½ cups ground pecans
- Powdered sugar

In large mixing bowl, beat butter, granulated sugar and vanilla until light and fluffy. Stir together flour, cocoa and salt in small bowl. Add to butter mixture; blend well. Stir in pecans. Refrigerate dough 1 hour or until firm enough to handle. Preheat oven to 375°F. Shape scant 1 tablespoon dough into log about 2½ inches long; place on ungreased cookie sheet. Shape each log into crescent, tapering ends. Bake 13 to 15 minutes or until set. Cool slightly; remove from cookie sheet to wire rack. Cool completely. Roll in powdered sugar. *Makes about 3½ dozen cookies*

Top to bottom: Maple Walnut Cookies, Peanut Butter Treats (page 294)

– Traditional –

PEANUT BUTTER SECRETS

COOKIES
- 1 CRISCO® Stick or 1 cup CRISCO all-vegetable shortening
- ¾ cup firmly packed brown sugar
- ½ cup granulated sugar
- ½ cup JIF® Creamy Peanut Butter
- 1 egg
- 1 teaspoon vanilla
- 2 cups all-purpose flour
- 1 teaspoon baking soda
- ½ teaspoon salt
- 40 to 45 chocolate-covered miniature peanut butter cups, unwrapped

GLAZE
- 1 teaspoon CRISCO® all-vegetable shortening
- 1 cup semi-sweet chocolate chips
- 2 tablespoons JIF® Creamy Peanut Butter

1. Preheat oven to 375°F. Grease cookie sheet with shortening.

2. For Cookies, combine shortening, brown sugar, granulated sugar and peanut butter in large bowl. Beat at medium speed of electric mixer until well blended. Beat in egg and vanilla.

3. Combine flour, baking soda and salt in small bowl. Mix into creamed mixture at low speed until just blended.

4. Form rounded teaspoonfuls of dough around each peanut butter cup. Enclose entirely. Place 2 inches apart on cookie sheet.

5. Bake 8 to 10 minutes or until cookies are just browned. Remove immediately to wire rack.

6. For Glaze, combine shortening, chocolate chips and peanut butter in microwave-safe cup. Microwave at 50% (MEDIUM). Stir after 1 minute. Repeat until smooth (or melt on rangetop in small saucepan on very low heat). Dip cookie tops in glaze. *Makes about 3½ dozen cookies*

QUICK CHOCOLATE MACAROONS

- 1 square BAKER'S® Unsweetened Chocolate
- 1⅓ cups BAKER'S® ANGEL FLAKE® Coconut
- ⅓ cup sweetened condensed milk
- ½ teaspoon vanilla

HEAT oven to 350°F.

MELT chocolate in large microwavable bowl on HIGH 1 to 2 minutes or until almost melted, stirring after each minute. **Stir until chocolate is completely melted.** Stir in coconut, condensed milk and vanilla. Drop from teaspoonfuls, 1 inch apart, onto well greased cookie sheets.

BAKE for 10 to 12 minutes or until set. Immediately remove from cookie sheets to cool on wire racks. *Makes about 2 dozen cookies*

Prep Time: 10 minutes
Baking Time: 10 to 12 minutes

Peanut Butter Secrets

— *Classic* —
CHIPS & CHUNKS

Peanut Butter Chocolate Chippers

1 cup creamy or chunky peanut butter
1 cup firmly packed light brown sugar
1 large egg
¾ cup milk chocolate chips
Granulated sugar

1. Preheat oven to 350°F.

2. Combine peanut butter, brown sugar and egg in medium bowl with mixing spoon until well blended. Add chips; mix well.

3. Roll heaping tablespoonfuls of dough into 1½-inch balls. Place balls 2 inches apart on *ungreased* cookie sheets.

4. Dip table fork into granulated sugar; press criss-cross fashion onto each ball, flattening to ½-inch thickness.

5. Bake 12 minutes or until set. Let cookies stand on cookie sheets 2 minutes. Remove cookies with spatula to wire racks; cool completely. Store tightly covered at room temperature or freeze up to 3 months. *Makes about 2 dozen cookies*

— Classic —

OATMEAL CANDIED CHIPPERS

- ¾ cup all-purpose flour
- ¾ teaspoon salt
- ½ teaspoon baking soda
- ¾ cup butter or margarine, softened
- ¾ cup granulated sugar
- ¾ cup firmly packed light brown sugar
- 3 tablespoons milk
- 1 large egg
- 2 teaspoons vanilla
- 3 cups uncooked quick-cooking or old-fashioned oats
- 1⅓ cups (10-ounce package) candy-coated semisweet chocolate chips*

*Or, substitute 1 cup (8-ounce package) candy-coated milk chocolate chips.

1. Preheat oven to 375°F. Grease cookie sheets; set aside.

2. Combine flour, salt and baking soda in small bowl.

3. Beat butter, granulated sugar and brown sugar in large bowl with electric mixer at medium speed until light and fluffy. Add milk, egg and vanilla; beat well. Add flour mixture. Beat at low speed until blended. Stir in oats and chips.

4. Drop dough by tablespoonfuls 2 inches apart onto prepared cookie sheets.**

**Or, use a small ice cream scoop (#80) filled with dough and pressed against side of bowl to level.

5. Bake 10 to 11 minutes or until edges are golden brown. Let cookies stand 2 minutes on cookie sheets. Remove cookies with spatula to wire racks; cool completely. Store tightly covered at room temperature or freeze up to 3 months.

Makes about 4 dozen cookies

CHOCOLATE-PEANUT COOKIES

- 1 cup butter or margarine, softened
- ¾ cup granulated sugar
- ¾ cup firmly packed light brown sugar
- 2 eggs
- 1 teaspoon vanilla
- 1 teaspoon baking soda
- ¼ teaspoon salt
- 2¼ cups all-purpose flour
- 2 cups chocolate-covered peanuts

Preheat oven to 375°F. Line cookie sheets with parchment paper or leave ungreased. Beat butter, granulated sugar, brown sugar, eggs and vanilla in large bowl with electric mixer until fluffy. Beat in baking soda and salt. Stir in flour to make stiff dough. Blend in chocolate-covered peanuts. Drop by rounded teaspoonfuls 2 inches apart onto cookie sheets. Bake 9 to 11 minutes or until just barely golden. *Do not overbake*. Remove to wire racks to cool.

Makes about 5 dozen cookies

Oatmeal Candied Chippers

— Classic —

CHOCOLATE CHIP SANDWICH COOKIES

COOKIES
- 1 package DUNCAN HINES® Chocolate Chip Cookie Mix
- 1 egg
- ⅓ cup CRISCO® Oil
- 3 tablespoons water

CREAM FILLING
- 1½ cups marshmallow creme
- ¾ cup butter or margarine, softened
- 2½ cups powdered sugar
- 1½ teaspoons vanilla extract

1. Preheat oven to 375°F.

2. **For Cookies,** combine cookie mix, egg, oil and water in large bowl. Stir until thoroughly blended. Drop by rounded teaspoonfuls 2 inches apart onto ungreased cookie sheets. Bake at 375°F for 8 to 10 minutes or until light golden brown. Cool 1 minute on cookie sheets. Remove to wire racks.

3. **For Cream Filling,** combine marshmallow creme and butter in large bowl. Add powdered sugar and vanilla extract, beating until smooth.

4. To assemble, spread bottoms of half the cookies with 1 tablespoon cream filling; top with remaining cookies. Press together to make sandwich cookies. Refrigerate to quickly firm the filling, if desired.

Makes about 24 sandwich cookies

TIP: After chilling the assembled cookies, wrap individually in plastic wrap. Store in the refrigerator until ready to serve.

QUICK CHOCOLATE SOFTIES

- 1 package (18.25 ounces) devil's food chocolate cake mix
- ⅓ cup water
- ¼ cup butter or margarine, softened
- 1 large egg
- 1 cup large vanilla baking chips
- ½ cup coarsely chopped walnuts

1. Preheat oven to 350°F. Lightly grease cookie sheets.

2. Combine cake mix, water, butter and egg in large bowl. Beat with electric mixer at low speed until moistened. Increase speed to medium; beat 1 minute. (Dough will be thick.) Stir in chips and walnuts with mixing spoon until well blended.

3. Drop heaping *teaspoonfuls* of dough 2 inches apart (for smaller cookies) or heaping *tablespoonfuls* of dough 3 inches apart (for larger cookies) onto prepared cookie sheets.

4. Bake 10 to 12 minutes or until set. Let cookies stand on cookie sheets 1 minute. Remove cookies with spatula to wire racks; cool completely. Store tightly covered at room temperature or freeze up to 3 months.

Makes about 2 dozen large or 4 dozen small cookies

Chocolate Chip Sandwich Cookies

– Classic –

OATMEAL SCOTCHIES

- 1¼ cups all-purpose flour
- 1 teaspoon baking soda
- ½ teaspoon salt
- ½ teaspoon ground cinnamon
- 1 cup (2 sticks) butter or margarine, softened
- ¾ cup granulated sugar
- ¾ cup packed brown sugar
- 2 eggs
- 1 teaspoon vanilla extract or grated peel of 1 orange
- 3 cups quick *or* old-fashioned oats
- 2 cups (12-ounce package) NESTLÉ® TOLL HOUSE® Butterscotch Flavored Morsels

COMBINE flour, baking soda, salt and cinnamon in small bowl. Beat butter, granulated sugar, brown sugar, eggs and vanilla in large mixing bowl until creamy. Gradually beat in flour mixture. Stir in oats and morsels. Drop by rounded tablespoons onto ungreased cookie sheets.

BAKE in preheated 375°F oven for 7 to 8 minutes for chewy cookies, 9 to 10 minutes for crisp cookies. Let stand for 2 minutes; remove to wire racks to cool completely. *Makes 4 dozen cookies*

CHOCO-SCUTTERBOTCH

- ⅔ CRISCO® Stick or ⅔ cup CRISCO all-vegetable shortening
- ½ cup firmly packed brown sugar
- 2 eggs
- 1 package DUNCAN HINES® Moist Deluxe Yellow Cake Mix
- 1 cup toasted rice cereal
- ½ cup milk chocolate chunks
- ½ cup butterscotch chips
- ½ cup semi-sweet chocolate chips
- ½ cup coarsely chopped walnuts or pecans

1. Preheat oven to 375°F.

2. Combine shortening and brown sugar in large bowl. Beat at medium speed of electric mixer until well blended. Beat in eggs.

3. Add cake mix gradually at low speed. Mix until well blended. Stir in cereal, chocolate chunks, butterscotch chips, chocolate chips and nuts with spoon until well blended. Shape dough into 1¼-inch balls. Place 2 inches apart on ungreased cookie sheet. Flatten slightly. Shape sides to form circle, if necessary.

4. Bake at 375°F for 7 to 9 minutes or until lightly browned around edges. Cool 2 minutes before removing to paper towels to cool completely.
Makes about 3 dozen cookies

Oatmeal Scotchies

— Classic —

Original Nestlé® Toll House® Chocolate Chip Cookies

- 2¼ cups all-purpose flour
- 1 teaspoon baking soda
- 1 teaspoon salt
- 1 cup (2 sticks) butter, softened
- ¾ cup granulated sugar
- ¾ cup firmly packed brown sugar
- 1 teaspoon vanilla extract
- 2 eggs
- 2 cups (12-ounce package) NESTLÉ® TOLL HOUSE® Semi-Sweet Chocolate Morsels
- 1 cup chopped nuts

COMBINE flour, baking soda and salt in small bowl. Beat butter, granulated sugar, brown sugar and vanilla in large mixing bowl. Add eggs one at a time, beating well after each addition; gradually beat in flour mixture. Stir in morsels and nuts. Drop by rounded tablespoons onto ungreased cookie sheets.

BAKE in preheated 375°F oven for 9 to 11 minutes or until golden brown. Let stand for 2 minutes; remove to wire racks to cool completely.

Makes about 5 dozen cookies

Cowboy Cookies

- ½ cup butter or margarine, softened
- ½ cup firmly packed light brown sugar
- ¼ cup granulated sugar
- 1 egg
- 1 teaspoon vanilla
- 1 cup all-purpose flour
- 2 tablespoons unsweetened cocoa
- ½ teaspoon baking powder
- ¼ teaspoon baking soda
- 1 cup uncooked rolled oats
- 1 cup (6 ounces) semisweet chocolate chips
- ½ cup raisins
- ½ cup chopped nuts

Preheat oven to 375°F. Lightly grease cookie sheets or line with parchment paper. Beat butter, brown sugar and granulated sugar in large bowl with electric mixer until blended. Add egg and vanilla; beat until fluffy. Combine flour, cocoa, baking powder and baking soda in small bowl; stir into creamed mixture with oats, chocolate chips, raisins and nuts. Drop dough by teaspoonfuls 2 inches apart onto prepared cookie sheets. Bake 10 to 12 minutes or until lightly browned around edges. Remove to wire racks to cool.

Makes about 4 dozen cookies

Original Nestlé® Toll House® Chocolate Chip Cookies

— Classic —

WHOLE GRAIN CHIPPERS

- 1 cup butter or margarine, softened
- 1 cup firmly packed light brown sugar
- ⅔ cup granulated sugar
- 2 eggs
- 1 teaspoon baking soda
- 1 teaspoon vanilla
- Pinch salt
- 1 cup whole wheat flour
- 1 cup all-purpose flour
- 2 cups uncooked rolled oats
- 1 package (12 ounces) semisweet chocolate chips
- 1 cup sunflower seeds

Preheat oven to 375°F. Lightly grease cookie sheets or line with parchment paper. Beat butter, brown sugar, granulated sugar and eggs in large bowl with electric mixer until light and fluffy. Beat in baking soda, vanilla and salt. Blend in flours and oats to make a stiff dough. Stir in chocolate chips. Shape rounded teaspoonfuls of dough into balls; roll in sunflower seeds. Place 2 inches apart on prepared cookie sheets. Bake 8 to 10 minutes or until firm. *Do not overbake.* Cool a few minutes on cookie sheets, then remove to wire racks to cool completely.
Makes about 6 dozen cookies

PEANUT BUTTER TREATS

- 1¼ cups firmly packed light brown sugar
- ¾ CRISCO® Stick or ¾ cup CRISCO all-vegetable shortening
- 2 tablespoons milk
- 1 tablespoon vanilla
- 1 egg
- 1¾ cups all-purpose flour
- 1 teaspoon salt
- ¾ teaspoon baking soda
- 2 cups (about 32) miniature peanut butter cups, unwrapped and quartered or coarsely chopped

1. Preheat oven to 375°F. Place sheets of foil on countertop for cooling cookies.

2. Place brown sugar, shortening, milk and vanilla in large bowl. Beat at medium speed of electric mixer until well blended. Add egg; beat well.

3. Combine flour, salt and baking soda in small bowl. Add to shortening mixture; beat at low speed just until blended. Stir in peanut butter cup quarters.

4. Drop dough by rounded measuring tablespoonfuls 3 inches apart onto ungreased cookie sheets.

5. Bake one cookie sheet at a time at 375°F for 8 to 10 minutes or until cookies are lightly browned. *Do not overbake.* Cool 2 minutes on cookie sheet. Remove cookies to foil to cool completely.
Makes about 3 dozen cookies

Whole Grain Chippers

– *Classic* –

ULTIMATE CHOCOLATE CHIP COOKIES

¾ CRISCO® Stick or ¾ cup CRISCO all-vegetable shortening
1¼ cups firmly packed brown sugar
2 tablespoons milk
1 tablespoon vanilla
1 egg
1¾ cups all-purpose flour
1 teaspoon salt
¾ teaspoon baking soda
1 cup semi-sweet chocolate chips
1 cup coarsely chopped pecans*

*You may substitute an additional ½ cup semi-sweet chocolate chips for the pecans.

1. Preheat oven to 375°F.

2. Combine shortening, sugar, milk and vanilla in large bowl. Beat at medium speed of electric mixer until well blended. Beat in egg.

3. Combine flour, salt and baking soda in small bowl. Mix into creamed mixture at low speed until just blended. Stir in chocolate chips and nuts.

4. Drop rounded tablespoonfuls of dough 3 inches apart onto ungreased cookie sheet.

5. Bake at 375°F for 8 to 10 minutes for chewy cookies (they will look light and moist—*do not overbake*), 11 to 13 minutes for crisp cookies. Cool 2 minutes on cookie sheet. Remove to wire rack. Cool completely.   *Makes about 3 dozen cookies*

Variations for Ultimate Chocolate Chip Cookies

DRIZZLE: Combine 1 teaspoon CRISCO® All-Vegetable Shortening and 1 cup semi-sweet chocolate chips or 1 cup white melting chocolate, cut into small pieces, in microwave-safe measuring cup. Microwave at 50% (MEDIUM). Stir after 1 minute. Repeat until smooth (or melt on rangetop in small saucepan on very low heat). To thin, add a little more shortening. Drizzle back and forth over cookie. Sprinkle with nuts before chocolate hardens, if desired. To quickly harden chocolate, place cookies in refrigerator for a few minutes.

CHOCOLATE DIPPED: Melt chocolate as directed for Drizzle. Dip one end of cooled cookie halfway up in chocolate. Sprinkle with finely chopped nuts before chocolate hardens. Place on waxed paper until chocolate is firm. To quickly harden chocolate, place cookies in refrigerator for a few minutes.

Clockwise from top: Old-Fashioned Oatmeal Cookies (page 274), Peanut Butter Sensations (page 268), Ultimate Chocolate Chip Cookies

Keepsake

BAR COOKIES

CHOCOLATE CHIP SHORTBREAD

½ cup butter, softened
½ cup sugar
1 teaspoon vanilla
1 cup all-purpose flour
¼ teaspoon salt
½ cup mini semisweet chocolate chips

Preheat oven to 375°F. Beat butter and sugar in large bowl with electric mixer at medium speed until light and fluffy. Beat in vanilla. Add flour and salt. Stir in chips.

Divide dough in half. Press each half into ungreased 8-inch round cake pan. Bake 12 minutes or until edges are golden brown. Score shortbread with sharp knife, taking care not to cut completely through shortbread. Make 8 wedges per pan.

Let pans stand on wire racks 10 minutes. Invert shortbread onto wire racks; cool completely. Break into wedges.

Makes 16 cookies

— Keepsake —

BAR COOKIES

Peachy Oatmeal Bars

CRUMB MIXTURE
- 1½ cups all-purpose flour
- 1 cup uncooked rolled oats
- ¾ cup margarine, melted
- ½ cup sugar
- 2 teaspoons almond extract
- ½ teaspoon baking soda
- ¼ teaspoon salt

FILLING
- ¾ cup peach or apricot preserves
- ⅓ cup flaked coconut

Preheat oven to 350°F.

For Crumb Mixture, combine all crumb mixture ingredients in large bowl of electric mixer. Beat at low speed, scraping bowl often, until mixture is crumbly, 1 to 2 minutes. *Reserve ¾ cup crumb mixture;* press remaining crumb mixture onto bottom of greased 9-inch square baking pan.

For Filling, spread preserves to within ½ inch of edge of crust; sprinkle with reserved crumb mixture and coconut. Bake for 20 to 25 minutes or until edges are lightly browned. Cool completely. Cut into bars.

Makes about 24 bars

Streusel Strawberry Bars

- 1 cup butter or margarine, softened
- 1 cup sugar
- 2 cups all-purpose flour
- 1 egg
- ¾ cup pecans, coarsely chopped
- 1 jar (10 ounces) strawberry or raspberry preserves

Preheat oven to 350°F. Combine butter and sugar in large mixing bowl. Beat at low speed, scraping bowl often, until well blended. Add flour and egg. Beat until mixture is crumbly, 2 to 3 minutes. Stir in pecans. Reserve 1 cup crumb mixture; press remaining crumb mixture onto bottom of greased 9-inch square baking pan. Spread preserves to within ½ inch of edge of crust. Crumble reserved crumb mixture over preserves. Bake for 40 to 50 minutes or until lightly browned. Cool completely. Cut into bars.

Makes about 24 bars

Top to bottom: Peachy Oatmeal Bars, Streusel Strawberry Bars

BAR COOKIES

CHOCOLATE CARAMEL PECAN BARS

- 2 cups butter, softened, divided
- ½ cup granulated sugar
- 1 large egg
- 2¾ cups all-purpose flour
- ⅔ cup firmly packed light brown sugar
- ¼ cup light corn syrup
- 2½ cups coarsely chopped pecans
- 1 cup semisweet chocolate chips

1. Preheat oven to 375°F. Grease 15×10-inch jelly-roll pan; set aside.

2. Beat 1 cup butter and granulated sugar in large bowl with electric mixer at medium speed until light and fluffy. Beat in egg. Add flour. Beat at low speed until blended. Pat dough into prepared pan.

3. Bake 20 minutes or until light golden brown.

4. While bars are baking, prepare topping. Combine remaining 1 cup butter, brown sugar and corn syrup in medium, heavy saucepan. Cook over medium heat until mixture boils, stirring frequently. Boil gently 2 minutes, without stirring. Quickly stir in pecans and spread topping evenly over base. Return to oven and bake 20 minutes or until dark golden brown and bubbling.

5. Immediately sprinkle chocolate chips evenly over hot caramel. Gently press chips into caramel topping with spatula. Loosen caramel from edges of pan with a thin spatula or knife.

6. Remove pan to wire rack; cool completely. Cut into 3×1½-inch bars. Store tightly covered at room temperature or freeze up to 3 months.

Makes 40 bars

ALMOND TOFFEE SQUARES

- 1 cup (2 sticks) margarine or butter, softened
- 1 cup firmly packed brown sugar
- 1 egg
- 1 teaspoon vanilla
- 2 cups all-purpose flour
- ¼ teaspoon salt
- 2 packages (4 ounces each) BAKER'S® GERMAN'S® Sweet Chocolate, broken into squares
- ½ cup toasted slivered almonds
- ½ cup lightly toasted BAKER'S® ANGEL FLAKE® Coconut

HEAT oven to 350°F.

BEAT margarine, sugar, egg and vanilla. Mix in flour and salt. Press into greased 13×9-inch pan.

BAKE for 30 minutes or until edges are golden brown. Remove from oven. Immediately sprinkle with chocolate squares. Cover with foil; let stand 5 minutes or until chocolate is softened.

SPREAD chocolate evenly over entire surface; sprinkle with almonds and coconut. Cut into squares while still warm. Cool on wire rack.

Makes about 26 squares

Chocolate Caramel Pecan Bars

— Keepsake —

Bar Cookies

LEMON NUT BARS

- 1⅓ cups all-purpose flour
- ½ cup firmly packed brown sugar
- ¼ cup granulated sugar
- ¾ cup butter
- 1 cup old-fashioned or quick oats, uncooked
- ½ cup chopped nuts
- 1 (8-ounce) package PHILADELPHIA BRAND® Cream Cheese, softened
- 1 egg
- 3 tablespoons lemon juice
- 1 tablespoon grated lemon peel

Preheat oven to 350°F. Stir together flour and sugars in medium bowl. Cut in butter until mixture resembles coarse crumbs. Stir in oats and nuts. Reserve 1 cup crumb mixture; press remaining crumb mixture onto bottom of greased 13×9-inch baking pan. Bake 15 minutes. Beat cream cheese, egg, juice and peel in small mixing bowl at medium speed with electric mixer until well blended. Pour over crust; sprinkle with reserved crumb mixture. Bake 25 minutes. Cool; cut into bars.

Makes about 36 bars

Prep Time: 30 minutes
Cook Time: 25 minutes

CHOCOLATE PECAN PIE BARS

- 1⅓ cups all-purpose flour
- 2 tablespoons plus ½ cup firmly packed light brown sugar, divided
- ½ cup (1 stick) cold butter or margarine
- 2 eggs
- ½ cup light corn syrup
- ¼ cup HERSHEY®S Cocoa
- 2 tablespoons butter or margarine, melted
- 1 teaspoon vanilla extract
- ⅛ teaspoon salt
- 1 cup coarsely chopped pecans

Preheat oven to 350°F. In large bowl, stir together flour and 2 tablespoons brown sugar. With pastry blender, cut in ½ cup butter until mixture resembles coarse crumbs; press onto bottom and about 1 inch up sides of ungreased 9-inch square baking pan. Bake 10 to 12 minutes or until set. Remove from oven. With back of spoon, lightly press crust into corners and against sides of pan. In small bowl, lightly beat eggs, corn syrup, remaining ½ cup brown sugar, cocoa, 2 tablespoons butter, vanilla and salt until well blended. Stir in pecans. Pour mixture over warm crust. Continue baking 25 minutes or until pecan filling is set. Cool completely in pan on wire rack. Cut into bars.

Makes about 16 bars

Lemon Nut Bars

Keepsake

Bar Cookies

CHUNKY MACADAMIA BARS

- ¾ cup (1½ sticks) butter or margarine, softened
- 1 cup firmly packed light brown sugar
- ½ cup granulated sugar
- 1 egg
- 1 teaspoon vanilla extract
- 2¼ cups all-purpose flour
- 1 teaspoon baking soda
- ¾ cup coarsely chopped macadamia nuts
- 1¾ cups (10-ounce package) HERSHEY®S Semi-Sweet Chocolate Chunks, divided
- Quick Vanilla Glaze (recipe follows)

Preheat oven to 375°F. In large mixing bowl, beat butter, brown sugar and granulated sugar until creamy. Add egg and vanilla; beat well. Add flour and baking soda; blend well. Stir in nuts and 1 cup chocolate chunks. Press dough onto bottom of ungreased 13×9×2-inch baking pan. Sprinkle with remaining ¾ cup chocolate chunks. Bake 22 to 25 minutes or until golden brown. Cool completely in pan on wire rack. Prepare Quick Vanilla Glaze; drizzle over top of bars. Allow glaze to set. Cut into bars. *Makes about 24 bars*

QUICK VANILLA GLAZE

- 1 cup powdered sugar
- 2 tablespoons milk
- ½ teaspoon vanilla extract

In small bowl, combine powdered sugar, milk and vanilla; stir until smooth and of desired consistency.

CHOCOLATE AMARETTO SQUARES

- ½ cup (1 stick) butter (do *not* use margarine), melted
- 1 cup sugar
- 2 eggs
- ½ cup all-purpose flour
- ⅓ cup HERSHEY®S Cocoa or HERSHEY®S European Style Cocoa
- 2 tablespoons almond flavored liqueur *or* ½ teaspoon almond extract
- 1¼ cups ground almonds
- Sliced almonds (optional)

Preheat oven to 325°F. Grease 8-inch square baking pan. In large bowl, beat butter and sugar until creamy. Add eggs, flour and cocoa; beat well. Stir in almond liqueur and ground almonds. Pour batter into prepared pan. Bake 35 to 40 minutes or just until set. Cool completely in pan on wire rack. Cut into squares. Garnish with sliced almonds, if desired. *Makes about 16 squares*

Clockwise from top: Chunky Macadamia Bars, Chocolate Amaretto Squares, Chocolate Pecan Pie Bars (page 304)

Keepsake

Bar Cookies

HEATH® BARS

- 1 cup butter, softened
- 1 cup firmly packed brown sugar
- 1 egg yolk
- 1 teaspoon vanilla
- 2 cups all-purpose flour
- 18 to 19 Original HEATH® English Toffee Snack Size Bars, crushed, divided
- ½ cup finely chopped pecans

Preheat oven to 350°F. In large bowl, with electric mixer, beat butter well; blend in brown sugar, egg yolk and vanilla. By hand, mix in flour, ⅔ cup Heath® Bars and nuts. Press into ungreased 15½×10½-inch jelly-roll pan.

Bake 18 to 20 minutes or until browned. Remove from oven and immediately sprinkle remaining Heath® Bars over top. Cool slightly; cut into bars while warm. *Makes about 48 bars*

LUSCIOUS LEMON BARS

CRUST
- ½ cup butter or margarine, softened
- ½ cup granulated sugar
  Grated peel of ½ SUNKIST® Lemon
- 1¼ cups all-purpose flour

LEMON LAYER
- 4 eggs
- 1⅔ cups granulated sugar
- 3 tablespoons all-purpose flour
- ½ teaspoon baking powder
  Grated peel of ½ SUNKIST® Lemon
  Juice of 2 SUNKIST® Lemons (6 tablespoons)
- 1 teaspoon vanilla extract
  Powdered sugar

For Crust, in medium bowl, cream together butter, granulated sugar and lemon peel. Gradually stir in flour to form a soft crumbly dough. Press evenly into bottom of aluminum foil-lined 13×9×2-inch baking pan. Bake at 350° for 15 minutes.

For Lemon Layer, while crust is baking, in large bowl, whisk or beat eggs well. Stir together granulated sugar, flour and baking powder. Gradually whisk sugar mixture into eggs. Whisk in lemon peel, juice and vanilla. Pour over hot crust. Return to oven. Bake for 20 to 25 minutes or until top is lightly browned. Cool. Using foil on two sides, lift out cookie base. Gently loosen foil along all sides. Cut into bars. Sprinkle with powdered sugar. *Makes about 3 dozen bars*

Heath® Bars

— Keepsake —

TRIPLE LAYER PEANUT BUTTER BARS

BASE
- 1¼ cups firmly packed light brown sugar
- ¾ cup creamy peanut butter
- ½ CRISCO® Stick or ½ cup CRISCO all-vegetable shortening
- 3 tablespoons milk
- 1 tablespoon vanilla
- 1 egg
- 1¾ cups all-purpose flour
- ¾ teaspoon baking soda
- ¾ teaspoon salt

PEANUT BUTTER LAYER
- 1½ cups powdered sugar
- 2 tablespoons creamy peanut butter
- 1 tablespoon CRISCO® all-vegetable shortening
- 3 tablespoons milk

CHOCOLATE GLAZE
- 2 squares (1 ounce each) unsweetened baking chocolate
- 2 tablespoons CRISCO® all-vegetable shortening

1. Preheat oven to 350°F. Grease 13×9-inch baking pan. Place wire rack on countertop.

2. For Base, place brown sugar, peanut butter, shortening, milk and vanilla in large bowl. Beat at medium speed of electric mixer until well blended. Add egg; beat just until blended.

3. Combine flour, baking soda and salt in small bowl. Add to shortening mixture; beat at low speed just until blended.

4. Press mixture onto bottom of prepared pan.

5. Bake at 350°F for 18 to 20 minutes or until wooden pick inserted in center comes out clean. *Do not overbake.* Cool completely on wire rack.

6. For Peanut Butter Layer, place powdered sugar, peanut butter, shortening and milk in medium bowl. Beat at low speed of electric mixer until smooth. Spread over base. Refrigerate 30 minutes.

7. For Chocolate Glaze, place chocolate and shortening in small microwave-safe bowl. Microwave at 50% (MEDIUM) for 1 to 2 minutes or until shiny and soft. Stir until smooth. Cool slightly. Spread over peanut butter layer. Refrigerate about 1 hour or until glaze is set. Cut into 3×1½-inch bars. Let stand 15 to 20 minutes at room temperature before serving.

Makes about 2 dozen bars

Triple Layer Peanut Butter Bars

Time-Honored BROWNIES

DECADENT BLONDE BROWNIES

- ½ cup butter or margarine, softened
- ¾ cup granulated sugar
- ¾ cup firmly packed light brown sugar
- 2 large eggs
- 2 teaspoons vanilla
- 1½ cups all-purpose flour
- 1 teaspoon baking powder
- ½ teaspoon salt
- 1 package (10 ounces) semisweet chocolate chunks
- 1 jar (3½ ounces) macadamia nuts, coarsely chopped

Preheat oven to 350°F. Beat butter, granulated sugar and brown sugar in large bowl with electric mixer at medium speed until light and fluffy. Beat in eggs and vanilla. Add combined flour, baking powder and salt. Stir until well blended. Stir in chocolate chunks and macadamia nuts. Spread evenly into greased 13×9-inch baking pan. Bake 25 to 30 minutes or until golden brown. Remove pan to wire rack; cool completely. Cut into 3¼×1½-inch bars. *Makes about 2 dozen brownies*

— Time-Honored —

BROWNIES

RASPBERRY FUDGE BROWNIES

- ½ cup butter or margarine
- 3 squares (1 ounce each) bittersweet chocolate*
- 2 eggs
- 1 cup sugar
- 1 teaspoon vanilla
- ¾ cup all-purpose flour
- ¼ teaspoon baking powder
- Dash salt
- ½ cup sliced or slivered almonds
- ½ cup raspberry preserves
- 1 cup (6 ounces) milk chocolate chips

*Bittersweet chocolate is available in specialty food stores. One square unsweetened chocolate plus 2 squares semisweet chocolate may be substituted.

Preheat oven to 350°F. Butter and flour 8-inch square baking pan. Melt butter and bittersweet chocolate in small, heavy saucepan over low heat. Remove from heat; cool. Beat eggs, sugar and vanilla in large bowl until light. Beat in chocolate mixture. Stir in flour, baking powder and salt until just blended. Spread ¾ of batter in prepared pan; sprinkle almonds over top. Bake 10 minutes. Remove from oven; spread preserves over almonds. Carefully spoon remaining batter over preserves, smoothing top. Bake 25 to 30 minutes or just until top feels firm. Remove from oven; sprinkle chocolate chips over top. Let stand a few minutes, then spread evenly over brownies. Cool completely. When chocolate is set, cut into squares.

Makes 16 brownies

WHITE CHOCOLATE CHUNK BROWNIES

- 4 squares (1 ounce each) unsweetened chocolate, coarsely chopped
- ½ cup butter or margarine
- 2 large eggs
- 1¼ cups granulated sugar
- 1 teaspoon vanilla
- ½ cup all-purpose flour
- ½ teaspoon salt
- 1 white baking bar (6 ounces), cut into ¼-inch pieces
- ½ cup coarsely chopped walnuts (optional)
- Powdered sugar for garnish

Preheat oven to 350°F. Melt unsweetened chocolate and butter in small, heavy saucepan over low heat, stirring constantly; set aside. Beat eggs in large bowl; gradually add granulated sugar, beating at medium speed about 4 minutes until very thick and lemon colored. Beat in chocolate mixture and vanilla. Beat in flour and salt just until blended. Stir in baking bar pieces and walnuts. Spread evenly into greased 8-inch square baking pan. Bake 30 minutes or until edges begin to pull away from sides of pan and center is set. Remove pan to wire rack; cool completely. Cut into 2-inch squares. Sprinkle with powdered sugar, if desired.

Makes about 16 brownies

Raspberry Fudge Brownies

Time-Honored

BROWNIES

TOFFEE BROWNIE BARS

CRUST
- ¾ cup butter or margarine, softened
- ¾ cup firmly packed brown sugar
- 1 egg yolk
- ¾ teaspoon vanilla extract
- 1½ cups all-purpose flour

FILLING
- 1 package (19.8 ounces) DUNCAN HINES® Chocolate Lovers' Fudge Brownie Mix
- 1 egg
- ⅓ cup water
- ⅓ cup CRISCO® Oil

TOPPING
- 1 package (12 ounces) milk chocolate chips, melted
- ¾ cup finely chopped pecans

1. Preheat oven to 350°F. Grease 15½×10½×1-inch jelly-roll pan.

2. For Crust, combine butter, brown sugar, egg yolk and vanilla extract in large bowl. Stir in flour. Spread in pan. Bake 15 minutes or until golden.

3. For Filling, combine brownie mix, egg, water and oil in large bowl. Stir with spoon until well blended, about 50 strokes. Spread over hot crust. Bake 15 minutes or until surface appears set. Cool 30 minutes.

4. For Topping, spread melted chocolate on top of brownie layer; garnish with pecans. Cool completely in pan on wire rack. Cut into bars.

Makes about 48 brownies

EXTRA MOIST & CHUNKY BROWNIES

- 1 (8-ounce) package cream cheese, softened
- 1 cup sugar
- 1 egg
- 1 teaspoon vanilla extract
- ¾ cup all-purpose flour
- 1 (4-serving size) package ROYAL® Chocolate or Dark 'n' Sweet Chocolate Pudding & Pie Filling
- 4 (1-ounce) semisweet chocolate squares, chopped

MICROWAVE DIRECTIONS: In large bowl, with electric mixer at high speed, beat cream cheese, sugar, egg and vanilla until smooth; blend in flour and pudding mix. Spread batter in greased 8×8×2-inch microwavable dish; sprinkle with chocolate. Microwave on HIGH (100% power) for 8 to 10 minutes or until toothpick inserted in center comes out clean, rotating dish ½ turn every 2 minutes. Cool completely in pan. Cut into squares.

Makes 16 squares

Toffee Brownie Bars

—Time-Honored—

BROWNIES

CARAMEL-LAYERED BROWNIES

- 4 squares BAKER'S® Unsweetened Chocolate
- ¾ cup (1½ sticks) margarine or butter
- 2 cups sugar
- 3 eggs
- 1 teaspoon vanilla
- 1 cup all-purpose flour
- 1 cup BAKER'S® Semi-Sweet Real Chocolate Chips
- 1½ cups chopped nuts
- 1 package (14 ounces) caramels
- ⅓ cup evaporated milk

HEAT oven to 350°F.

MICROWAVE chocolate and margarine in large microwavable bowl on HIGH 2 minutes or until margarine is melted. **Stir until chocolate is completely melted.**

STIR sugar into melted chocolate mixture. Mix in eggs and vanilla until well blended. Stir in flour. Remove 1 cup of batter; set aside. Spread remaining batter in greased 13×9-inch pan. Sprinkle with chips and 1 cup of the nuts.

MICROWAVE caramels and milk in same bowl on HIGH 4 minutes, stirring after 2 minutes. Stir until caramels are completely melted and smooth. Spoon over chips and nuts, spreading to edges of pan. Gently spread reserved batter over caramel mixture. Sprinkle with the remaining ½ cup nuts.

BAKE for 40 minutes or until toothpick inserted into center comes out with fudgy crumbs. **Do not overbake.** Cool in pan; cut into squares.

Makes about 24 brownies

BLONDE BRICKLE BROWNIES

- 1⅓ cups all-purpose flour
- ½ teaspoon baking powder
- ¼ teaspoon salt
- 2 eggs
- ½ cup granulated sugar
- ½ cup firmly packed brown sugar
- ⅓ cup butter or margarine, melted
- 1 teaspoon vanilla
- ¼ teaspoon almond extract
- 1 package (6 ounces) BITS 'O BRICKLE®, divided
- ½ cup chopped pecans (optional)

Preheat oven to 350°F. Grease 8-inch square baking pan. Mix flour with baking powder and salt; set aside. In large bowl, beat eggs well. Gradually beat in granulated sugar and brown sugar until thick and creamy. Add butter, vanilla and almond extract; mix well. Gently stir in flour mixture until moistened. Fold in ⅔ cup Bits 'O Brickle® and nuts. Pour into prepared pan.

Bake 30 minutes. Remove from oven; immediately sprinkle remaining Bits 'O Brickle® over top. Cool completely in pan on wire rack. Cut into squares.

Makes about 16 brownies

Blonde Brickle Brownies

BROWNIES

COCONUT CROWNED CAPPUCCINO BROWNIES

- 6 squares (1 ounce each) semisweet chocolate, coarsely chopped
- 1 tablespoon freeze-dried coffee
- 1 tablespoon boiling water
- ¾ cup all-purpose flour
- ¾ teaspoon ground cinnamon
- ½ teaspoon baking powder
- ¼ teaspoon salt
- ½ cup sugar
- ¼ cup butter or margarine, softened
- 3 large eggs, divided
- ¼ cup whipping cream
- 1 teaspoon vanilla
- ¾ cup flaked coconut, divided
- ½ cup semisweet chocolate chips, divided

1. Preheat oven to 350°F. Grease 8-inch square baking pan; set aside.

2. Melt chocolate squares in small, heavy saucepan over low heat, stirring constantly; set aside. Dissolve coffee in boiling water in small cup; set aside.

3. In small bowl, combine flour, cinnamon, baking powder and salt.

4. Beat sugar and butter in large bowl with electric mixer at medium speed until light and fluffy. Beat in 2 eggs, 1 at a time, scraping down side of bowl after each addition. Beat in chocolate mixture and coffee mixture until well combined. Add flour mixture. Beat at low speed until well blended. Spread batter evenly into prepared pan.

5. For topping, combine cream, remaining 1 egg and vanilla in small bowl; mix well. Stir in ½ cup coconut and ¼ cup chips. Spread evenly over brownie base; sprinkle with remaining ¼ cup coconut and chips.

6. Bake 30 to 35 minutes or until coconut is browned and center is set. Remove pan to wire rack; cool completely. Cut into 2-inch squares. Store tightly covered at room temperature or freeze up to 3 months. *Makes 16 brownies*

Coconut Crowned Cappuccino Brownies

Time-Honored

BROWNIES

CHOCOLATEY ROCKY ROAD BROWNIES

BROWNIES
- 1 cup butter or margarine
- 4 squares (1 ounce each) unsweetened chocolate
- 1½ cups granulated sugar
- 1 cup all-purpose flour
- 3 eggs
- 1½ teaspoons vanilla
- ½ cup salted peanuts, chopped

FROSTING
- ¼ cup butter or margarine
- 1 (3-ounce) package cream cheese
- 1 square (1 ounce) unsweetened chocolate
- ¼ cup milk
- 2¾ cups powdered sugar
- 1 teaspoon vanilla
- 2 cups miniature marshmallows
- 1 cup salted peanuts

For Brownies, preheat oven to 350°F. In 3-quart saucepan, combine 1 cup butter and 4 squares chocolate. Cook over medium heat, stirring constantly, until melted, 5 to 7 minutes. Add granulated sugar, flour, eggs and 1½ teaspoons vanilla; mix well. Stir in ½ cup chopped peanuts. Spread into greased 13×9-inch baking pan. Bake 20 to 25 minutes or until brownie starts to pull away from sides of pan. Cool completely.

For Frosting, in 2-quart saucepan, combine ¼ cup butter, cream cheese, 1 square chocolate and milk. Cook over medium heat, stirring occasionally, until melted, 6 to 8 minutes. Remove from heat; add powdered sugar and 1 teaspoon vanilla; beat with hand mixer until smooth. Stir in marshmallows and 1 cup peanuts. Immediately spread over cooled brownies. Cool completely; cut into bars. Store in refrigerator. *Makes about 4 dozen brownies*

Chocolatey Rocky Road Brownies

─ *Grandkids'* ─
DELIGHTS

CHOCOLATE CHIP LOLLIPOPS

1 package DUNCAN HINES® Chocolate Chip Cookie Mix
1 egg
⅓ cup CRISCO® Oil
2 tablespoons water
Flat ice cream sticks
Assorted decors

1. Preheat oven to 375°F.

2. Combine cookie mix, egg, oil and water in large bowl. Stir until thoroughly blended. Shape dough into 32 (1-inch) balls. Place balls 3 inches apart on ungreased cookie sheets. Push ice cream stick into center of each ball. Flatten dough ball with hand to form round lollipop. Decorate by pressing decors onto dough. Bake at 375°F for 8 to 9 minutes or until light golden brown. Cool 1 minute on cookie sheets. Remove to wire racks. Cool completely. Store in airtight container.

Makes 2½ to 3 dozen cookies

Grandkids' Delights

PEANUT BUTTER BEARS

- 1 cup SKIPPY® Creamy Peanut Butter
- 1 cup MAZOLA® Margarine, softened
- 1 cup firmly packed brown sugar
- ⅔ cup KARO® Light or Dark Corn Syrup
- 2 eggs
- 4 cups all-purpose flour, divided
- 1 tablespoon baking powder
- 1 teaspoon ground cinnamon (optional)
- ¼ teaspoon salt

In large bowl, with mixer at medium speed, beat peanut butter, margarine, brown sugar, corn syrup and eggs until smooth. Reduce speed; beat in 2 cups of the flour, the baking powder, cinnamon and salt. With spoon, stir in remaining 2 cups flour. Wrap dough in plastic wrap; refrigerate 2 hours.

Preheat oven to 325°F. Divide dough in half; set aside half. On floured surface, roll out half the dough to ⅛-inch thickness. Cut with floured bear cookie cutter. Repeat with remaining dough. Bake on ungreased cookie sheets 10 minutes or until lightly browned. Remove from cookie sheets; cool completely on wire rack. Decorate as desired.

Makes about 3 dozen bears

Prep Time: 35 minutes, plus chilling
Bake Time: 10 minutes, plus cooling

NOTE: Use scraps of dough to make bear faces. Make one small ball of dough for muzzle. Form 3 smaller balls of dough and press gently to create eyes and nose; bake as directed. If desired, use frosting to create paws, ears and bow ties.

MARSHMALLOW KRISPIE BARS

- 1 package (19.8 ounces) DUNCAN HINES® Chocolate Lovers' Fudge Brownie Mix
- 1 package (10½ ounces) miniature marshmallows
- 1½ cups semi-sweet chocolate chips
- 1 cup JIF® Creamy Peanut Butter
- 1 tablespoon butter or margarine
- 1½ cups crisp rice cereal

1. Preheat oven to 350°F. Grease bottom of 13×9×2-inch baking pan.

2. Prepare and bake brownies following package directions for original recipe. Remove from oven. Sprinkle marshmallows on hot brownies. Return to oven. Bake for 3 minutes longer.

3. Place chocolate chips, peanut butter and butter in medium saucepan. Cook on low heat, stirring constantly, until chips are melted. Add rice cereal; mix well. Spread mixture over marshmallow layer. Refrigerate until chilled. Cut into bars.

Makes 24 bars

Peanut Butter Bears

Grandkids' Delights

PEANUT BUTTER PIZZA COOKIES

- 1 package DUNCAN HINES® Peanut Butter Cookie Mix
- 1 egg
- ¼ cup CRISCO® Oil
- 1 tablespoon water
- Sugar
- 1 container (16 ounces) DUNCAN HINES® Creamy Homestyle Chocolate Frosting
- Cashews
- Candy-coated chocolate pieces
- Gumdrops, halved
- Flaked coconut
- ½ bar (2 ounces) white chocolate baking bar
- 1½ teaspoons CRISCO® all-vegetable shortening

1. Preheat oven to 375°F.

2. Combine cookie mix, peanut butter packet from Mix, egg, oil and water in large bowl. Stir until thoroughly blended. Shape into 12 (2-inch) balls (about 3 level tablespoons each). Place balls 3½ inches apart on ungreased cookie sheets. Flatten with bottom of large glass dipped in sugar to make 3-inch circles. Bake at 375°F for 9 to 11 minutes or until set. Cool 1 minute on cookie sheets. Remove to wire racks. Cool completely.

3. Frost cookies with Chocolate frosting. Decorate with cashews, candy pieces, gumdrops and coconut. Melt white chocolate and shortening in small saucepan on low heat, stirring constantly, until smooth. Drizzle over cookies.

Makes 12 large cookies

CRUMBLE BARS

- ½ cup butter or margarine
- 1 cup all-purpose flour
- ¾ cup quick-cooking oats, uncooked
- ⅓ cup firmly packed light brown sugar
- ½ teaspoon salt
- ½ teaspoon baking soda
- ½ teaspoon vanilla extract
- 4 MILKY WAY® Bars (2.15 ounces each), each cut into 8 slices

Preheat oven to 350°F. Lightly grease 8×8×2-inch baking pan; set aside.

Melt butter in large saucepan. Remove from heat; stir in flour, oats, sugar, salt, baking soda and vanilla. Blend until crumbly. Press ⅔ of mixture into prepared pan. Arrange Milky Way® Bar slices in pan to within ½ inch from edges. Finely crumble remaining mixture over the Milky Way® Bars. Bake 20 to 25 minutes or until edges are golden brown. Cool in pan on wire rack. Cut into bars or squares to serve. *Makes 12 to 16 bars*

Peanut Butter Pizza Cookies

Grandkids' Delights

WATERMELON SLICES

- 1 package **DUNCAN HINES® Golden Sugar Cookie Mix**
- 1 egg
- ¼ cup **CRISCO® Oil**
- 1½ tablespoons water
- 12 drops red food coloring
- 5 drops green food coloring
- Chocolate sprinkles

1. Combine cookie mix, egg, oil and water in large bowl. Stir until thoroughly blended; reserve ⅓ cup dough.

2. For red cookie dough, combine remaining dough with red food coloring. Stir until evenly tinted. On waxed paper, shape dough into 12-inch-long roll with one side flattened. Cover; refrigerate with flat side down until firm.

3. For green cookie dough, combine reserved ⅓ cup dough with green food coloring in small bowl. Stir until evenly tinted. Place between 2 layers of waxed paper. Roll dough into 12×4-inch rectangle. Refrigerate for 15 minutes.

4. Preheat oven to 375°F.

5. To assemble, remove green dough rectangle from refrigerator. Remove top layer of waxed paper. Trim edges along both 12-inch sides. Remove red dough log from refrigerator. Place red dough log, flattened side up, along center of green dough. Mold green dough up to edge of flattened side of red dough. Remove bottom layer of waxed paper. Trim excess green dough, if necessary.

6. Cut chilled roll with flat side down into ¼-inch-thick slices with sharp knife. Place 2 inches apart on ungreased cookie sheets. Sprinkle chocolate sprinkles on red dough for seeds. Bake at 375°F for 7 minutes or until set. Cool 1 minute on cookie sheets. Remove to wire racks. Cool completely. Store between layers of waxed paper in airtight container. *Makes 3 to 4 dozen cookies*

TIP: To make neat, clean slices, use unwaxed dental floss.

Watermelon Slices

Grandkids'

DELIGHTS

CHOCOLATEY PEANUT BUTTER GOODIES

COOKIES
- 1 CRISCO® Stick or 1 cup CRISCO all-vegetable shortening
- 4 cups (1 pound) powdered sugar
- 1½ cups JIF® Extra Crunchy Peanut Butter
- 1½ cups graham cracker crumbs

FROSTING
- 1 tablespoon CRISCO® all-vegetable shortening
- 1⅓ cups semi-sweet chocolate chips

1. **For Cookies,** combine shortening, powdered sugar, peanut butter and crumbs in large bowl with spoon. Spread evenly on bottom of 13×9-inch baking pan.

2. **For Frosting,** combine shortening and chocolate chips in small microwave-safe bowl. Microwave at 50% (MEDIUM). Stir after 1 minute. Repeat until smooth (or melt on rangetop in small saucepan on very low heat). Spread over top of cookie mixture. Cool at least 1 hour or until chocolate hardens. Cut into 2×1½-inch bars.

Makes 3 dozen bars

P. B. GRAHAM SNACKERS

- ½ CRISCO® Stick or ½ cup CRISCO all-vegetable shortening
- 2 cups powdered sugar
- ¾ cup JIF® Creamy Peanut Butter
- 1 cup graham cracker crumbs
- ½ cup semi-sweet chocolate chips
- ½ cup graham cracker crumbs, crushed peanuts or chocolate sprinkles (optional)

1. Combine shortening, powdered sugar and peanut butter in large bowl. Beat at low speed of electric mixer until well blended. Stir in 1 cup crumbs and chocolate chips. Cover and refrigerate 1 hour.

2. Form dough into 1-inch balls. Roll in ½ cup crumbs, peanuts or sprinkles for a fancier cookie. Cover and refrigerate until ready to serve.

Makes about 3 dozen cookies

Top to bottom: P.B. Graham Snackers and Chocolatey Peanut Butter Goodies

Old-World Holiday Treats

GOLDEN KOLACKY

½ cup butter, softened
4 ounces cream cheese, softened
1 cup all-purpose flour
Fruit preserves

Combine butter and cream cheese in large bowl; beat until smooth. Gradually add flour to butter mixture, blending until soft dough forms. Divide dough in half; wrap each half in plastic wrap. Refrigerate until firm.

Preheat oven to 375°F. Roll out dough, ½ at a time, on floured surface to ⅛-inch thickness. Cut into 3-inch squares. Spoon 1 teaspoon preserves in center of each square. Bring up two opposite corners to center; pinch together tightly to seal. Fold sealed tip to one side; pinch to seal. Place 1 inch apart on ungreased cookie sheets. Bake for 10 to 15 minutes or until lightly browned. Remove to wire racks; cool completely.

Makes about 2½ dozen cookies

Old-World Holiday Treats

WALNUT CHRISTMAS BALLS

- 1 cup California walnuts
- ⅔ cup powdered sugar, divided
- 1 cup butter or margarine, softened
- 1 teaspoon vanilla
- 1¾ cups all-purpose flour
- Chocolate Filling (recipe follows)

Preheat oven to 350°F. In food processor or blender, process walnuts with 2 tablespoons sugar until finely ground. In large bowl, cream butter and remaining sugar. Beat in vanilla. Add flour and ¾ cup walnut mixture; beat until blended. Roll dough into about 3 dozen walnut-size balls. Place 2 inches apart on ungreased cookie sheets.

Bake 10 to 12 minutes or until just golden around edges. Remove to wire racks to cool completely. Prepare Chocolate Filling. Place generous teaspoonful of filling on flat side of half the cookies. Top with remaining cookies, flat side down, forming sandwiches. Roll chocolate edges of cookies in remaining ground walnuts.
Makes about 1½ dozen sandwich cookies

CHOCOLATE FILLING: Chop 3 squares (1 ounce each) semisweet chocolate into small pieces; place in food processor or blender with ½ teaspoon vanilla. In small saucepan, heat 2 tablespoons *each* butter or margarine and whipping cream over medium heat until hot; pour over chocolate. Process until chocolate is melted, turning machine off and scraping sides as needed. With machine running, gradually add 1 cup powdered sugar; process until smooth.

Favorite recipe from **Walnut Marketing Board**

BANANA CRESCENTS

- ½ cup DOLE® Chopped Almonds, toasted
- 6 tablespoons sugar, divided
- ½ cup margarine, cut into pieces
- 1½ cups plus 2 tablespoons all-purpose flour
- ⅛ teaspoon salt
- 1 extra-ripe, medium DOLE® Banana, peeled
- 2 to 3 ounces semisweet chocolate chips

Pulverize almonds with 2 tablespoons sugar in food processor.

Beat margarine, almond mixture, remaining 4 tablespoons sugar, flour and salt.

Puree banana; add to batter and mix until well blended.

Using 1 tablespoon batter, roll into log then shape into crescent. Place on ungreased cookie sheet. Bake in 375°F oven 25 minutes or until golden. Cool on wire rack.

Melt chocolate in microwavable dish at 50% power 1½ to 2 minutes, stirring once. Dip ends of cookies in chocolate. Refrigerate until chocolate hardens.
Makes 2 dozen cookies

Banana Crescents

Old-World

Holiday Treats

GLAZED SUGAR COOKIES

COOKIES
- 1 package DUNCAN HINES® Golden Sugar Cookie Mix
- 1 egg
- ¼ cup CRISCO® Oil
- 1 teaspoon water

GLAZE
- 1½ cups sifted powdered sugar
- 2 to 3 tablespoons water or milk
- ¾ teaspoons vanilla extract
- Food coloring
- Red and green sugar crystals, nonpareils or cinnamon candies

1. Preheat oven to 375°F.

2. For Cookies, combine cookie mix, egg, oil and water in large bowl. Stir thoroughly until blended. Roll dough to ¼-inch thickness on lightly floured surface. Cut dough into desired shapes using floured cookie cutters. Place cookies 2 inches apart on ungreased cookie sheets. Bake at 375°F for 7 to 8 minutes or until edges are light golden brown. Cool 1 minute on cookie sheets. Remove to wire racks. Cool completely.

3. For Glaze, combine powdered sugar, water and vanilla extract in medium bowl. Beat until smooth. Tint glaze with food coloring, if desired. Brush glaze on each cookie with a clean pastry brush. Sprinkle each cookie with sugar crystals, nonpareils or cinnamon candies before glaze sets. Allow glaze to set before storing between layers of waxed paper in air-tight container.

Makes 4 dozen cookies

TIP: Use Duncan Hines® Creamy Homestyle Vanilla Frosting for a quick glaze. Heat frosting in opened container in microwave oven at HIGH (100% power) for 10 to 15 seconds. Stir well. Spread on cookies and decorate as desired before frosting sets.

Glazed Sugar Cookies

DANISH RASPBERRY RIBBONS

COOKIES
- 1 cup butter, softened
- ½ cup granulated sugar
- 1 large egg
- 2 tablespoons milk
- 2 tablespoons vanilla
- ¼ teaspoon almond extract
- 2 to 2⅔ cups all-purpose flour, divided
- 6 tablespoons seedless raspberry jam

GLAZE
- ½ cup sifted powdered sugar
- 1 tablespoon milk
- 1 teaspoon vanilla

1. For Cookies, beat butter and granulated sugar in bowl with mixer at medium speed until fluffy. Beat in egg, 2 tablespoons milk, 2 tablespoons vanilla and almond extract until blended.

2. Gradually add 1½ cups flour. Beat at low speed until well blended. Stir in additional flour with spoon until stiff dough forms. Wrap in plastic wrap and refrigerate until firm, 30 minutes or overnight.

3. Preheat oven to 375°F. Cut dough into 6 pieces. Rewrap 3 pieces; refrigerate. With floured hands, shape each dough piece into 12-inch-long, ¾-inch-thick rope.

4. Place ropes 2 inches apart on *ungreased* cookie sheets. Make a ¼-inch-deep groove down center of each rope with handle of wooden spoon. (Ropes flatten to ½-inch-thick strips.)

5. Bake 12 minutes. Spoon 1 tablespoon jam along each groove. Bake 5 to 7 minutes longer or until strips are light golden brown. Cool strips 15 minutes on cookie sheets.

6. For Glaze, place powdered sugar, 1 tablespoon milk and 1 teaspoon vanilla in small bowl; stir until smooth. Drizzle Glaze over strips; let stand 5 minutes to dry. Cut strips at 45° angle into 1-inch slices. Cool cookies completely on wire racks. Repeat with remaining dough. Store tightly covered between sheets of waxed paper at room temperature. *Makes about 5½ dozen cookies*

Danish Raspberry Ribbons

— Old-World —

HOLIDAY TREATS

PEANUT BUTTER CUT-OUTS

- ½ cup **SKIPPY® Creamy Peanut Butter**
- 6 tablespoons **MAZOLA® Margarine or butter, softened**
- ½ cup **firmly packed brown sugar**
- ⅓ cup **KARO® Light or Dark Corn Syrup**
- 1 **egg**
- 2 cups **all-purpose flour, divided**
- 1½ teaspoons **baking powder**
- 1 teaspoon **ground cinnamon (optional)**
- ⅛ teaspoon **salt**

In large bowl, with mixer at medium speed, beat peanut butter, margarine, brown sugar, corn syrup and egg until smooth. Reduce speed; beat in 1 cup flour, baking powder, cinnamon and salt. With spoon, stir in remaining 1 cup flour.

Divide dough in half. Between two sheets of waxed paper on large cookie sheets, roll each half of dough to ¼-inch thickness. Refrigerate until firm, about 1 hour.

Preheat oven to 350°F. Remove top piece of waxed paper. With floured cookie cutters, cut dough into shapes. Place on ungreased cookie sheets. Bake 10 minutes or until lightly browned. *Do not overbake.* Let stand on cookie sheets 2 minutes. Remove from cookie sheets; cool completely on wire racks. Reroll dough trimmings and cut. Decorate as desired. *Makes about 5 dozen cookies*

NOTE: Use scraps of dough to create details on cookies.

BAVARIAN COOKIE WREATHS

- 3½ cups **unsifted all-purpose flour**
- 1 cup **sugar, divided**
- 3 teaspoons **grated orange peel, divided**
- ¼ teaspoon **salt**
- 1⅓ cups **butter or margarine**
- ¼ cup **Florida orange juice**
- ⅓ cup **finely chopped blanched almonds**
- 1 **egg white beaten with 1 teaspoon water**
- **Prepared frosting (optional)**

Preheat oven to 400°F. In large bowl, mix flour, ¾ cup sugar, 2 teaspoons orange peel and salt. Using pastry blender, cut in butter and orange juice until mixture holds together. Knead few times and press into a ball.

Shape dough into ¾-inch balls; lightly roll each ball on floured board into a 6-inch-long strip. Using two strips, twist together to make a rope. Pinch ends of rope together to make a wreath; place on lightly greased baking sheet.

In shallow dish, mix almonds, remaining ¼ cup sugar and 1 teaspoon orange peel. Brush top of each wreath with egg white mixture and sprinkle with sugar-almond mixture.

Bake 8 to 10 minutes or until lightly browned. Remove to wire racks; cool completely. Frost, if desired. *Makes 5 dozen cookies*

Favorite recipe from **Florida Department of Citrus**

Peanut Butter Cut-Outs

342

Old-World

Holiday Treats

CHOCOLATE CHIP RUGALACH

- 1 cup (2 sticks) butter or margarine, slightly softened
- 2 cups all-purpose flour
- 1 cup vanilla ice cream, softened
- ½ cup strawberry jam
- 1 cup BAKER'S® Semi-Sweet Real Chocolate Chips
- 1 cup finely chopped nuts
- Powdered sugar

BEAT butter and flour. Beat in ice cream until well blended. Divide dough into 4 balls; wrap each in waxed paper. Refrigerate until firm, about 1 hour.

HEAT oven to 350°F. Roll dough, one ball at a time, on floured surface into 11×6-inch rectangle, about ⅛ inch thick. Spread with 2 tablespoons of the jam; sprinkle with ¼ cup of the chips and ¼ cup of the nuts. Roll up lengthwise as for jelly roll. Place on ungreased cookie sheet. Cut 12 diagonal slits in roll, being careful not to cut all the way through. Repeat with the remaining dough.

BAKE for 35 minutes or until golden brown. Cool 5 minutes on cookie sheet. Cut through each roll; separate pieces. Finish cooling on wire racks. Sprinkle with powdered sugar, if desired.

Makes 4 dozen pieces

Prep Time: 30 minutes
Chill Time: 1 hour
Baking Time: 35 minutes

CHOCOLATE ALMOND SHORTBREAD

- ¾ cup (1½ sticks) butter or margarine, softened
- 1¼ cups powdered sugar
- 6 squares BAKER'S® Semi-Sweet Chocolate, melted, cooled
- 1 teaspoon vanilla
- 1 cup all-purpose flour
- ¼ teaspoon salt
- 1 cup toasted ground blanched almonds
- ½ cup toasted chopped almonds

HEAT oven to 250°F.

BEAT butter and sugar until light and fluffy. Stir in chocolate and vanilla. Mix in flour, salt and ground almonds.

PRESS dough into 12×9-inch rectangle on ungreased cookie sheet. Sprinkle with chopped almonds; press lightly into dough.

BAKE for 45 to 50 minutes or until set. Cool on cookie sheet; cut into bars. *Makes about 36 bars*

Prep Time: 30 minutes
Baking Time: 45 to 50 minutes

Top to bottom: Chocolate Almond Shortbread, Chocolate Chip Rugalach

LINZER SANDWICH COOKIES

- 1⅓ cups all-purpose flour
- ¼ teaspoon baking powder
- ¼ teaspoon salt
- ¾ cup sugar
- ½ cup butter, softened
- 1 large egg
- 1 teaspoon vanilla
- Seedless raspberry jam

1. Combine flour, baking powder and salt in small bowl.

2. Beat sugar and butter in medium bowl with electric mixer at medium speed until light and fluffy. Beat in egg and vanilla. Gradually add flour mixture. Beat at low speed until dough forms.

3. Form dough into 2 discs; wrap in plastic wrap and refrigerate 2 hours or until firm.

4. Preheat oven to 375°F. Working with 1 disc at a time, unwrap dough and place on lightly floured surface. Roll out dough with lightly floured rolling pin.

5. Cut dough into desired shapes with floured cookie cutters. Cut out equal numbers of each shape. (If dough becomes soft, cover and refrigerate several minutes before continuing.)

6. Cut 1-inch centers out of half the cookies of each shape. Gently press dough trimmings together; reroll and cut out more cookies. Place cookies 1½ to 2 inches apart on *ungreased* cookie sheets.

7. Bake 7 to 9 minutes or until edges are lightly browned. Let cookies stand on cookie sheet 1 to 2 minutes. Remove cookies with spatula to wire racks; cool completely. To assemble cookies, spread 1 teaspoon jam on flat side of whole cookies, spreading almost to edges. Place cookies with holes, flat-side down, on jam. Store tightly covered at room temperature or freeze up to 3 months.

Makes about 2 dozen cookies

WALNUT–BRANDY SHORTBREAD

- 1 cup butter
- ½ cup firmly packed brown sugar
- ⅛ teaspoon salt
- 2 tablespoons brandy
- 1 cup all-purpose flour
- 1 cup finely chopped toasted California walnuts
- Granulated sugar

Cream butter with brown sugar and salt in large bowl; mix in brandy. Gradually add flour; stir in walnuts. Spread in ungreased 9-inch square pan. Refrigerate 30 minutes.

Pierce mixture all over with fork. Bake at 325°F about 55 minutes or until dark golden brown. If dough puffs up during baking, pierce again with fork. Sprinkle lightly with granulated sugar and cool. Cut into squares with sharp knife.

Makes 36 squares

Favorite recipe from **Walnut Marketing Board**

Linzer Sandwich Cookies

Acknowledgments

The publisher would like to thank the companies and organizations listed below for the use of their recipes and photographs in this publication.

Alltrista Corporation Kerr Brands®
American Lamb Council
Best Foods Division, CPC International Inc.
Blue Diamond Growers
California Tree Fruit Agreement
Canned Food Information Council
Canned Fruit Promotion Service
Chef Paul Prudhomme's Magic Seasoning Blends®
Colorado Potato Administrative Committee
Del Monte Corporation
Dole Food Company, Inc.
Florida Department of Agriculture & Consumer Services, Bureau of Seafood and Aquaculture
Florida Department of Citrus
Florida Tomato Committee
Golden Grain/Mission Pasta
Heinz U.S.A.
Hershey Foods Corporation
Hunt-Wesson, Inc.
The HV Company
Kellogg Company
Kraft Foods, Inc.
Lawry's® Foods, Inc.
Leaf®, Inc.
Lipton™
M & M/MARS
McIlhenny Company

MOTT'S® Inc., a division of Cadbury Beverages Inc.
Nabisco, Inc.
National Broiler Council
National Cattlemen's Beef Association
National Dairy Board
National Honey Board
National Pork Producers Council
National Turkey Federation
Nestlé USA
Newman's Own, Inc.®
North Dakota Barley Council
North Dakota Wheat Commission
Perdue Farms Incorporated
The Procter & Gamble Company
Quaker® Kitchens
Reckitt & Colman Inc.
Riviana Foods Inc.
Sargento® Foods Inc.
Southeast United Dairy Industry Association, Inc.
StarKist® Seafood Company
The Sugar Association, Inc.
Sunkist Growers
Uncle Ben's Rice
USA Dry Pea & Lentil Council
Walnut Marketing Board
Washington Apple Commission

Index

A
Acorn Squash with Maple Butter, 30
Almond Blueberry Muffins, 188
Almond Toffee Squares, 302
Angel Hair Carbonara, 150
Apple
  Apple-Buttermilk Pie, 90
  Apple Butter Spice Muffins, 186
  Apple Cheddar Muffins, 14
  Apple Cheddar Scones, 220
  Apple Oat Bran Muffins, 240
  Apple Ring Coffee Cake, 200
  Apple Sauce Cinnamon Rolls, 228
  Golden Apple Cheesecake, 94
  Golden Apple Cheese Muffins, 190
  Golden Apple Sour Cream Muffins, 254
  Golden Chicken Normandy-Style, 60
  Mott's® Luscious Lemon Lite Muffins, 233
  Oatmeal Apple Cookies, 268
  Oatmeal Apple Cranberry Scones, 234
  Sausage Skillet Dinner, 44
  Savory Pork & Apple Stir-Fry, 106
  Tomato Ginger Apple Salad, 36
Apricot-Pear Strudel, 86
Artichokes
  Buffet Chicken Medley, 127
  Company Crab, 76
  Fresh Vegetable Lasagna, 156
  Oyster-Artichoke Pan Roast, 76
  Spinach Bake, 26

Asparagus
  Chicken and Ham with Rice, 54
  Fancy Chicken Puff Pie, 62
  Sausage & Pasta Primavera, 178

B
Bacon
  Bacon Brunch Buns, 10
  Basque Bean Casserole, 174
  Deluxe Potato Bake, 156
  Okra-Bacon Casserole, 27
  Savory Pumpkin Bacon Muffins, 217
  Spinach Bake, 26
  Zesty Catfish Bake, 68
Baked Country Cured Ham, 40
Baked Doughnuts with Cinnamon Glaze, 250
Baked Fish with Potatoes and Onions, 74
Baked Potato Spears, 34
Baked Rigatoni with Sausage, 144
Baked Rockfish Veracruz, 130
Bananas
  Banana Breakfast Muffins, 200
  Banana Crescents, 336
  Banana-Honey Muffins, 192
  Banana Nut Bread, 236
  Black Bottom Banana Cream Pie, 87
  Caribbean Vegetarian Curry, 163
  Classic Banana Bread, 20
  Healthy Banana-Walnut Muffins, 202
  Mini Muffins, 243
  Poppy Seed Bread, 20
  Sesame Crunch Banana Muffins, 230

Basque Bean Casserole, 174
Bavarian Cookie Wreaths, 342
Bayou Jambalaya, 18
Beans
  Basque Bean Casserole, 174
  Beef Tamale Pie, 172
  Caribbean Vegetarian Curry, 163
  Chicken Risotto, 178
  Chili Bean Ragoût, 160
  Family Baked Bean Dinner, 48
  Lamb & Pork Cassoulet, 50
  Minestrone Soup, 18
  Quick & Easy Chili, 17
  Southwestern Beef and Bean Lasagna, 102
  Texas-Style Deep-Dish Chili Pie, 42
  "Wild" Black Beans, 163
Beef
  Beef Bourguignon, 100
  Beef Tamale Pie, 172
  Cider Stew, 100
  Corned Beef, Potato and Pepper Hash, 44
  Countdown Casserole, 110
  French Beef Stew, 168
  Hickory Beef Kabobs, 38
  Meat and Potato Pie, 105
  Oriental Beef and Broccoli, 170
  Spicy Barbecue Beef, 50
  T-Bone Steaks with Vegetable Kabobs, 48
  Texas-Style Beef Brisket, 52
  Texas-Style Deep-Dish Chili Pie, 42
  Vegetable Beef Pot Pie, 104

Index

Beef, Ground
    Chili Meatloaf & Potato Casserole, 108
    Chili Wagon Wheel Casserole, 148
    Crazy Lasagna Casserole, 150
    Mini Meat Loaves & Vegetables, 106
    Old-Fashioned Beef Pot Pie, 108
    Oriental Beef & Noodle Toss, 176
    Patchwork Casserole, 40
    Quick & Easy Chili, 17
    String Pie, 46
Berry Cobbler, 84
Biscuits
    Chive Whole Wheat Drop Biscuits, 242
    Country Biscuits, 184
    Flakey Southern Biscuits, 16
    Herb-Cheese Biscuit Loaf, 212
Biscuit-Topped Tuna Bake, 132
Black Bottom Banana Cream Pie, 87
Blazing Bandito Veggie Medley, 158
Blonde Brickle Brownies, 318
Blueberry
    Almond Blueberry Muffins, 188
    Berry Cobbler, 84
    Blueberry Crunch Muffins, 242
    Blueberry Muffins, 236
    Blueberry Yogurt Muffins, 224
    Peach Cobbler, 88
    Streusel-Topped Blueberry Muffins, 248
    Wild Rice Blueberry Muffins, 238
Brazilian Corn and Shrimp Moqueca Casserole, 175

Breads, Quick
    Banana Nut Bread, 236
    Classic Banana Bread, 20
    Cornsticks, 17
    Golden Hearty Cornbread, 16
    Orange Pecan Bread, 10
    Peanut Butter Mini Chip Loaves, 260
    Poppy Seed Bread, 20
    Spice-Prune Loaf, 238
Breads, Yeast
    Apple Sauce Cinnamon Rolls, 228
    Bacon Brunch Buns, 10
    Baked Doughnuts with Cinnamon Glaze, 250
    Cinnamon Buns, 188
    Cinnamon-Raisin Bread, 256
    Cloverleaf, 216
    Crescents, 216
    Dinner Rolls, 216
    Fan-Tans, 217
    Maple Nut Twist, 196
    Marble Swirl Bread, 214
    Refrigerator Sweet Yeast Dough, 190
    Sweet Yeast Dough, 190
    Thyme-Cheese Bubble Loaf, 206
    Whole Wheat Herb Bread, 226
Broccoli
    Broccoli Casserole with Crumb Topping, 164
    Cheddar Broccoli Corn Bake, 30
    Harvest Vegetable Scallop, 162
    Herb-Baked Fish & Rice, 78
    Oriental Beef and Broccoli, 170
    Sesame Chicken and Vegetable Stir-Fry, 117
    Vegetable Risotto, 158
    "Wildly" Delicious Casserole, 127

Brownies
    Blonde Brickle Brownies, 318
    Caramel-Layered Brownies, 318
    Chocolatey Rocky Road Brownies, 322
    Coconut Crowned Cappuccino Brownies, 320
    Decadent Blonde Brownies, 312
    Extra Moist & Chunky Brownies, 316
    Raspberry Fudge Brownies, 314
    Toffee Brownie Bars, 316
    White Chocolate Chunk Brownies, 314
Buffet Chicken Medley, 127
Bulgur
    Chicken Tabbouleh, 117
    Tabbouleh, 154
Buttermilk Oatmeal Scones, 186

C
Cajun-Style Green Beans, 26
Cakes
    Golden Apple Cheesecake, 94
    Karen Ann's Lemon Cake, 90
    Old-Fashioned Upside-Down Cake, 87
California Apricot-Cherry Cornmeal Cobbler, 94
Caramel-Layered Brownies, 318
Caraway Cheese Muffins, 218
Caribbean Vegetarian Curry, 163
Carrot Zucchini Muffins, 232
Casseroles
    Angel Hair Carbonara, 150
    Baked Fish with Potatoes and Onions, 74
    Baked Rigatoni with Sausage, 144
    Basque Bean Casserole, 174
    Beef Tamale Pie, 172
    Biscuit-Topped Tuna Bake, 132
    Brazilian Corn and Shrimp Moqueca Casserole, 175

Index

Casseroles *(continued)*
  Broccoli Casserole with Crumb Topping, 164
  Buffet Chicken Medley, 127
  Cheddar Broccoli Corn Bake, 30
  Chesapeake Crab Strata, 80
  Chicken & Wild Rice, 122
  Chicken Tetrazzini, 114
  Chilaquiles, 175
  Chili Meatloaf & Potato Casserole, 108
  Chili Wagon Wheel Casserole, 148
  China Choy Quiche, 180
  Company Crab, 76
  Corn and Chicken Casserole, 126
  Corn Pudding Soufflé, 36
  Countdown Casserole, 110
  Country Chicken Dinner, 140
  Crab and Corn Enchilada Casserole, 138
  Dairyland Confetti Chicken, 66
  Deluxe Potato Bake, 156
  Double Spinach Bake, 164
  Down-Home Corn and Chicken Casserole, 58
  Easy Three Cheese Tuna Soufflé, 136
  Enchiladas Suisse, 174
  Enlightened Macaroni and Cheese, 146
  Family Baked Bean Dinner, 48
  Fancy Chicken Puff Pie, 62
  Fresh Vegetable Casserole, 22
  Harvest Vegetable Scallop, 162
  Herb-Baked Fish & Rice, 78
  Homestyle Tuna Pot Pie, 128
  Lamb & Pork Cassoulet, 50
  Layered Chicken & Vegetable Bake, 126
  Louisiana Seafood Bake, 70

Casseroles *(continued)*
  Meat and Potato Pie, 105
  Mexican Cheese-Rice Pie, 170
  Okra-Bacon Casserole, 27
  Old-Fashioned Beef Pot Pie, 108
  Old-Fashioned Tuna Noodle Casserole, 78
  One-Dish Chicken 'n' Rice, 118
  Original Green Bean Casserole, 166
  Orzo Casserole, 172
  Oyster-Artichoke Pan Roast, 76
  Pastitso, 148
  Patchwork Casserole, 40
  Pizza Pasta, 152
  Polish Reuben Casserole, 146
  Potato Gorgonzola Gratin, 162
  Prize Potluck Casserole, 110
  Savory Chicken & Biscuits, 116
  Shepherd's Pie, 52
  Shrimp Casserole, 132
  Shrimp in Angel Hair Pasta Casserole, 70
  Shrimp Noodle Supreme, 144
  Spinach Bake, 26
  String Pie, 46
  Surfer's Seafood Casserole, 134
  Swiss Vegetable Medley, 166
  Tasty Turkey Pot Pie, 56
  Texas-Style Deep-Dish Chili Pie, 42
  Turkey Cottage Pie, 60
  Turkey-Tortilla Bake, 116
  Vegetable Beef Pot Pie, 104
  "Wild" Black Beans, 163
  "Wildly" Delicious Casserole, 127
  Wisconsin Swiss Linguine Tart, 142
  Zucchini Tomato Bake, 160

Cauliflower
  Cheddar Chowder, 14
  Fresh Vegetable Casserole, 22
  Cheddar Broccoli Corn Bake, 30
  Cheddar Chowder, 14
  Cheese and Nut Scones, 210
Cherry
  California Apricot-Cherry Cornmeal Cobbler, 94
  Cherry Coconut Cheese Coffee Cake, 198
  Chesapeake Crab Strata, 80
Chicken
  Chicken & Wild Rice, 122
  Chicken Tetrazzini, 114
  Chicken Vegetable Skillet, 124
  Country Chicken Dinner, 140
  Dairyland Confetti Chicken, 66
  Enchiladas Suisse, 174
  Fancy Chicken Puff Pie, 62
  Grilled Roaster with International Basting Sauces, 64
  Layered Chicken & Vegetable Bake, 126
  Microwaved Garlic and Herb Chicken, 114
  Paella a la Española, 180
  Sesame Chicken and Vegetable Stir-Fry, 117
  "Wildly" Delicious Casserole, 127
Chicken, Cut-Up
  Chicken Bourguignonne, 122
  Chicken Fiesta, 124
  Corn and Chicken Casserole, 126
  Down-Home Corn and Chicken Casserole, 58
  Golden Chicken Normandy-Style, 60
Chicken Breasts
  Buffet Chicken Medley, 127
  Chicken and Ham with Rice, 54

Index

Chicken Breasts *(continued)*
   Chicken Milano, 176
   Chicken Ragoût, 118
   Chicken Risotto, 178
   Chicken Tabbouleh, 117
   One-Dish Chicken 'n' Rice, 118
   Orange Ginger Chicken & Rice, 112
   Savory Chicken & Biscuits, 116
Chilaquiles, 175
Chili Bean Ragoût, 160
Chili Meatloaf & Potato Casserole, 108
Chili Wagon Wheel Casserole, 148
China Choy Quiche, 180
Chive Whole Wheat Drop Biscuits, 242
Chocolate *(see also* **Chocolate Chips, Cocoa***)*
   Almond Toffee Squares, 302
   Black Bottom Banana Cream Pie, 87
   Caramel-Layered Brownies, 318
   Chocolate Almond Shortbread, 344
   Chocolate-Caramel Sugar Cookies, 270
   Chocolate Filling, 336
   Chocolate-Peanut Cookies, 286
   Chocolate Pumpkin Muffins, 252
   Chocolate Sugar Cookies, 270
   Chocolatey Rocky Road Brownies, 322
   Choco-Scutterbotch, 290
   Coconut Crowned Cappuccino Brownies, 320
   Crumble Bars, 328
   Extra Moist & Chunky Brownies, 316

Chocolate *(continued)*
   Jam-Filled Chocolate Sugar Cookies, 270
   Marshmallow Krispie Bars, 326
   Oatmeal Candied Chippers, 286
   Oreo® Muffins, 260
   Peanut Butter Pizza Cookies, 328
   Quick Chocolate Macaroons, 282
   Quick Chocolate Softies, 288
   Raspberry Fudge Brownies, 314
   Swiss Mocha Treats, 276
   Toffee Brownie Bars, 316
   Triple Layer Peanut Butter Bars, 310
   Walnut Christmas Balls, 336
   Walnut Macaroons, 276
   White Chocolate Chunk Brownies, 314
   White Chocolate Chunk Muffins, 262
Chocolate Chips
   Banana Crescents, 336
   Caramel-Layered Brownies, 318
   Chocolate Caramel Pecan Bars, 302
   Chocolate Chip Lollipops, 324
   Chocolate Chip Rugalach, 344
   Chocolate Chip Sandwich Cookies, 288
   Chocolate Chip Shortbread, 298
   Chocolate-Dipped Almond Horns, 266
   Chocolatey Peanut Butter Goodies, 332
   Choco-Scutterbotch, 290
   Chunky Macadamia Bars, 306
   Coconut Crowned Cappuccino Brownies, 320
   Cowboy Cookies, 292
   Decadent Blonde Brownies, 312
   Drizzle, 296

Chocolate Chips *(continued)*
   Marshmallow Krispie Bars, 326
   Mini Crumbcakes, 258
   Mint Chocolate Chip Muffins, 248
   Original Nestlé® Toll House® Chocolate Chip Cookies, 292
   P.B. Graham Snackers, 332
   Peanut Butter Chocolate Chippers, 284
   Peanut Butter Mini Chip Loaves, 260
   Peanut Butter Secrets, 282
   Peanut Chocolate Surprise Pie, 82
   Quick Chocolate Softies, 288
   Raspberry Fudge Brownies, 314
   Toffee Brownie Bars, 316
   Topping, 258
   Ultimate Chocolate Chip Cookies, 296
   Whole Grain Chippers, 294
Choco-Scutterbotch, 290
Chunky Macadamia Bars, 306
Cider Stew, 100
Cinnamon Buns, 188
Cinnamon-Date Scones, 192
Cinnamon-Raisin Bread, 256
Classic Banana Bread, 20
Cloverleaf, 216
Cocoa
   Chocolate Amaretto Squares, 306
   Chocolate Pecan Pie Bars, 304
   Cocoa Pecan Crescents, 280
   Cocoa Snickerdoodles, 272
   Cowboy Cookies, 292
   White Chocolate Chunk Muffins, 262
Coconut
   Almond Toffee Squares, 302
   Cherry Coconut Cheese Coffee Cake, 198

Index

Coconut *(continued)*
    Coconut Crowned Cappuccino Brownies, 320
    Marvelous Macaroons, 86
    Peachy Oatmeal Bars, 300
    Quick Chocolate Macaroons, 282
    Walnut Macaroons, 276

Coffee Cakes
    Apple Ring Coffee Cake, 200
    Cherry Coconut Cheese Coffee Cake, 198
    Maple Nut Twist, 196

Company Crab, 76
Confetti Topping, 66

Cookies, Bar
    Almond Toffee Squares, 302
    Chocolate Almond Shortbread, 344
    Chocolate Amaretto Squares, 306
    Chocolate Caramel Pecan Bars, 302
    Chocolate Chip Shortbread, 298
    Chocolate Pecan Pie Bars, 304
    Chocolatey Peanut Butter Goodies, 332
    Chunky Macadamia Bars, 306
    Crumble Bars, 328
    Heath® Bars, 308
    Lemon Nut Bars, 304
    Luscious Lemon Bars, 308
    Marshmallow Krispie Bars, 326
    Peachy Oatmeal Bars, 300
    Streusel Strawberry Bars, 300
    Triple Layer Peanut Butter Bars, 310
    Walnut-Brandy Shortbread, 346

Cookies, Drop
    Chocolate Chip Sandwich Cookies, 288
    Chocolate-Peanut Cookies, 286

Cookies, Drop *(continued)*
    Cocoa Snickerdoodles, 272
    Cowboy Cookies, 292
    Maple Walnut Cookies, 280
    Marvelous Macaroons, 86
    Oatmeal Apple Cookies, 268
    Oatmeal Candied Chippers, 286
    Oatmeal Scotchies, 290
    Old-Fashioned Oatmeal Cookies, 274
    Original Nestlé® Toll House® Chocolate Chip Cookies, 292
    Peanut Butter Sensations, 268
    Peanut Butter Treats, 294
    Quick Chocolate Macaroons, 282
    Quick Chocolate Softies, 288
    Raspberry Almond Sandwich Cookies, 274
    Spicy Pumpkin Cookies, 272
    Ultimate Chocolate Chip Cookies, 296
    Walnut Macaroons, 276

Cookies, Rolled
    Chocolate Chip Rugalach, 344
    Glazed Sugar Cookies, 338
    Golden Kolacky, 334
    Linzer Sandwich Cookies, 346
    Peanut Butter Cut-Outs, 342
    Ultimate Sugar Cookies, 278
    Watermelon Slices, 330

Cookies, Shaped
    Banana Crescents, 336
    Bavarian Cookie Wreaths, 342
    Chocolate-Caramel Sugar Cookies, 270
    Chocolate Chip Lollipops, 324
    Chocolate-Dipped Almond Horns, 266
    Chocolate Sugar Cookies, 270
    Choco-Scutterbotch, 290
    Cocoa Pecan Crescents, 280
    Danish Raspberry Ribbons, 340

Cookies, Shaped *(continued)*
    Jam-Filled Chocolate Sugar Cookies, 270
    P.B. Graham Snackers, 332
    Peanut Butter Bears, 326
    Peanut Butter Chocolate Chippers, 284
    Peanut Butter Pizza Cookies, 328
    Peanut Butter Secrets, 282
    Swiss Mocha Treats, 276
    Walnut Christmas Balls, 336
    Whole Grain Chippers, 294

Corn
    Brazilian Corn and Shrimp Moqueca Casserole, 175
    Cheddar Broccoli Corn Bake, 30
    Chicken Fiesta, 124
    Chili Bean Ragoût, 160
    Chili Meatloaf & Potato Casserole, 108
    Corn and Chicken Casserole, 126
    Corn Pudding Soufflé, 36
    Corn Relish, 32
    Crab and Corn Enchilada Casserole, 138
    Creamy Corn au Gratin, 24
    Down-Home Corn and Chicken Casserole, 58
    Fresh Corn with Adobe Butter, 28
    Golden Hearty Cornbread, 16
    Hickory Beef Kabobs, 38
    "Wild" Black Beans, 163

Corned Beef, Potato and Pepper Hash, 44
Cornmeal Dumplings, 12
Cornmeal Sticks, 208
Cornsticks, 17
Countdown Casserole, 110
Country Biscuits, 184

Index

Country Chicken Dinner, 140
Country-Style Potato Salad, 24
Cowboy Cookies, 292
Crab
   Chesapeake Crab Strata, 80
   Company Crab, 76
   Crab and Corn Enchilada Casserole, 138
   Surfer's Seafood Casserole, 134
Cranberry
   Cranberry Oat Bran Muffins, 240
   Oatmeal Apple Cranberry Scones, 234
Crazy Lasagna Casserole, 150
Creamy Baked Mashed Potatoes, 27
Creamy Corn au Gratin, 24
Crescents, 216
Crispy Catfish Nuggets with Creole Sauce, 77
Crumble Bars, 328
Crunch Topping, 243

D
Dairyland Confetti Chicken, 66
Danish Raspberry Ribbons, 340
Decadent Blonde Brownies, 312
Deluxe Potato Bake, 156
Desserts
   Apricot-Pear Strudel, 86
   Berry Cobbler, 84
   California Apricot-Cherry Cornmeal Cobbler, 94
   Peach Cobbler, 88
   Praline Pumpkin Tart, 92
Dilled Salmon Supper, 72
Dinner Rolls, 216
Double Spinach Bake, 164
Down-Home Corn and Chicken Casserole, 58
Drizzle, 296

E
Easy Three Cheese Tuna Soufflé, 136
Eggplant
   Blazing Bandito Veggie Medley, 158
   Zucchini Tomato Bake, 160
Enchiladas Suisse, 174
Enlightened Macaroni and Cheese, 146
Extra Moist & Chunky Brownies, 316

F
Family Baked Bean Dinner, 48
Fancy Chicken Puff Pie, 62
Fan-Tans, 217
Feta-Dill Muffins, 212
Fish (*see also* **Tuna**)
   Baked Fish with Potatoes and Onions, 74
   Baked Rockfish Veracruz, 130
   Crispy Catfish Nuggets with Creole Sauce, 77
   Dilled Salmon Supper, 72
   Herb-Baked Fish & Rice, 78
   Louisiana Seafood Bake, 70
   Seafood Gumbo, 130
   Zesty Catfish Bake, 68
Five-Fruit Granola Scones, 194
Flakey Southern Biscuits, 16
French Beef Stew, 168
Fresh Corn with Adobe Butter, 28
Fresh Lemon Meringue Pie, 88
Fresh Vegetable Casserole, 22
Fresh Vegetable Lasagna, 156
Frostings and Glazes
   Lemony Frosting, 90
   Lemony Glaze, 254
   Quick Vanilla Glaze, 306
Fruity Dressing, 74

G
Gingerbread Pear Muffins, 246
Glazed Strawberry Lemon Streusel Muffins, 254
Glazed Sugar Cookies, 338
Glazed Sweet Potatoes and Turnips, 28
Golden Apple Cheesecake, 94
Golden Apple Cheese Muffins, 190
Golden Apple Sour Cream Muffins, 254
Golden Chicken Normandy-Style, 60
Golden Hearty Cornbread, 16
Golden Kolacky, 334
Graham Muffins, 198
Green Beans
   Cajun-Style Green Beans, 26
   Chicken Milano, 176
   Cider Stew, 100
   Green Beans with Pine Nuts, 28
   Original Green Bean Casserole, 166
Grilled Recipes
   Grilled Roaster with International Basting Sauces, 64
   Hickory Beef Kabobs, 38
   T-Bone Steaks with Vegetable Kabobs, 48
   Texas-Style Beef Brisket, 52
   Vegetable Kabobs, 48

H
Ham
   Angel Hair Carbonara, 150
   Baked Country Cured Ham, 40
   Bayou Jambalaya, 18
   Ham with Fruited Mustard Sauce, 46
   Potato & Cheddar Soup, 8
   Wonderfully Flavored Skillet Greens, 33

Index

Harvest Vegetable Scallop, 162
Healthy Banana-Walnut Muffins, 202
Hearty Barbecue Dip, 34
Heath® Bars, 308
Herb and Cheddar Scones, 210
Herb-Baked Fish & Rice, 78
Herb-Cheese Biscuit Loaf, 212
Hickory Beef Kabobs, 38
Homestyle Tuna Pot Pie, 128
Honey Currant Scones, 202
Honey Muffins, 252

I
Indian Corn Muffins, 222

J
Jam-Filled Chocolate Sugar Cookies, 270

K
Karen Ann's Lemon Cake, 90

L
Lamb & Pork Cassoulet, 50
Layered Chicken & Vegetable Bake, 126
Lemon
  Fresh Lemon Meringue Pie, 88
  Glazed Strawberry Lemon Streusel Muffins, 254
  Lemon-Garlic Shrimp, 136
  Lemon Nut Bars, 304
  Lemon Poppy Seed Muffins, 258
  Lemon Streusel Topping, 254
  Lemony Frosting, 90
  Lemony Glaze, 254
  Luscious Lemon Bars, 308
  Mott's® Luscious Lemon Lite Muffins, 233
Linzer Sandwich Cookies, 346
Louisiana Seafood Bake, 70
Luscious Lemon Bars, 308

M
Maple Nut Twist, 196
Maple Walnut Cookies, 280
Marble Swirl Bread, 214
Marshmallow Krispie Bars, 326
Marvelous Macaroons, 86
Meat and Potato Pie, 105
Mexican Cheese-Rice Pie, 170
Microwaved Garlic and Herb Chicken, 114
Minestrone Soup, 18
Mini Crumbcakes, 258
Mini Meat Loaves & Vegetables, 106
Muffins
  Almond Blueberry Muffins, 188
  Apple Butter Spice Muffins, 186
  Apple Cheddar Muffins, 14
  Apple Oat Bran Muffins, 240
  Banana Breakfast Muffins, 200
  Banana-Honey Muffins, 192
  Blueberry Crunch Muffins, 242
  Blueberry Muffins, 236
  Blueberry Yogurt Muffins, 224
  Caraway Cheese Muffins, 218
  Carrot Zucchini Muffins, 232
  Chocolate Pumpkin Muffins, 252
  Cranberry Oat Bran Muffins, 240
  Feta-Dill Muffins, 212
  Gingerbread Pear Muffins, 246
  Glazed Strawberry Lemon Streusel Muffins, 254
  Golden Apple Cheese Muffins, 190
  Golden Apple Sour Cream Muffins, 254
  Graham Muffins, 198
  Healthy Banana-Walnut Muffins, 202
  Honey Muffins, 252

Muffins *(continued)*
  Indian Corn Muffins, 222
  Lemon Poppy Seed Muffins, 258
  Mini Crumbcakes, 258
  Mini Muffins, 243
  Mint Chocolate Chip Muffins, 248
  Mott's® Best Ever Strawberry Muffins, 226
  Mott's® Luscious Lemon Lite Muffins, 233
  Newton Muffins, 244
  Orange-Almond Muffins, 188
  Oreo® Muffins, 260
  Pesto Surprise Muffins, 210
  Pineapple-Raisin Muffins, 194
  Quick Nectarine Oat Muffins, 246
  Salsa Muffins, 208
  Savory Pumpkin Bacon Muffins, 217
  Sesame Crunch Banana Muffins, 230
  Squash Muffins, 218
  Streusel-Topped Blueberry Muffins, 248
  Toffee Crunch Muffins, 262
  Tomato-Carrot Muffin Tops, 220
  White Chocolate Chunk Muffins, 262
  Wild Rice Blueberry Muffins, 238
Mushrooms
  Chicken Ragoût, 118
  Orzo Casserole, 172
  Zucchini Tomato Bake, 160

N
Navajo Lamb Stew with Cornmeal Dumplings, 12
Newton Muffins, 244

Index

Nuts
  Almond Blueberry Muffins, 188
  Almond Toffee Squares, 302
  Apple Butter Spice Muffins, 186
  Apple Ring Coffee Cake, 200
  Banana Crescents, 336
  Banana Nut Bread, 236
  Bavarian Cookie Wreaths, 342
  Caramel-Layered Brownies, 318
  Cheese and Nut Scones, 210
  Chicken & Wild Rice, 122
  Chocolate Almond Shortbread, 344
  Chocolate Amaretto Squares, 306
  Chocolate Caramel Pecan Bars, 302
  Chocolate-Caramel Sugar Cookies, 270
  Chocolate Chip Rugalach, 344
  Chocolate-Dipped Almond Horns, 266
  Chocolate-Peanut Cookies, 286
  Chocolate Pecan Pie Bars, 304
  Chocolatey Rocky Road Brownies, 322
  Choco-Scutterbotch, 290
  Chunky Macadamia Bars, 306
  Classic Banana Bread, 20
  Cocoa Pecan Crescents, 280
  Cowboy Cookies, 292
  Decadent Blonde Brownies, 312
  Green Beans with Pine Nuts, 28
  Healthy Banana-Walnut Muffins, 202
  Heath® Bars, 308
  Jam-Filled Chocolate Sugar Cookies, 270
  Lemon Nut Bars, 304
  Maple Nut Twist, 196

Nuts *(continued)*
  Maple Walnut Cookies, 280
  Old-Fashioned Oatmeal Cookies, 274
  Orange-Almond Muffins, 188
  Orange Pecan Bread, 10
  Original Nestlé® Toll House® Chocolate Chip Cookies, 292
  Peanut Chocolate Surprise Pie, 82
  Praline Pumpkin Tart, 92
  Praline Topping, 92
  Quick Chocolate Softies, 288
  Raspberry Almond Sandwich Cookies, 274
  Raspberry Fudge Brownies, 314
  Spicy Pumpkin Cookies, 272
  Streusel Strawberry Bars, 300
  Toffee Brownie Bars, 316
  Topping, 258
  Ultimate Chocolate Chip Cookies, 296
  Walnut-Brandy Shortbread, 346
  Walnut Christmas Balls, 336
  Walnut Macaroons, 276

O
Oats
  Buttermilk Oatmeal Scones, 186
  Carrot Zucchini Muffins, 232
  Cocoa Snickerdoodles, 272
  Cowboy Cookies, 292
  Crumble Bars, 328
  Lemon Nut Bars, 304
  Mott's® Luscious Lemon Lite Muffins, 233
  Oatmeal Apple Cookies, 268
  Oatmeal Apple Cranberry Scones, 234
  Oatmeal Candied Chippers, 286
  Oatmeal Scotchies, 290
  Old-Fashioned Oatmeal Cookies, 274

Oats *(continued)*
  Peachy Oatmeal Bars, 300
  Quick Nectarine Oat Muffins, 246
  Sesame Crunch Banana Muffins, 230
  Whole Grain Chippers, 294
Okra-Bacon Casserole, 27
Old-Fashioned Beef Pot Pie, 108
Old-Fashioned Carrot Soup, 16
Old-Fashioned Cole Slaw, 34
Old-Fashioned Oatmeal Cookies, 274
Old-Fashioned Tuna Noodle Casserole, 78
Old-Fashioned Upside-Down Cake, 87
One-Dish Chicken 'n' Rice, 118
Orange
  Bavarian Cookie Wreaths, 342
  Glazed Sweet Potatoes and Turnips, 28
  Orange-Almond Muffins, 188
  Orange Ginger Chicken & Rice, 112
  Orange Pecan Bread, 10
  Raisin Scones, 210
Oreo® Muffins, 260
Oriental Beef and Broccoli, 170
Oriental Beef & Noodle Toss, 176
Original Green Bean Casserole, 166
Original Nestlé® Toll House® Chocolate Chip Cookies, 292
Orzo Casserole, 172
Oyster-Artichoke Pan Roast, 76

P
Paella a la Española, 180
Parma Dip, 34
Parmesan Garlic Twists, 211

Index

Pasta
- Angel Hair Carbonara, 150
- Baked Rigatoni with Sausage, 144
- Blazing Bandito Veggie Medley, 158
- Chicken Tetrazzini, 114
- Chili Wagon Wheel Casserole, 148
- Country Chicken Dinner, 140
- Crazy Lasagna Casserole, 150
- Double Spinach Bake, 164
- Enlightened Macaroni and Cheese, 146
- Fresh Vegetable Lasagna, 156
- Old-Fashioned Tuna Noodle Casserole, 78
- Oriental Beef & Noodle Toss, 176
- Orzo Casserole, 172
- Pastitso, 148
- Pizza Pasta, 152
- Polish Reuben Casserole, 146
- Sausage & Pasta Primavera, 178
- Seafood Pasta Salad, 74
- Shrimp in Angel Hair Pasta Casserole, 70
- Shrimp Noodle Supreme, 144
- Skillet Pasta Roma, 152
- Southwestern Beef and Bean Lasagna, 102
- String Pie, 46
- Wisconsin Swiss Linguine Tart, 142

Pastitso, 148
Patchwork Casserole, 40
P.B. Graham Snackers, 332

Peach
- Peach Cobbler, 88
- Peach Spread, 243
- Peachy Oatmeal Bars, 300
- Pickled Peaches, 84

Peanut Butter
- Chocolatey Peanut Butter Goodies, 332
- Marshmallow Krispie Bars, 326
- P.B. Graham Snackers, 332
- Peanut Butter Bears, 326
- Peanut Butter Chocolate Chippers, 284
- Peanut Butter Cut-Outs, 342
- Peanut Butter Mini Chip Loaves, 260
- Peanut Butter Pizza Cookies, 328
- Peanut Butter Secrets, 282
- Peanut Butter Sensations, 268
- Peanut Butter Treats, 294
- Triple Layer Peanut Butter Bars, 310

Peanut Chocolate Surprise Pie, 82

Pear
- Apricot-Pear Strudel, 86
- Gingerbread Pear Muffins, 246
- Pear Scones, 232

Peas
- Angel Hair Carbonara, 150
- Biscuit-Topped Tuna Bake, 132
- Homestyle Tuna Pot Pie, 128
- Minestrone Soup, 18
- Old-Fashioned Beef Pot Pie, 108
- Quick and Easy Tuna Rice with Peas, 77

Pesto Surprise Muffins, 210
Pickled Peaches, 84

Pies
- Apple-Buttermilk Pie, 90
- Black Bottom Banana Cream Pie, 87
- Fresh Lemon Meringue Pie, 88
- Peanut Chocolate Surprise Pie, 82

Pineapple
- Family Baked Bean Dinner, 48
- Ham with Fruited Mustard Sauce, 46
- Marvelous Macaroons, 86
- Old-Fashioned Upside-Down Cake, 87
- Pineapple-Raisin Muffins, 194

Pizza Pasta, 152
Polish Reuben Casserole, 146
Poppy Seed Bread, 20

Pork (*see also* **Bacon, Ham, Sausage**)
- Pork Roast with Corn Bread & Oyster Stuffing, 42
- Savory Pork & Apple Stir-Fry, 106

Potatoes
- Baked Fish with Potatoes and Onions, 74
- Baked Potato Spears, 34
- Beef Bourguignon, 100
- Cheddar Chowder, 14
- Chili Meatloaf & Potato Casserole, 108
- Corned Beef, Potato and Pepper Hash, 44
- Countdown Casserole, 110
- Country-Style Potato Salad, 24
- Creamy Baked Mashed Potatoes, 27
- Deluxe Potato Bake, 156
- Fresh Vegetable Casserole, 22
- Harvest Vegetable Scallop, 162
- Meat and Potato Pie, 105
- Minestrone Soup, 18
- Mini Meat Loaves & Vegetables, 106
- Navajo Lamb Stew with Cornmeal Dumplings, 12
- Patchwork Casserole, 40
- Potato & Cheddar Soup, 8
- Potato Gorgonzola Gratin, 162

Index

Potatoes *(continued)*
   Sausage Skillet Dinner, 44
   Shepherd's Pie, 52
   Turkey Cottage Pie, 60
   Vegetable Kabobs, 48
Potluck Pockets, 62
Praline Pumpkin Tart, 92
Praline Topping, 92
Prize Potluck Casserole, 110
Pumpkin
   Chocolate Pumpkin Muffins, 252
   Indian Corn Muffins, 222
   Praline Pumpkin Tart, 92
   Pumpkin-Ginger Scones, 222
   Savory Pumpkin Bacon Muffins, 217
   Spicy Pumpkin Cookies, 272

Q
Quick & Easy Chili, 17
Quick and Easy Tuna Rice with Peas, 77
Quick Chocolate Macaroons, 282
Quick Chocolate Softies, 288
Quick Dills, 33
Quick Nectarine Oat Muffins, 246
Quick Vanilla Glaze, 306

R
Raisins
   Banana Breakfast Muffins, 200
   Cinnamon-Raisin Bread, 256
   Cowboy Cookies, 292
   Mott's® Luscious Lemon Lite Muffins, 233
   Old-Fashioned Oatmeal Cookies, 274
   Pineapple-Raisin Muffins, 194
   Raisin Scones, 210
   Spicy Pumpkin Cookies, 272
   Squash Muffins, 218

Raspberry
   Berry Cobbler, 84
   Danish Raspberry Ribbons, 340
   Linzer Sandwich Cookies, 346
   Raspberry Almond Sandwich Cookies, 274
   Raspberry Fudge Brownies, 314
Refrigerator Sweet Yeast Dough, 190

S
Salads
   Country-Style Potato Salad, 24
   Old-Fashioned Cole Slaw, 34
   Seafood Pasta Salad, 74
   Tomato Ginger Apple Salad, 36
Salsa Muffins, 208
Sauces, Savory
   Special Sauce, 52
   Spicy Tomato Sauce, 138
Sausage
   Baked Rigatoni with Sausage, 144
   Basque Bean Casserole, 174
   Chicken Fiesta, 124
   Family Baked Bean Dinner, 48
   Lamb & Pork Cassoulet, 50
   Polish Reuben Casserole, 146
   Prize Potluck Casserole, 110
   Sausage & Pasta Primavera, 178
   Sausage Skillet Dinner, 44
   Skillet Pasta Roma, 152
Savory Chicken & Biscuits, 116
Savory Pork & Apple Stir-Fry, 106
Savory Pumpkin Bacon Muffins, 217
Scones
   Apple Cheddar Scones, 220
   Buttermilk Oatmeal Scones, 186
   Cheese and Nut Scones, 210
   Cinnamon-Date Scones, 192
   Five-Fruit Granola Scones, 194
   Herb and Cheddar Scones, 210
   Honey Currant Scones, 202

Scones *(continued)*
   Oatmeal Apple Cranberry Scones, 234
   Pear Scones, 232
   Pumpkin-Ginger Scones, 222
   Raisin Scones, 210
   Scones, 210
   Wheat Germ Scones, 191
Seafood Gumbo, 130
Seafood Pasta Salad, 74
Sesame Chicken and Vegetable Stir-Fry, 117
Sesame Crunch Banana Muffins, 230
Sesame Crunch Topping, 230
Shepherd's Pie, 52
Shrimp
   Bayou Jambalaya, 18
   Brazilian Corn and Shrimp Moqueca Casserole, 175
   Lemon-Garlic Shrimp, 136
   Louisiana Seafood Bake, 70
   Paella a la Española, 180
   Seafood Pasta Salad, 74
   Shrimp Casserole, 132
   Shrimp in Angel Hair Pasta Casserole, 70
   Shrimp in Cajun Red Gravy, 80
   Shrimp Noodle Supreme, 144
   Surfer's Seafood Casserole, 134
   Thai-Style Tuna Fried Rice, 134
Skillet Pasta Roma, 152
Soups
   Cheddar Chowder, 14
   Minestrone Soup, 18
   Old-Fashioned Carrot Soup, 16
   Potato & Cheddar Soup, 8
   Seafood Gumbo, 130
Southwestern Beef and Bean Lasagna, 102
Special Sauce, 52
Spice-Prune Loaf, 238
Spicy Barbecue Beef, 50

Index

Spicy Pumpkin Cookies, 272
Spicy Tomato Sauce, 138
Squash
   Acorn Squash with Maple Butter, 30
   Blazing Bandito Veggie Medley, 158
   Carrot Zucchini Muffins, 232
   Minestrone Soup, 18
   Squash Muffins, 218
   Vegetable Risotto, 158
   Zucchini Tomato Bake, 160
Stews
   Beef Bourguignon, 100
   Cider Stew, 100
   French Beef Stew, 168
   Navajo Lamb Stew with Cornmeal Dumplings, 12
Stir-Fries
   Lemon-Garlic Shrimp, 136
   Oriental Beef and Broccoli, 170
   Savory Pork & Apple Stir-Fry, 106
   Sesame Chicken and Vegetable Stir-Fry, 117
   Thai-Style Tuna Fried Rice, 134
Strawberry
   Chocolate Chip Rugalach, 344
   Glazed Strawberry Lemon Streusel Muffins, 254
   Mott's® Best Ever Strawberry Muffins, 226
   Streusel Strawberry Bars, 300
   Streusel-Topped Blueberry Muffins, 248
String Pie, 46
Success in a Skillet, 98
Surfer's Seafood Casserole, 134
Sweetened Whipped Cream, 92
Sweet Yeast Dough, 190
Swiss Mocha Treats, 276
Swiss Vegetable Medley, 166

T
Tabasco® Corn Bread Wedges, 217
Tabbouleh, 154
Tasty Turkey Pot Pie, 56
Tasty Turkey Roll, 63
T-Bone Steaks with Vegetable Kabobs, 48
Texas-Style Beef Brisket, 52
Texas-Style Deep-Dish Chili Pie, 42
Thai-Style Tuna Fried Rice, 134
Three-Egg Meringue, 88
Thyme-Cheese Bubble Loaf, 206
Toffee Brownie Bars, 316
Toffee Crunch Muffins, 262
Tomato-Carrot Muffin Tops, 220
Tomato Ginger Apple Salad, 36
Toppings
   Confetti Topping, 66
   Crunch Topping, 243
   Drizzle, 296
   Lemon Streusel Topping, 254
   Peach Spread, 243
   Praline Topping, 92
   Sesame Crunch Topping, 230
   Sweetened Whipped Cream, 92
   Three-Egg Meringue, 88
   Topping, 258
Triple Layer Peanut Butter Bars, 310
Tuna
   Biscuit-Topped Tuna Bake, 132
   Easy Three Cheese Tuna Soufflé, 136
   Homestyle Tuna Pot Pie, 128
   Old-Fashioned Tuna Noodle Casserole, 78
   Quick and Easy Tuna Rice with Peas, 77
   Thai-Style Tuna Fried Rice, 134
   Tuna with Peppercorns on a Bed of Greens, 72

Turkey
   Potluck Pockets, 62
   Success in a Skillet, 98
   Tasty Turkey Pot Pie, 56
   Tasty Turkey Roll, 63
   Turkey Cottage Pie, 60
   Turkey-Tortilla Bake, 116

U
Ultimate Chocolate Chip Cookies, 296
Ultimate Sugar Cookies, 278

V
Vegetable Beef Pot Pie, 104
Vegetable Kabobs, 48
Vegetable Risotto, 158

W
Walnut-Brandy Shortbread, 346
Walnut Christmas Balls, 336
Walnut Macaroons, 276
Watermelon Slices, 330
Wheat Germ Scones, 191
White Chocolate Chunk Brownies, 314
White Chocolate Chunk Muffins, 262
Whole Grain Chippers, 294
Whole Wheat Herb Bread, 226
Whole Wheat Popovers, 204
"Wild" Black Beans, 163
"Wildly" Delicious Casserole, 127
Wild Rice Blueberry Muffins, 238
Wisconsin Swiss Linguine Tart, 142
Wonderfully Flavored Skillet Greens, 33

Z
Zesty Catfish Bake, 68
Zucchini Tomato Bake, 160

METRIC CONVERSION CHART

VOLUME MEASUREMENTS (dry)

1/8 teaspoon = 0.5 mL
1/4 teaspoon = 1 mL
1/2 teaspoon = 2 mL
3/4 teaspoon = 4 mL
1 teaspoon = 5 mL
1 tablespoon = 15 mL
2 tablespoons = 30 mL
1/4 cup = 60 mL
1/3 cup = 75 mL
1/2 cup = 125 mL
2/3 cup = 150 mL
3/4 cup = 175 mL
1 cup = 250 mL
2 cups = 1 pint = 500 mL
3 cups = 750 mL
4 cups = 1 quart = 1 L

VOLUME MEASUREMENTS (fluid)

1 fluid ounce (2 tablespoons) = 30 mL
4 fluid ounces (1/2 cup) = 125 mL
8 fluid ounces (1 cup) = 250 mL
12 fluid ounces (1 1/2 cups) = 375 mL
16 fluid ounces (2 cups) = 500 mL

WEIGHTS (mass)

1/2 ounce = 15 g
1 ounce = 30 g
3 ounces = 90 g
4 ounces = 120 g
8 ounces = 225 g
10 ounces = 285 g
12 ounces = 360 g
16 ounces = 1 pound = 450 g

DIMENSIONS

1/16 inch = 2 mm
1/8 inch = 3 mm
1/4 inch = 6 mm
1/2 inch = 1.5 cm
3/4 inch = 2 cm
1 inch = 2.5 cm

OVEN TEMPERATURES

250°F = 120°C
275°F = 140°C
300°F = 150°C
325°F = 160°C
350°F = 180°C
375°F = 190°C
400°F = 200°C
425°F = 220°C
450°F = 230°C

BAKING PAN SIZES

Utensil	Size in Inches/Quarts	Metric Volume	Size in Centimeters
Baking or Cake Pan (square or rectangular)	8×8×2	2 L	20×20×5
	9×9×2	2.5 L	22×22×5
	12×8×2	3 L	30×20×5
	13×9×2	3.5 L	33×23×5
Loaf Pan	8×4×3	1.5 L	20×10×7
	9×5×3	2 L	23×13×7
Round Layer Cake Pan	8×1½	1.2 L	20×4
	9×1½	1.5 L	23×4
Pie Plate	8×1¼	750 mL	20×3
	9×1¼	1 L	23×3
Baking Dish or Casserole	1 quart	1 L	—
	1½ quart	1.5 L	—
	2 quart	2 L	—